T0331006

*Collecting in the Twenty-First Century*

# Collecting in the Twenty-First Century

## From Museums to the Web

Edited by
Johannes Endres and Christoph Zeller

 CAMDEN HOUSE
Rochester, New York

First published 2022
by Camden House

Camden House is an imprint of Boydell & Brewer Inc.
668 Mt. Hope Avenue, Rochester, NY 14620, USA
and of Boydell & Brewer Limited
PO Box 9, Woodbridge, Suffolk IP12 3DF, UK
www.boydellandbrewer.com

ISBN-13: 978-1-57113-970-2

**Library of Congress Cataloging-in-Publication Data**

CIP data is available from the Library of Congress.

The publisher has no responsibility for the continued existence
or accuracy of URLs for external or third-party internet websites
referred to in this book and does not guarantee that any content
on such websites is, or will remain, accurate or appropriate.

This publication is printed on acid-free paper.
Printed in the United States of America.

# Contents

# Part III. Virtuality

# Part IV. Economics

# Introduction: Collecting in the Digital Age

*Christoph Zeller*

THIS BOOK IS DEDICATED to the concept of "collecting" and its shifting meanings in a digital context. It explores in what ways individual collectors and collecting institutions such as archives, museums, and libraries have espoused various forms of data processing; it offers insights into the practice of collecting as a cultural phenomenon and how this practice changes in an era in which computers are ubiquitous and the Internet dominates our time; and it discusses what is being collected in the digital domain, why digital objects are different from non-digital ones, and what it means when we "collect data." Its essays and case studies examine the practice of collecting in a digital context from the perspectives of art historians, media and cultural-studies scholars, preservationists, museum theorists, librarians, and computer scientists.

The Western idea of "collection" signifies an intentional and selective accumulation of like elements, may they be physical objects or ideas and experiences. The all-encompassing meaning of "collecting," correspondingly, ranges from shopping lists to address books, from remembering days past to focusing on the here and now, and from sorting comestibles to tracking debts. Almost unfathomable in its breadth, "collecting" requires conceptual framing to avoid its use as an imprecise, hollowed-out metaphor. Such frames have been outlined in the past to think about "collecting," but they failed to capture the idea of collecting in all its multifaceted manifestations. As a result, each of these preliminary and heterogenous frames exist largely in isolation from one another. For example, psychologists point to the prominent role of collecting in the development of the self and stress the mirroring of subjects and collected objects; historians emphasize the sociopolitical circumstances in which collecting rose to prominence among cultural elites; and economists investigate the significance of collecting in consumer societies, considering the cycles of "acquisition, possession, and disposition" of goods that constitute and dissolve what is called a "collection."[1] Each of these unique conceptual

---

1    Russell W. Belk, *Melanie Wallendorf, John F. Sherry, Jr., and Morris B. Holbrook*, "Collecting in a Consumer Culture," in *Highways and Buyways:*

frameworks, however, introduces an additional feature of collecting, namely the role of influential agents—members of the nobility, wealthy merchants, naturalists, curators, gallery owners, librarians, and archivists—who began to collect for the benefit of the collection. Although collectors undeniably grow in status and knowledge through their collections, the most dramatic changes concern the collection and its objects. With each object added, the semiotic fabric of a collection changes; and in turn, each object acquires a different meaning through the collection. In other words, at various points in history, collecting was no longer seen as merely an intentional process of selection designed to increase the prestige of the collector, to amaze and to educate an audience, or to preserve things of the past, but also became a strategy to re-assign meaning and to create a new order: the order of a collection. According to the logic of collecting, a chair is no longer a piece of furniture—commonly with a back and seat supported by four legs, built to seat a person—but an object that derives its meaning from its position within the hierarchy of like, intentionally selected elements, say, other chairs or a set of furniture from a specific era. Together, intentionality, selectivity, and reassignment of meaning determine what can be understood as collecting from high culture to mass markets and from individuals to institutions. By defining collecting as an intentional process of selection that recontextualizes objects and provides new meaning to them excludes those shopping lists, address books, and photo albums so long as they serve the purpose of efficient shopping, recording addresses, or remembering past events.

Technological innovations such as personal computers, the Internet, wearables, and cloud computing (since 2010) have dramatically changed the way we work, trade, shop, communicate, learn, teach, and entertain ourselves. Moreover, the introduction of these technologies challenges the notion of collecting altogether. What scholars call the "digital revolution"[2]—the gradual shift from mechanical and analog electronic technology to digital technology since the invention of the point-contact

---

*Naturalistic Research from the Consumer Behaviour Odyssey*, ed. Russell Belk (Provo, UT: Association for Consumer Research, 1991), 178–215, here 180.

2    In 2014, Dirk Helbing, Professor of Computational Social Science, wrote: "We are in the middle of a digital revolution—a third industrial revolution after the one turning agricultural societies into industrial ones, and these into service societies. This will fundamentally transform our economy and lead us into the 'digital society.'" Helbing, *Thinking Ahead: Essays on Big Data, Digital Revolution, and Participatory Market Society* (Cham, Switzerland: Springer, 2015). While most business-related publications consider the entrepreneurial possibilities of the digital revolution, Helbing and other social and media studies scholars highlight the problems this revolution has already and will continue to bring about: extensive surveillance, loss of jobs, disregard of ethical boundaries with the use of AI, and the formation of market monopolies, to name a few.

transistor in 1947, a semi-conductor that led to the development of digital computers—culminated in the beginning of the "digital age" in 2002, when digital storage surpassed its analog counterpart. Between 1986 and 2007, the world's "general-purpose computing capacity grew at an annual rate of 58%," its "capacity for bidirectional telecommunication grew at 28% a year," and its capacity to store information digitally grew by 23%.[3] During the same period, digitally stored information vastly outpaced analog information storage and expanded its share from just 1% in 1986 to 96% in 2007. This significant increase of storage, computation, and communication capacity resulted in a paradox: information is not only stored, processed, and transmitted at higher rates, but it also permanently expands in volume. Collecting in a digital context no longer denotes a process of intentionally selecting from a given set of objects but is instead a process of data production. What is called "collecting" describes the (often) indiscriminate accumulation of large quantities of data and, thus, is more accurately captured by the verb "amassing." While amassed data is frequently reorganized to be sold, to serve as intelligence, or to help scientific progress, its purpose is no longer to be allocated to a collection, that is, to be collected for the purpose of collecting.

Notwithstanding the vagaries of its usage, the term "collecting" now encapsulates, on the one hand, what can be found on library shelves, in museum exhibition rooms, and in a person's living room cabinet, including, for example, philatelic treasures or jars of sand from visited beaches; on the other hand, "collecting" signifies everything that was created in a digital environment, pertains to an algorithmic formula, and is commonly called a "digital object." Based on a 2012 proposition by the Consultative Committee for Space Data Systems (CCSDS), Laura Molloy defines a "digital object" as "an object composed of a set of bit sequences"; an algorithmically prompted bitstream that "appears to the user as a digital file," while to those who do not use computer code, it appears as a visually or audibly separated or separable unit, such as a group of pixels or a photo, a letter or word in an HTML document, an entire folder or a single document, a whole melody or a single note: "Some digital objects can be simple, like a text file. Video, being composed of multiple elements (video track, audio track, container file, and possibly others) may be considered a complex digital object."[4] Contrary to what everyday language

---

3   Martin Hilbert and Priscila López. "The World's Technological Capacity to Store, Communicate, and Compute Information," *Science* 332, no. 6025 (2011), DOI: 10.1126/science.1200970.

4   Laura Molloy, "Digital Objects—What Are They and Why Should We Manage Them," Blog Entry, Oxford Internet Institute, August 24, 2017, https://www.oii.ox.ac.uk/blog/digital-objects-what-are-they-and-why-should-we-manage-them/.

implies, digital objects lack materiality and can neither be "opened" nor "found" like objects in the physical world. Instead, they must be actualized (by a prompt) and performed (by algorithms) in order to be seen or heard. Many digital objects today populate the Internet, a reservoir of nearly everything in mathematical code, which allows an immaterial stream of bits to be actualized. We encounter many digital objects in a day on screen and often create new ones when we shoot photos, write text, send emails, and visit websites. In most cases, we do not intentionally select digital objects and re-assign meaning to them, although some specific digital objects' sole purpose is to be collected, such as a non-fungible token. Non-fungible tokens (NFTs) are stored data that achieves uniqueness by means of blockchain technology, i.e., digital ledgers consisting of users and timestamps. NFTs can be original (digital) artworks that were created for the sole purpose of being unique and sold to collectors, or they can be any other kind of digital objects, for example photos, emails, and pieces of code that are reissued in the form of an NFT. Collectors are willing to pay high sums of money for the unique quality of an NFT, likening them to artworks, but focusing solely on the monetary equivalent that was paid for the acquisition of an NFT. In this case, the amount of money signifies a shift in meaning of an NFT at the moment it changes from one collector to another. This is why an NFT fulfills the features of traditional collecting as an intentionally selected object with a reassignedmeaning.

The rise of information technology as the most powerful economic social force cannot be separated from new practices of collecting. What we call "collecting data"—the amassing of data for the purpose of generating profits—takes center stage in creating jobs, as well as stimulating innovation and scientific progress. But it also results in the erosion of privacy, the ubiquity of surveillance, the political and economic disenfranchisement of citizens, and the solidification of corporate interests. Most importantly, collecting skills themselves are in the process of changing. Age-old practices of collecting—the ability to intentionally select and arrange objects to assign new meaning within the composition of a collection—are confronted by new dexterities that have emerged in the past decades. At present, collecting institutions, collectors, objects, and the way we collect are equally linked to and affected by information technology. Collecting inherently presupposes individuals' rudimentary expertise in the use of digital devices, the mastery of databases, and the assessment of large amounts of information. Not only tech companies, but also collecting institutions have perfected these skills. While common notions of collecting derive from the division of *naturalia* and *artificalia* that drove Renaissance collectors' fascination for "exotic" objects in their "cabinet of wonder," from museums' tasks to portraying the greatness of nations in the nineteenth century, and from today's desire to generate lasting experiences through mass exhibitions, collecting institutions have long since come to embrace the advantages of digital technology, which include increased access to their archives' holdings, and welcoming a growing number of "visitors" to their virtual locales rather than to their brick-and-mortar counterparts.

This book outlines five aspects of collecting that touch upon the shifting landscape of technology itself and how these aspects in turn impact cultural practices of collecting: *storage, surveillance, authenticity, knowledge,* and *destruction.*

1. Museum and archive storage have grown along with ever-evolving data storing capabilities. For the stored information to be usable, accessibility is key: searching the Internet requires not only an inquisitive mind but also tools such as search engines. The Internet, interpreted numerically, has surpassed what visionary engineer and inventor Vannevar Bush conceived of as humanity's cultural memory with his hypothetical "memex" machine as early as 1945. Similar to the Internet and the cloud, Bush's "memex is a device in which an individual stores all his books, records, and communications, and which is mechanized so that it may be consulted with exceeding speed and flexibility. It is an enlarged intimate supplement to his memory" and, thus, "frees" him for other activities.[5] In Bush's vision, collecting is outsourced to a device that stores all of one's information.

2. To access the modern rendering of Bush's "memex" storage—the Internet—collectors pay a price: that of being collected. Search engines generate profits by selling individualized data packages to advertisers. Companies such as Google and many others need to "know" their users. User data is the Internet's currency, users' attention its principle, and changes in user behavior its endgame.[6] In this context, "collecting" means "compiling through surveillance." Large amounts of individual data are compiled in order to to improve the ability of artificial intelligence (AI) to anticipate and influence our actions, acquisitions, and communications.[7] However, programmed to increase efficiency and profitability,

---

5    Vannevar Bush, "As We May Think," *Atlantic* (July 1945), www.theatlantic.com/magazine/archive/1945/07/as-we-may-think/303881/.

6    See Jaron Lanier, *Who Owns the Future?* (New York: Simon & Schuster, 2014); Tim Wu, *The Attention Merchants: The Epic Scramble to Get inside our Heads* (New York: Knopf, 2017).

7    Hector Postigo, *The Digital Rights Movement* (Cambridge, MA, and London: MIT Press, 2012); Wendy Brown, *Undoing the Demos: Neoliberalism's Stealth Revolution* (New York: Zone Books, 2015).

different forms of artificial intelligence are no less biased than the algorithms by which their creators breathed life into them.[8] In a digital environment, collectors, i.e., those who intentionally select items and assign a new meaning to them, have become desired objects themselves and contribute, even if only inadvertently, to the collection of data and the increasing revenue that catapulted technology corporations to the top of the most valuable worldwide.

3.  Algorithms are sequences of computable instructions that we perceive on screen: to name just one example, they might be in the form of illuminated pixels that visualize what lies dormant on hard drives and in the cloud. Accordingly, digital objects are said to be representations of mathematical procedures, but what exactly is represented and thus what we catch sight of remains unclear. Is what we see on screen a visual representation of a hidden code; is the actual code a representation of that which can be seen on screen; or does that which is seen on screen represent a physical object somewhere else? Digital objects, say, a photo of Pieter Bruegel the Elder's *Netherlandish Proverbs* (1559) are editable and distributable reproductions, or, more precisely, streams of bits that are simultaneously unique and themselves reproducible by the millions. Originality no longer seems to be a defining category for digital objects. Instead, collectors seek their objects' authentication—a process of ascribing the status of uniqueness. NFTs are such objects: in essence innumerably reproducible and yet at the same time encrypted through blockchain technology and, thus, unique. Most digital objects lack authentication. Although these objects may be considered "original," they can still be reproduced, with each reproduction being indistinguishable from one another and, hence, identical. Such digital objects do not require an empirical, tangible equivalent or a retractable source (unless they are NFTs that seek authentication on purpose). Consequently, objects change their nature once translated into numbers and so do their collecting institutions as agents that operate in both a physical and a virtual state.

---

8    Cailin O'Connor and James Owen Weatherall, *The Misinformation Age: How False Beliefs Spread* (New Haven, CT: Yale University Press, 2019); Cathy O'Neil, *Weapons of Math Destruction: How Big Data Increases Inequality and Threatens Democracy* (New York: Crown, 2016); Virginia Eubanks, *Automating Inequality: How High-Tech Tools Profile, Police, and Punish the Poor* (New York: St. Martin' 2017).

4.  Overshadowed by AI's analytical skills, the rapidity with which new technologies such as quantum computation produce results, and the ruthlessness of the exploitative practices of "surveillance capitalism," our understanding of knowledge is significantly altered if computation is the predominant tool of scientific exploration and economic evaluation.[9] Whereas critical analysis, self-evaluation, and emotional intelligence conventionally define knowledge, our understanding of this concept is no longer separated from the output of self-learning machine intelligence. Throughout the history of collecting, collectors were learned individuals whose "system of objects"[10] informed their selection, acquisition, and ordering of new goods. With every object, the range of knowledge increased. Breakthroughs in digital data processing during the last third of the twentieth century finally helped probability and statistical expertise to gain in prominence and secure a leading position in knowledge production.

5.  Destruction is the antagonist of all collecting archives, analog and digital alike. Indeed, the preservation of digital objects faces constant threats: hacking, data corruption, and ultimately system failure may lead to an irretrievable loss of data. Such moments of data destruction undermine any effort to salvage digital mediums that are far less reliable than, say, paper, papyrus, and stone. And whereas physical collections of objects may survive hundreds, maybe even thousands of years, destruction is the constant companion of digital collections.

## Storage

In recent decades, philosophers and scholars described "collecting" as an innate, anthropological feature of humanity,[11] emphasized its relation to religious rituals,[12] portrayed the collector as driven by passion

---

9    Shoshana Zuboff, *The Age of Surveillance Capitalism: The Fight for a Human Future at the New Frontier of Power* (New York: PublicAffairs, 2019).

10    Jean Baudrillard, *The System of Objects*, trans. James Benedict (London: Verso, 2005).

11    Manfred Sommer, *Sammeln: Ein philosophischer Versuch* (Frankfurt am Main: Suhrkamp, 1999).

12    Krzysztof Pomian, *Collectors and Curiosities: Paris and Venice, 1500–1800*, trans. Elizabeth Wiles-Portier (Cambridge: Polity, 1990), 13: "Our museums owe their name to the ancient temples of the Muses . . . Once the object crossed the threshold of the sacred enclosure, it entered into a domain which was strictly opposed to utilitarian activities."

and desire,[13] showed the interplay of market mechanisms and psychological dispositions that surface in every collection,[14] and focused on the origins of collecting rather than its future.[15] But few considered the all-encompassing changes that the arrival of the Internet and an increase of storage capacity generated (see Peter M. McIsaac in this volume pertaining to changes in collecting institutions' exhibition practices due to ever-changing technological advances).[16] Before the turn of the millennium, Tim Berners-Lee's proposition of the World Wide Web project in 1989[17] and its physical introduction in 1990 with a browser of the same name[18] took off and was soon the all-in-one social, scientific, and economic magic orb. This was the time when another form of collecting would take shape, namely the amassing of data. An unfathomable increase in storage capacity made it possible for Internet corporations to begin to amass data for future use.

Parallel to their data sales to advertisers, companies such as Google, Apple, and Amazon offer cloud storage for an ever-increasing amount of data. The storage capacities offered by data storage centers will keep growing at an exceedingly rapid pace, along with revenues.[19] The growth of storage—a word that is derived from Latin *instaurare* = "to set up, renew,

---

13   See Werner Muensterberger, *Collecting: An Unruly Passion. Psychological Perspectives* (San Diego: Harcourt, Brace, 1994).

14   See Baudrillard, *The System of Objects.*

15   Anke te Heesen, *The World in a Box: The Story of an Eighteenth-Century Picture Encyclopedia*, trans. Ann M. Hentschel (Chicago: University of Chicago Press, 2002); Philipp Blom, *To Have and to Hold: An Intimate History of Collectors and Collecting* (Woodstock: Overlook, 2004); James Delburgo, *Collecting in the World: Hans Sloane and the Origins of the British Museum* (Cambridge, MA.: The Belknap Press of Harvard University Press, 2017); Oliver Impey and Arthur MacGregor, *The Origins of Museums: The Cabinet of Curiosities in Sixteenth- and Seventeenth Century Europe* (Oxford: Ashmolean Museum and University of Oxford, 2017); George H. Schwartz, *Collecting the Globe: The Salem East India Marine Society Museum* (Amherst: University of Massachusetts Press, 2020).

16   Boris Groys offers some of the earliest and to this day most profound considerations on the impact of digital technology on collecting, for example in *Logik der Sammlung: Am Ende des musealen Zeitalters* (Munich: Hanser, 1997).

17   CERN, "Tim Berners-Lee's proposal," http://info.cern.ch/Proposal.html.

18   Tim Berners-Lee, "The WorldWideWeb Browser," www.w3.org/People/Berners-Lee/WorldWideWeb.html.

19   Storage was expected to grow from 880 exabytes in 2016 to an estimated 2,300 exabytes in 2021 (with one exabyte equaling one billion gigabytes), see Statista, "Data Storage Capacity Worldwide from 2016 to 2021, by Segment" (March 2018), www.statista.com/statistics/638593/worldwide-data-center-storage-capacity-cloud-vs-traditional/. During roughly the same time period, profit margins were projected to rise from $130.1 billion in 2016 to an estimated $274.3 billion in 2022; see Statista, "Revenue from Big Data and Business

restore" and Old French *estorer* = "to build, erect, reconstruct"—comes with an increased flow of revenue which is topped only by the flow of information itself. This flow of information is captured by words that otherwise would not have entered the public consciousness and which do not adequately illustrate the extent of computable mathematical equivalents and what they mean in daily operations—tera- ($10^{12}$), peta- ($10^{15}$), exa- ($10^{18}$), zetta- ($10^{21}$), and yottabyte ($10^{24}$). The amount of information that was transmitted worldwide reached an estimated 2.8 zettabytes in 2002, surpassed 30 zettabytes in 2019,[20] and will grow to 160 zettabytes in 2025.[21]

The ongoing race to create the fastest and most powerful computer worldwide, with Fujitsu's Fugaku currently leading,[22] will soon prove to be futile if predictions of engineers are correct and a recently introduced type of computational technology becomes more widely available, overcoming current cost and logistical limitations. The next generation of computers will not need to default to either 0 or 1 in their basic processing operations but will consider both options at the same time. Rather than abiding by the laws of mathematics, these quantum computers will follow the laws of physics. "Superposition," the simultaneous representation of quantum states, and "quantum entanglement," the interdependence of a pair or group of particles once separated or put into relation to each other, are the dominant factors of quantum computing:

> Quantum computers aren't just about doing things faster or more efficiently. They'll let us do things that we couldn't even have dreamed of without them. Things that even the best supercomputer just isn't capable of . . . Quantum computers will find a use anywhere where there's a large, uncertain[,] complicated system that needs to be simulated. That could be anything from predicting the financial markets to improving weather forecasts, modeling the behavior of

---

Analytics Worldwide from 2015 to 2022" (April 2019), www.statista.com/statistics/551501/worldwide-big-data-business-analytics-revenue/.

20  BBC, "Byte-Sized Graphic Guide to Data Storage" (2013), www.bbc.com/future/article/20130621-byte-sized-guide-to-data-storage.

21  David Rynsel, John Gantz, and John Rydning, "The Digitization of the World: From Edge to Core," in *Data Age 2025*, ed. Seagate, November 2018, www.seagate.com/files/www-content/our-story/trends/files/idc-seagate-data-age-whitepaper.pdf.

22  Don Clark, "Japanese Supercomputer Is Crowned World's Speediest," *New York Times* (June 22, 2020), www.nytimes.com/2020/06/22/technology/japanese-supercomputer-fugaku-tops-american-chinese-machines.html?searchResultPosition=1.

individual electrons, or using quantum computing to understand quantum physics.[23]

Although not yet widely in use, quantum computers are used to develop new material, anticipate complicated chemical reactions, set standards in cryptography, and develop new products—"from new materials for batteries in electric cars, through to better and cheaper drugs, or vastly improved solar panels."[24] Google currently uses quantum computers to model artificial intelligence—with outcomes that no human brain could understand or recreate, a phenomenon known as "quantum supremacy."[25] The tremendous acceleration of processing speed will doubtlessly change the way data is collected. Quantum computers—ones that already exist as well as those that will soon be built—process vast amounts of data in a fraction of time compared to conventional computers. With increasing processing speed, statistical operations will likely expand the range of applications. Once-dormant data will serve a functional purpose and thus will no longer receive its meaning from the "collection"; such data, according to our definition, will not be "collected" any longer, but instead will be amassed, mined, retrieved, and, most importantly, created.

Parallel to the development of super- and quantum computers, the search for new solutions to store vast amounts of data is inevitable and will likely impact what is still referred to "data collecting." Scientists predict that DNA will be the key to maintaining and retrieving information in the future. With four rather than two options compared to traditional computational systems—the nucleobases cytosine (C), guanine (G), adenine (A), and thymine (T)—the polynucleotide acid chain in form of a double-helix "stands out as an especially attractive alternative [to established storage technologies]. For example, using DNA for data storage offers density of up to $10^{18}$ bytes per $mm^3$, approximately six orders of magnitude denser than the densest media available today. The sheer density also facilitates preservation of the data in molecules for long periods of time at low energy costs."[26] Considering the half-life of DNA of 521 years, DNA

---

23  Amit Katwala, "Quantum Computers Will Change the World (If They Work)," *Wired*, (March 5, 2020), www.wired.co.uk/article/quantum-computing-explained.

24  Amit Katwala, "Quantum Computers."

25  Edwin Pednault, John Gunnels & Dmitri Maslov, and Jay Gambetta, "On Quantum Supremacy," *IBM Research Blog* (October 21, 2019), www.ibm.com/blogs/research/2019/10/on-quantum-supremacy/.

26  Luis Ceze, Jeff Nivala, and Karin Strauss, "Molecular Digital Data Storage Using DNA," *Nature Reviews Genetics* 20 (May 8, 2019), www.nature.com/articles/s41576-019-0125-3. In 2016, Microsoft, together with researchers at the University of Washington, introduced a fully automated DNA storage device—a milestone for the proliferation and commercial use of DNA storage. See

lasts much longer than any known digital medium, particularly if the fast reproduction cycle of new technologies is taken into account. Scholars estimate that frozen DNA might persist for thousands of years and, as a result, would easily surpass the durability of paper and be comparable only to one other "old" storage medium: stone. The lack of durability of current digital storage technology is a major obstacle for preservation in libraries and archives and a reason for their ongoing skepticism about fully digital holdings (see below under "Destruction and Preservation"). Indeed, not only the durability, but also the density of DNA storage is extraordinary: "Capable of storing 215 petabytes (215 million gigabytes) in a single gram of DNA, the system could, in principle, store every bit of datum ever recorded by humans in a container about the size and weight of a couple of pickup trucks."[27] The content of this storage would dwarf every individual "collection" of data and each person's homegrown archive. At the same time, the seeming abundance of storage is rapidly outstripped by the ever-growing production of information that would be needed to be categorized, indexed, and made accessible.[28]

What seems to be an infinite increase of data transmission speed and the amount of storage is ultimately limited to natural resources. Both the Internet and the cloud require a "physical infrastructure consisting of phone lines, fiber optics, satellites, cables on the ocean floor, and vast warehouses filled with computers, which consume huge amounts of water and energy and reside within national and legal jurisdiction."[29] Data is neither "the new oil"[30]—although data's exploitation, like oil, contributes

---

Jennifer Langston, "With a 'Hello,' Microsoft and UW Demonstrate First Fully Automated DNA Data Storage," *Microsoft Innovation Stories* (March 21, 2019), https://news.microsoft.com/innovation-stories/hello-data-dna-storage/. Shortly after, Yaniv Erlich and Dina Zielinski from the New York Genome Center registered a breakthrough in the algorithmic transmission of binary code to DNA format and vice versa—an important step to connect existing with a developing technology, see Yaniv Erlich and Dina Zielinski, "DNA Fountain Enables a Robust and Efficient Storage Architecture," *bioRxiv* (December 7, 2017), www.biorxiv.org/content/10.1101/074237v4.

27  Robert F. Service, "DNA Could Store All the World's Data in One Room," *Science* (March 2, 2017), www.sciencemag.org/news/2017/03/dna-could-store-all-worlds-data-one-room.

28  César Hidalgo, *Why Information Grows: The Evolution of Order, from Atoms to Economies* (New York: Basic Books, 2017).

29  James Bridle, *New Dark Age: Technology and the End of the Future* (London and New York: Verso, 2019), 7.

30  Clive Humby, a mathematician and entrepreneur, famously stated in 2006 that "data is the new oil," further describing it as raw material that needs refinement: see Michael Palmer, "Data is the New Oil," *ANA Marketing Maestros*, blog (November 2006), https://ana.blogs.com/maestros/2006/11/data_is_the_new.html.

to the emission of greenhouse gases—nor should the cloud be seen as an immaterial sphere, as much as its figurative description suggests the opposite (see Edward Dawson's considerations in this book on the physical aspects of data collecting). The metaphor "cloud" dismisses the material nature of information transmission and evokes instead an elevated "location" of knowledge where divine beings reside, surrounded by an air of impenetrability and protected by mysticism: no one knows what could be found within the cloud, but everyone could potentially visit and access its vast pool of information. Yet the cloud remains conspicuously mundane despite its undeniably useful and permanently expanding storage offerings. Its only "secret" is the unparalleled amount of information that it harbors and, in theory, makes accessible. While the network that forms the cloud could serve as the "most advanced, civilisation-scale tool for introspection our species has built thus far," dealing with this network means to step into a "Borgesian infinite library and all the inherent contradictions contained within it: a library that will not converge and continually refuses to cohere."[31]

Often cited by media theorists, Jorge Luis Borges's novella *The Library of Babel* (1941) is understood today as an allegorical anticipation of what is now known as the Internet and the cloud. Borges describes the universe itself as "composed of an indefinite, perhaps infinite number of hexagonal galleries" (113) of books that contain each and every bit of information: "For every rational line of forthright statement there are leagues of senseless cacophony, verbal nonsense, and incoherency" (114). The sheer amount of information necessarily remains unintelligible and indecipherable. Having *all* information within reach is as good as having *none*. No longer could we count on web search engines to actually "find" information. In a scenario of ubiquitous and all-encompassing availability of data, "collecting" information would necessarily be indistinguishable from "producing" information: the very act of collecting in a digital environment is an act of composition and re-composition of data for different purposes (Nikolaus Wegmann offers insights into analog/digital knowledge production in this volume). Each search online amounts to the creation of information. Every search result is generated by a new prompt, channeling electronic impulses in altering variations and constellations. Search engines are intrinsically performative in that they feed information about the search itself back into new searches and thus modify the results with new input and additional energy. Information (or its raw material: data) is by no means "retrieved," "extracted," "mined," or "harvested," as the most common entrepreneurial metaphors suggest, but generated.

---

31   Bridle, *New Dark Age*, 249.

## Collecting and Being Collected

"Collecting" data and information is the result of creating and performing—rather than intentionally selecting, acquiring, and arranging—objects that are disassociated from their former context and receive new meaning through the collection. Objects that are collected in a digital environment ultimately consist of data and information. In opposition to its daily linguistic application as a "mass-noun used to denote any amount of data,"[32] information connotes an aggregate state that is different from that of data. Information is selected, processed, and organized data. Accordingly, data should be deemed "raw" and "given," quite in sync with its etymological origin from the Latin past participle *datum*=that which is given[33] and its infinitive *dare*="to give." Broadly speaking, "data" denotes a given fact as the basis for calculation in mathematical operations. Euclid uses the notion *dedomena* (Δεδομένα) to propose the solution of 94 geometrical problems, all of which start with "given that" in a book with the same title (*Dedomena*, c. 300 BCE, or *Data* in its Latin version). Dedomena has a "proto-epistemic" gist, "that is, data before they are epistemically interpreted. As 'fractures in the fabric of being' they can only be posited as an external anchor of our information, for dedomena are never accessed or elaborated independently of a *level of abstraction*."[34] To "abstract" data derives from the scientific custom of observation, suggesting that nature's "truths" always include a subjective perspective. It does not come as a surprise that the word "data" gained prominence during a phase of breakthroughs in mathematics during the mid-twentieth century, which led to the emergence of a variety of theories that sought to distinguish data as mere numerical "facts" from "information" as a descriptor of the way data, now as a mass noun, turns into valuable intelligence, particularly in the emerging fields of information technology and media studies. The conflation of data and information, as understandable as it is misleading, disguises the complex levels of sophistication when dealing with information. To this day, several theories of "information" compete and are dependent on the context in which the notion is used. Generally, information can be understood as processed data, while processing data (i.e., filtering, selecting, organizing) serves

---

32 Pieter Adriaans, "Information," in *Stanford Encyclopedia of Philosophy* (Spring 2019), ed. Edward N. Zalta, https://plato.stanford.edu/entries/information/.

33 In German, *Datum* designates what is commonly referred to in English as "date" such as in the precise day of a year, hence, that "which is given" in numerical terms regarding a calendar.

34 Luciano Floridi, "Semantic Conceptions of Information," in *Stanford Encyclopedia of Philosophy* (Spring 2019), ed. Edward N. Zalta, https://plato.stanford.edu/entries/information-semantic/#1.3.

the reduction of uncertainty. Although following the doctrine of objectivity based on mathematical logic, information maintains a considerable subjective component. Probability, uncertainty, and a subjective element in mathematical calculations are key features of Claude Shannon and Warren Weaver's information theory, which heavily builds on the concept of entropy. Shannon explains complexity reduction through negative exclusion; "meaning" does not exist in his equation. Rather, information is not simply what is transmitted, but only that which is "unlikely" to appear as a result of said transmission and hence "new" in opposition to that which can probably be expected in a certain set of data. Entropy, a principle that is codified in the Second Law of Thermodynamics and applied in Shannon and Weaver's *Mathematical Theory of Information* (1948/49),[35] indicates a tendency of permanent diffusion of particles in a system, with high entropy equaling low energy and high likelihood, whereas low entropy equals high energy and low likelihood. Shannon's concept of binary code, based on the rules of statistical probability, guarantees an efficient and fast transfer of information. What is "probable," then, may be neglected as "noise"—another important conceptual part of Shannon and Weaver's theory. The likelihood of "redundant" organized data, however, only comes at the price of what psychologists, sociologists, and behavioral economists call "cognitive" or "information bias," that is, subjective attempts to reduce uncertainty through a distinct attachment to what an individual already knows. Information bias enters Shannon's mathematical model through logarithms (to capture probability) and algorithms (to compute data according to a stringent set of logical operations) in order to process information independent of "content" and "meaning." The subjective factor in Shannon's equation remains an unknown variable.

Yet this unknown variable is already built in when programmers use algorithms and imbue them with their subjective views, whether they are scientists or employees of tech corporations. Considering the role of digital technology in an economic environment where tech companies are the most valuable in the world, most algorithms are clearly created around neoliberal principles. Efficiency, profitability, deregulation, and the formation of monopolies are given priority in the coding of wealth-generating computer programs. Such algorithms treat personal data like a common good, similar to air and water, profit from its use, but do not share the gains with those who created such data. Efficiency is attained by the size of the processing power and an infrastructure that is guarded from

---

35  Claude Shannon, "A Mathematical Theory of Communication," *Bell System Technical Journal* 27, no. 3 (1948): 379–423; and Claude Shannon and Warren Weaver, *The Mathematical Theory of Communication* (Urbana: University of Illinois Press, 1949).

others (except when they pay for it), profitability is at the core of turning alleged "raw material" (unclaimed data) into financial gain, deregulation is the basis for tech corporations to stake out their operating area, and monopolies are the ultimate shield against competition and government intervention. Companies such as Google and Facebook use algorithms to "extract" (that is, produce) personal data and to analyze it with high accuracy. "Predictive analytics" not only allows machines to determine individuals' political, religious, culinary, aesthetic, and sexual preferences, their race, gender, and consumer behavior, and their location, driving patterns, and family connections; algorithms also readily anticipate our very actions and place the products we are supposed to want right in front of our eyes.[36] The scandal around Cambridge Analytica's illegal usage of personal information from 50 million Facebook users in an attempt to manipulate voters in the 2016 US election is but one example of companies that exploit our fascination with and indiscriminate use of technology. Combined with facial recognition software—routinely used by Facebook to create additional information about the habits and behaviors of its users—and other forms of data "collecting," for example through so-called cookies, the Internet has turned as much into a marketplace as it is a control and policing instrument.[37] Collectors—those who created their own profiles on any given social media platform (and that is almost all of us) with, for example, personal pictures and files—have become collectibles whose data is assembled and processed in real time. The conflation of data and information begins with the biased use of mathematical "facts" (Euclid). It is not easy to decide where data is still factual and where it is not already processed and, hence, information (Shannon).

Biases are amplified by self-learning algorithms such as in artificial intelligence—with consequences in the real world where jobs, loans, or benefits may be hard to come by. Shoshana Zuboff created the notion of "surveillance capitalism" to describe the exploitation of personal data to maximize corporate profit, the elimination of privacy standards, and the wealth gap between today's information elite and an excluded majority of users who are deprived of their rights and separated from any surplus that their own data generates:

---

36 More on the role of algorithms can be found in, among others, Ed Finn, *What Algorithms Want: Imagination in the Age of Computing* (Cambridge, MA: MIT Press, 2017); Terrence J. Sejnowski, *The Deep Learning Revolution* (Cambridge, MA: MIT Press, 2018).

37 See, for example, Seb Franklin, *Control: Digitality as Cultural Logic* (Cambridge, MA: MIT Press, 2015). Similarly, Zygmunt Bauman and David Lyon describe the temptation of permanent observation through technological devices, *Liquid Surveillance: A Conversation* (Cambridge: Polity, 2013).

Surveillance capitalism commandeered the wonders of the digital world to meet our needs for effective life, promising the magic of unlimited information and a thousand ways to anticipate our needs and ease the complexities of our harried lives. We welcomed it into our hearts and homes with our own rituals of hospitality . . . Under this new regime, the precise moment at which our needs are met is also the precise moment at which our lives are plundered for behavioral data, and all for the sake of others' gain. The result is a perverse amalgam of empowerment inextricably layered with diminishment. In the absence of a decisive societal response that constrains or outlaws this logic of accumulation, surveillance capitalism appears poised to become the dominant form of capitalism in our time.[38]

In the Western world and many rising economies, digital technology and the use of the Internet are inescapable even for those who have limited access. Legal procedures, job applications, and money transfers often rely on such technology. Every action online produces data that is instantly analyzed and added to the user profile information (UPI) of each person who ever accessed the Internet. Gatekeepers "collect" data with great purposefulness; users hand their personal data over, more often involuntarily than not. The alleged sharing of information, that is, its exploitation, exposes the ambiguous meaning of "data collecting" itself. Under the conditions of machine-driven analytics, "collecting" has become a denomination that substitutes the economic realities of an uncompromising bargain with the false image of a leisurely activity to express one's personality. However, where information is produced by tech corporations based on data that belongs to others, individuals have more to lose than to gain upon accessing the Internet: every "find" in an online search produces revenue for others (see Roberto Simanowski and Douglas C. Schmidt on surveillance capitalism in this volume).

The connection of economic interests and collecting is not new, although it is magnified in a digital environment. In his book *Collecting in a Consumer Society* (1995), Canadian economist Russell W. Belk details the concurrent rise of the museum and department store alongside increasingly refined techniques of exhibition. Both the museum and the department store competed with traditional locales of exhibition, for example, religious sites such as churches, for attention: "Early department stores have been called cathedrals, temples, dreamworlds, and palaces of consumption. They extend the lavish display and magical atmosphere of the exposition to everyday consumer goods and the simultaneous development of these two forms of spectacle involved imitation in both

---

38  Zuboff, *The Age of Surveillance Capitalism*, 53.

directions."[39] Collecting is an economic transaction, one that requires collectors to pay a monetary equivalent for a commodity that is deemed valuable in a competitive market: "It is no accident that auctions are a popular means of selling collectibles, for nowhere else is this competitive spirit likely to be more of a public spectacle and lead 'many collectors to abandon logical decisions and self-restraint in favor of competition and, not inconceivably, exhibitionistic grandeur.'"[40] What consumer goods and collectibles share is that they are on display. Typical locales for displaying goods and collectibles are, besides auctions and department stores as mentioned above, museums, private collections, and fairs.[41] Commonly, those who are interested in goods and collectibles must visit these locales. However, in a digital environment, this scenario is turned inside out: digital objects "move" on screens while "visitors" remain tied to their place in front of a two-dimensional surface and become themselves objectified "goods" in a market of surveillance. The screen has taken on the function of a showcase in a museum or a department store. Not only do "visitors" of online museum pages contemplate what they see, but they are being observed by the museum in the sense that their data is collected through cookies. What is on screen is only a fraction of what happens underneath the surface: what we see on display is secretly ordered through tags that are embedded in codes and prompted by computational operations. In a digital environment, not everyone is a collector, but everyone's data is collected.

## Original, Reproduction, and Copy

Behind each collection is the desire to liberate objects from their fraying daily use and to transfer them into a permanent state, Aleida Assmann claims. The collected object would be the "exception" that offers a glimpse at that which is absent and forever lost.[42] (On the connection of memory and collecting see Clifford Anderson in this volume.) Objects, according to this definition, are figurative in the sense of ancient rhetoric. Their "language" is not different from the symbolic linguistic tools of

---

39  Russell W. Belk, *Collecting in a Consumer Society* (London: Routledge, 1995), 18.

40  Belk, *Collecting in a Consumer Society*, 68 (with reference to Muensterberger, *Collecting*, 247).

41  In some cases, scarcity itself is used to appeal to customers/collectors, for example through the production of limited-edition "collector's items."

42  Aleida Assmann, "Sammeln, Sammlungen, Sammler," in *Erleben, Erleiden, Erfahren: Die Konstitution sozialen Sinns jenseits instrumenteller Vernunft*, ed. Kay Junge, Daniel Suber, and Gerold Gerber (Bielefeld: transcript, 2008), 345–53, here 345.

communication. Institutions of collecting capture their meaning and treat each object as a synecdoche—a figure of speech in which a part stands for an entirety. The "pars pro toto" referentiality of an object is of transcending allure to the observer who, through the setting of the institution—be it a museum, a gallery, an archive, or a library—is aware of the object's peculiarity. Undeniably, the object's *raison d'être* is its representational nature in those locales. This is most obvious in artworks. With the rare exception of art that is produced solely for the pleasure of production, only to end up in a drawer or be destroyed afterwards, artworks are produced to be shown, most as designer goods to accentuate an interior design, few solely for the purpose of being, one day, exhibited in a museum, thus representing the entirety of what Pierre Bourdieu calls the "field of cultural production."[43] Uniqueness, in that sense, is as artificial as it is an abstract concept, one that can be better understood, as another French theorist, Jean Baudrillard, claims, if we consider the interdependence of series and exclusivity. Unknowingly, Baudrillard foreshadows the meaning of seriality for digital objects.[44] It is in no small part owing to the concept of seriality in relation to a perceived uniqueness that we can distinguish empirical from digital objects.

Digital objects do not represent the empirical world but instead refer to a numerical formula, Lev Manovich argues.[45] They exist as code and materialize because of prompts that enable electrical impulses to run through computer hardware and, if it is the built-in design of a digital object, to charge pixels on a screen. Pixels are the smallest physical parts and building blocks of images in a digital setting, standardized on a high-quality computer screen at a level of, for example, $1920 \times 1080 = 2{,}073{,}600$ pixels. Most people think of digital objects as visible elements much like the ones that populate computer games or websites, both of which require an interplay of numerous such objects at once. That they appear on screen is probably the most prominent feature of digital objects, but this feature is only one part of digital objects' manifold manifestations (on sound as a conceptual model for specific digital objects, see Rolf J. Goebel in this book). According to computer scientists, "object-oriented programming" develops data structures "consisting of a collection of appropriate variables." The product is a composition of mathematical procedures that belong to a specific class with "private instance variables,"

---

43   Pierre Bourdieu, *The Field of Cultural Production: Essays on Art and Literature*, ed. and introduced by Randal Johnson (New York: Columbia University Press, 1993), 29–73.

44   Baudrillard, *The System of Objects*, 100.

45   "A new media object can be described formally. For instance, an image or shape can be described using a mathematical function . . . A new media object is subject to algorithmic manipulation" and is, by definition, "*programmable*," Lev Manovich, *The Language of New Media* (Cambridge, MA: MIT Press 2001), 27.

with each class being defined by the "properties of the objects."[46] As a result, digital objects may not have visual qualities at all but instead simply reside within a code that is embedded in a larger mathematical design, that is, an algorithm.

A definition of a digital object as "numerical representation" (Manovich) may not sufficiently explain the difference between what is represented (invisible code, electric impulses, and illuminated pixels) and what materializes on screen as a stand-in for something else (a tree on a screen for the idea of trees, a specific tree, or a specific message such as a warning against deforestation). An example may demonstrate the issues that come with the concept of representation. A high-resolution digital photo of Caravaggio's *Judith Beheading Holofernes* (c. 1598–99 or 1602) would not fit the definition of a reproduction in the strict sense of the word. The painting is neither represented by the photo (because what we see on screen refers to a mathematical formula, as Manovich explains), nor is the photo, as a digital object, solely represented by its code (as to exceed Manovich's conclusion). Rather, the photo is first "translated" into a specific mathematical formula that can be archived or stored on a hard drive, flash drive, or in the cloud. To see the photo, its file would need to be opened by a prompt, and the consecutive mathematical formula (or: code) would then trigger electric impulses to visualize the photo through pixels. The photo of Caravaggio's painting is the result of a process whose potential is inscribed in code and stored on a computer to wait for its actualization. Each picture on screen is, as a condition of digital media, fleeting, instable or limited in time and space to wait for another actualization, possibly on a different computer. Much like the human memory evokes pictures of the past in one's current state of mind, mixed with the circumstances with which they are remembered, the digital photo is a new creation each time it is displayed on screen because the electric impulses that visualize the code are never exactly the same, irrespective of their similitude with former actualizations of the code (even if it were only the time or the location that would change). That is why even Caravaggio's painting, although the object itself appears to be the exact same artwork, constantly changes its meaning and hence its nature depending on its use in specific contexts, such as to show students an ideal of late Renaissance art or to accompany a Bible exegesis of the deuterocanonical book of Judith (13:7–9).

Since "representation" does not apply in connection with digital renderings of the empirical world, we can no longer consider digital objects as originals in the sense of one-time creations that transcend

---

46 Butterfield et al., "Object-oriented Programming," *A Dictionary of Computer Science*, www-oxfordreference-com.proxy.library.vanderbilt.edu/view/10.1093/acref/9780199688975.001.0001/acref-9780199688975-e-6550#.

what is represented due to their figurative meaning. They do not offer a glimpse into that which is absent and forever lost (Assmann) and are by no means a synecdoche, a "pars pro toto" illustration, but rather new creations that are triggered with each user prompt. The owner of an original Caravaggio painting may see different features represented in it. The painting appears as an original artwork. A digital object, in contrast, is "original" each time it is performed. As a result, the concept of originality is void of meaning, inaccurate at best and superfluous for the most part. Performing the same code with its electric impulses and computational processes, albeit in a uniquely new context each time it is performed, does not refer to an original, but to a multitude of originals, however different they may be. Collectors of digital objects do not collect "originals," but instead focus on their objects' authenticity. A digital object—that is, anything that is created within a digital environment and remains digital in essence, be it a photo, a text, a website, or a separately recognizable feature of a website—becomes authentic if a traceable numerical addendum completes the object's code. In this sense, we could understand digital objects with Jannis Kallinikos, Alexi Aaltonen, and Attila Marton as digitally created units that promote "editability, interactivity, openness, and distributedness."[47] At the same time, digital objects are indexed in such a way that their recognizability and authenticity is guaranteed.

The following may serve as an illustration: for librarians and archivists the distributivity and editability of digital objects poses problems as much as it opens up opportunities. From the standpoint of preservation, a copy that is indistinguishable from an "original" would be a nightmare and a blessing at once. What if an "original" document was edited and then reinjected into an archive or, as its largest iteration, the Internet itself? Readers and viewers may hardly see a difference, or they may quote from different versions of a text without knowing about the co-existence of, possibly, conflicting content. Art historians may interpret digital visual art differently according to their copy at hand. To guarantee the authenticity of a digital object, commonly with the purpose of its preservation, such an object needs to be made unique through a digital signature, a numerical key that would unmistakably clarify that it is what it claims to be. Only a digital signature assures that the origin, authorship, and editing of a

---

47    The authors suggest an arithmetic design of digital objects that would secure their authenticity and simplify their storage and indexicality. The ultimate goal, however, would be no less than an overhaul of the Internet's entire structure to eliminate corporate interests through search prompts and promote a free and fair distribution of objects beyond the goal of maximizing profit margins—a decidedly activist agenda of rather utopian scope. Jannis Kallinikos, Alexi Aaltonen, and Attila Marton, "A Theory of Digital Objects," *First Monday* 15, no. 6 (2010), https://journals.uic.edu/ojs/index.php/fm/article/download/3033/2564.

book are verifiable.[48] If such markers are in place, librarians and archivists no longer have to worry about physical copies, because digital versions (or: objects) could easily be distributed, not only among libraries but also among users. As addenda to an already existing code, such markers seem artificial though, established after the fact and created with the sole purpose of marking an object similar to an imprimatur. Nevertheless, digital signatures along with the now "legitimized" distribution of a near-infinite number of copies open up new opportunities and change the tasks of libraries and archives. Focusing on rare and unique books or specific areas of research might be a viable response to the deluge of information and rising number of circulating digital objects (see Michael Knoche in this volume). Libraries as well as archives have long since begun to reconceptualize themselves as service-oriented institutions and to occupy a strategic societal place in an environment of online learning, reading, viewing, and listening. They see themselves as a "mediator for search and access, but also for preparing information from databases and other resources."[49] Digitized material will likely surpass—in quantity—printed material and other tangible matter in the future even if, to give just one prominent example, of the 170 million objects that the Library of Congress now holds, only approximately 10 percent have so far been transformed into a computable format and, thus, become digital objects.

The Internet, a place for self-representation as much as it is a sphere of experimentation and commerce, supports an imagined uniqueness (Baudrillard) of digital objects in its own way. Every click on every website, every search, view, and action is observed by Internet corporations through log-in prompts and "cookies" and traced back to a computer's Internet Protocol (IP) address: "The Internet registers every moment when a certain piece of data is clicked on, liked, disliked, transferred or transformed. Accordingly, a digital image can never be merely copied (as an analogue, mechanically reproducible image can), but is always newly

---

48   Charles Cullen, "Authentication of Digital Objects: Lessons from a Historian's Perspective," in *Authenticity in a Digital Environment*, ed. Abby Smith (Arlington, TX: Council on Library and Information Resources, 2000), www.clir.org/pubs/reports/pub92/cullen/. Steven Conn presents a different approach to objects from the perspective of a critique of the changing role of museums, not the changing character of objects. Conn argues that events supplant experience and learning. He advocates for maintaining museums' traditional role of preserving and displaying physical objects. Conn, *Do Museums Still Need Objects?* (Philadelphia: University of Pennsylvania Press, 2010).

49   Veit Köppen, Department Head, IT-Applications, Otto-von-Guericke University, Magdeburg, quoted in *The End of Wisdom? The Future of Libraries in a Digital Age*, ed. David Baker and Wendy Evans (Amsterdam: Elsevier, 2017), 29.

staged or performed."[50] Unique as these activities may be, their meaning is lost in the sheer amount of Internet traffic. Artists, always ahead of markets and, thus setting the trend, have chosen two responses to escape what appears to be the conundrum of original and cópy, that is, that no "copies" exist in an environment that no longer recognizes "originals" (but only authentic/non-authentic, distributable objects). Many of them see the Internet as a site of documentation where the production of art merges with personal activities online (as Boris Groys argues in this volume) or they produce artworks that are specifically designed for an online art market.[51] While in 2018 the highest-priced artwork thus far was the virtual picture of a rose called *Forever Rose* that sold for $1 million, divided by ten different shareholders who each acquired 10 percent of the artwork, NFTs stand for a new chapter in collecting digital objects. Mike Winkelman, a South Carolina graphic designer who goes by his nom de plume, "Beeple," sold his work *Everydays: The First 5000 Days* at Christie's for $69.3 million.[52] Beeple's work is not only the most expensive NFT ever sold (and the most expensive digital artwork, too), but also the most expensive work ever sold by a living artist.

Collectibles based solely on blockchain technology, "a long cryptographically complex string of numbers and letters" and thus tradable solely in cryptocurrency, NFTs have become more than a trend. A playing card from a digital blockchain game—the Hyperion Mythic card—sold in the same year as the *Forever Rose* for almost 146 ethereum (or ETH, a blockchain currency that is frequently used in NFT transactions) which equaled at that time roughly $54,000.[53] Blockchain currencies are not subject to control by nation-states. They rely on acceptance by a wider community, but also seek authenticity through a unique digital signature (created by a large group of "signatories" for each blockchain unit). The process of authentication through the sheer number of individuals' digital consent guarantees their stability. Even though they exist only in a digital environment, their authentication has consequences in

---

50   Boris Groys, *In the Flow* (London: Verso, 2016), 185.

51   This online art market—one where art is produced digitally and also sold online—is not to be confused with an online marketplace where empirical objects are bought and sold online. According to the statistics web portal Statista, the value of the latter grew from $3.1 billion in 2013 to $12.4 billion in 2020. Statista, "Total Online Sales of the Art and Antiques Markets Worldwide from 2013 to 2020" (July 19, 2021), https://www-statista-com.proxy.library.vanderbilt.edu/statistics/886776/online-art-and-antiques-market-total-global-sales/.

52   Beeple shot pictures daily (= everydays) for 13 years and created an assemblage of these digital pictures that were sold as one lot at Christie's.

53   Zach Hines, "The Weird Wild and Expensive World of Blockchain Art," *engadget* (August 30, 2018), www.engadget.com/2018-08-30-cryptokitties-gods-unchained-blockchain-art.html.

non-digital contexts, because the authentication requires an enormous amount of energy.

Similar to cryptocurrencies, blockchain artworks are defined by their performative character much like any other digital object that is prompted to appear on screen; and as much as conventional money is based on the principle of artificial scarcity to avoid currency devaluation and, often hand in hand with it, an inflation of prices, digital artworks, too, rely on their limited distribution to maintain their value. For example, thirteen of the twenty most expensive NFTs are CryptoPunks,[54] a specific kind of algorithm-based art image that began to be offered by Larva Labs in New York in 2017. Limited in number and with proof of ownership that is stored on the ethereum blockchain, their verifiable scarcity sets their value on the digital marketplace. "CryptoPunk #7804, a computer-generated avatar of a teal-colored, pipe-smoking alien wearing a hat and sunglasses was sold on March 11, 2021 for 4,200 ethereum, which equates to approximately $7.5 million, setting a record for the highest amount paid for a punk as the digital collectibles marketplace continues its meteoric rise."[55] Whether their features are comparable to traditional artworks or not, the relative rarity of NFTs makes them highly attractive for collectors.

What distinguishes empirical from digital objects such as NFTs is the unique digital environment that requires a specific infrastructure and use of energy. More precisely, digital objects cannot actually be "found" in a collection. They are, in a more precise way, created with every prompt that makes them appear on screen. Accordingly, digital collections no longer consist of things but of numbers, patterns, and impulses. A collector of digital objects either holds the exclusive rights to use a code that transforms electricity into light and sound waves—while an artist certifies the artwork's origin and ownership by the buyer—or, in case of NFTs, a collector is registered as the authentic owner of a digital object with help of blockchain cryptography.

## Machine Intelligence and Human Culture

Digital technology has been used by collecting institutions for quite some time. Museums, libraries, and archives were among the first to benefit from processing and ordering large amounts of data through

---

54  Statista, "Most Expensive Non-Fungible Token (NFT) Sales Worldwide as of March 16, 2021," https://www-statista-com.proxy.library.vanderbilt.edu/statistics/1222113/top-nft-projects-worldwide/.

55  Tommy Beer, "Pipe-Smoking Alien CryptoPunk NFT Sells for $7.5 Million," *Forbes* (March 11, 2021), https://www.forbes.com/sites/tommybeer/2021/03/11/pipe-smoking-alien-cryptopunk-nft-sells-for-75-million/?sh=2236e8cd5c56.

new technological achievements. For Ross Parry the integration of digital technology in museums has become a historical fact, so much so that he assigns the notion of the "post-digital" to current museum practices, alluding to the all-pervasiveness of computation.[56] Accordingly, Haidy Geismar holds that digital objects should neither be defined by the idea of "immateriality," nor by such concepts as "abstraction, inauthenticity and sociality." From her anthropological perspective, the "dialogues between digital technologies and museum collections" reveal "how digital objects are used to constitute reality effects."[57] By exploring the transformative impact of actual experiences on museum visitors, Geismar even goes so far as to say that "*the digital does not exist* . . . Rather, by observing the digital as another kind of thing in the world, we may begin to understand how the digital encompasses a plethora of different representational forms, techniques and technologies that work in different ways to develop different kinds of object lessons."[58] Guided by a focus on "object lessons," that is, "arguments about the world made through things" that are "educational, performative and fundamentally material,"[59] her approach dismisses any distinction between material and immaterial, figurative and concrete, original and copy, or cause and impact. Quite in opposition to Geismar's alleged indifference of the digital and museum visitors to objects' digital nature, visitors are deeply affected by the digitization of objects—so much so that it is precisely the digital nature of some objects that attracts them to museums. Visitors' experiences greatly depend on information that is increasingly presented through screens and apps. Geismar admits that these "screens and apps render the collections that are scanned, augmented and socially framed more colourful, brighter, more tactile and more accessible than the same objects that lie still, either in their cases, hidden away with low lighting, or in the museum storerooms barely accessible to the public."[60] What she does not admit is that the same kind of enhanced object experience through digital media has become the main attraction for many museum-goers. Screens have turned into physical objects and apps into digital ones that are on display alongside traditional museum collectibles, as, for example, Gwyneira Isaac maintains.[61]

---

56  Ross Parry, "The End of the Beginning: Normativity in the Postdigital Museum," *Museum Worlds: Advances in Research* 1 (2013): 24–39.

57  Haidy Geismar, *Museum Object Lessons for the Digital Age* (London: UCL Press, 2018), 19.

58  Geismar, *Museum Object Lessons for the Digital Age*, 112 (italics in the original text).

59  Geismar, *Museum Object Lessons for the Digital Age*, XV.

60  Geismar, *Museum Object Lessons for the Digital Age*, 21.

61  Gwyneira Isaac, "Technology Becomes the Object: The Use of Electronic Media at the National Museum of the American Indian," *Journal of Material*

Technology corporations, like tech enthusiasts, expect consumer goods to become computing units that communicate with each other through the much-anticipated Internet of things (IoT). Once homes and cars, refrigerators and TV sets, toothbrushes and glasses are connected, the information that they gather is as important as their function in our everyday lives: to give shelter and to transport, to store food and to entertain, to attend to hygiene and to help us to see. In a world where every physical object is dominated by an algorithmic regime and co-exists next to its digital doppelganger, digital and physical objects depend on each other. Although Walter Benjamin knew that the "period, the region, the craftsmanship, the former ownership," in other words, "the whole background of an item adds up to a magic encyclopedia whose quintessence is the fate of [an] object,"[62] in a digital environment the collected object—whether digital or physical—is already viewed as information itself. Seen through the lens of machine intelligence, physical objects are but the result of a translation into numerical nomenclature and mathematical procedure. To humans, however, they are part of a "magic encyclopedia" because the commodities of digital labor, mediated through coding and technology, surface—much in the way Karl Marx describes commodities in general doing—as depersonalized forms of the social relations of production:

> The commodity form, and the value-relation of the products of labor within which it appears, have absolutely no connection with the physical nature of the commodity and the material relations arising out of this. It is nothing but the definite social relation between men themselves which assumes here, for them, the fantastic form of a relation between things. In order, therefore, to find an analogy we must take flight into the misty realm of religion. There the products of the human brain appear as autonomous figures endowed with a life of their own, which enter into relations both with each other and with the human race.[63]

To Marx, our quasi-religious relationship to *objects* (or: commodities) disguises social relationships. Similarly, and one step further, our quasi-religious relationship to *digital objects* disguises our relationship to the

---

*Culture* 13, no. 3 (2008): 287–310.

62  Walter Benjamin, "Unpacking My Library: A Talk about Collecting," in *Selected Writings*, vol. 2, 1927–34, ed. Michael W. Jennings, Howard Eiland, and Gary Smith, trans. Rodney Livingstone (Cambridge, MA: The Belknap Press of Harvard University Press, 1999), 486–93, here 487. Benjamin's essay first appeared on July 17, 1931, in vol. 7, no. 29 of *Die literarische Welt* (pages 3–5).

63  Karl Marx, *Capital*, vol. 1, trans. Ben Fowkes (Harmondsworth, UK: Penguin/New Left Review 1976), 165.

materiality of computation (hardware, electricity). While to Marx wage labor itself is a form of "fetishism" which is "inseparable from the production of commodities,"[64] we fetishize the devices that "charm" two-dimensional digital objects to appear before our eyes.

The mutually dependent relationship between human labor and machine intelligence increases in complexity if we take into account that the algorithms we create are self-learning and aim to change human behavior. This means that the more sophisticated computer networks become, the more we will develop behaviors these algorithms teach us; and the more feedback we provide, the more efficient AIs become in changing us even further. More specifically, media technology and its platforms not only sell human attention, as Tim Wu shows, but seek to change social behavior at large.[65] Social media companies as well as Internet providers collect behavioral data, feed algorithms, apply predictive analytics, and ultimately change the behavior of users with the purpose of creating product loyalty and dependency. Users become addicted through the pings and visual signals that indicate gains in social currency—"likes" of posts, pictures, or videos; received emails or text messages that underscore their status; promotions and "rewards" that enhance their connectivity, and "click-bait" that promises tremendous payoff. Devices that vibrate, blink, and beep, Internet pages that beam, light up, or display pop-up messages, are irresistible because they release the neurotransmitters dopamine and serotonin, commonly associated with motivational satisfaction, well-being, or "happiness." The unknown consequences of the introduction of a new technology with all of its benefits, but also with all its pitfalls and perils, led Nicholas Carr to wonder in what way the Internet is the setup for a neurological experiment that exploits the brain's neuroplasticity and results in the loss of critical thought.[66] Another way to assess the downside of digital technology is evident in the increasing number of related forms of addiction (for example, shopping addiction, gambling disorder, texting while driving, addiction to pornography, and so on).[67] Many individuals seem to have lost the ability to live without digital

---

64 Karl Marx, *Capital*, 165.

65 See Tim Wu, *The Attention Merchants*, and Jaron Lanier: *Ten Arguments for Deleting Your Social Media Accounts Right Now* (London: Picador, 2019).

66 Nicholas Carr, *The Shallows: What the Internet Is Doing to Our Brains* (New York: W. W. Norton, 2010), as well as *The Glass Cage: Automation and Us* (New York: W. W. Norton, 2014). Similarly critical is Evgeny Morozov, *To Save Everything, Click Here: The Folly of Technological Solutionism* (New York: PublicAffairs, 2013).

67 Cf. chapter 4, "Potential Negative Impact of Internet and Technology Use and Patterns of Use," in *The Oxford Handbook of Mental Health*, ed. Marc N. Potenza, Kyle A. Faust, and David Faust (New York: Oxford University Press, 2020), online.

devices, can hardly separate themselves from them, and may visit technology detox retreats.

Perhaps more important is the growing inability to distinguish valuable from valueless information on the Internet and to recognize credible and reject implausible sources of information. As a collection of information, the Internet as a whole can be seen in a tradition that delineates "collecting" as a precondition for knowledge production.[68] With information being an intentionally administered and curated commodity, the Internet should not be seen simply as a "vast repository of knowledge" that serves the enlightenment of humanity, but instead has become on many levels a means to redraw knowledge in the era of "post-truth" and "alternative facts." Machine intelligence, tainted by human biases, distributes messages tailored to further entrench individuals in their echo chambers. As the populace is unable to escape the relentless exposure to algorithms' quantitative assessment of human behavior, machine intelligence is already a danger to the *demos*, much in the way neoliberalism poses a threat to democracy.[69] Bridle highlights how governance is relegated to algorithms: "Reading a book, listening to music, researching and learning: these and many other activities are increasingly governed by algorithmic logics and policed by opaque and hidden computational processes. Culture is itself a code/space"—an environment inseparable from computation, augmentation, and manipulation.[70] What once, in the eyes of early Internet enthusiasts, seemed to promise a democratic model for the "sharing" of gained knowledge—a collection of everyone's wisdom about everything—has become a pool of information, brimming with product propaganda and conspiracy theories that dilute factual knowledge to a point that this knowledge seems insignificant. The forced retreat of quality gatekeepers—journalists, scientists, experts in all areas—has given rise to amateurs and dilettantes who promote opinions instead of facts, analyses, and expertise.[71]

Ardent defenders of the Internet's many undeniable advantages hold that collecting has always been a process of selection and that choosing information online is not different from selecting objects out of a reservoir of goods, even if the selection process is different and less cumbersome today in a digital environment than, say, during the mid-eighteenth century, when the catalog of Sir Hans Sloane's collection of around 200,000 pieces—"complete with large and exotic stuffed animals and

---

68   Anke te Heesen and E. C. Spary, "Sammeln als Wissen," in *Sammeln als Wissen: Das Sammeln und seine wissenschaftsgeschichtliche Bedeutung*, ed. Anke te Heesen and E. C. Spary (Göttingen: Wallstein, 2001), 7–21.

69   See Brown, *Undoing the Demos*.

70   Bridle, *New Dark Age*, 39.

71   Roberto Simanowski, *Stumme Medien: Vom Verschwinden der Computer in Bildung und Gesellschaft* (Berlin: Matthes & Seitz, 2018), 13–14.

entire boats"—surpassed forty volumes as early as 1742.[72] The use of a catalog of this size limits (quick) access to the objects themselves and, ultimately, to the knowledge that can be derived from the study of one of these objects. Today, the sheer size of the Internet requires a catalog that includes the World Wide Web, while the access to information necessarily depends on the functionality of this catalog. Search engines—run by algorithms that in equal parts offer information to their users and collect information about them—filter information through data processing. This form of computation primes any kind of knowledge that is to be gained from the Internet. Although knowledge is still the result of careful individual selection processes that rest upon analysis, critical inquiry, and emotional intelligence, the technology-based paradigm of "knowing" must take metrics into account. The capitulation to and reliance on metrics is mirrored in cultural debates, when "knowing" is said to be severed from humanistic traditions and is instead tied to economic principles that instrumentalize education as a means for commercial ends. Not critical analysis but practical education, not intelligence but efficiency, not empathy but profitability are its goals.

Indeed, knowledge may be seen as a problematic term itself. Despite its occasional overlap with information, the etymology of "knowledge" has to do with a) the capacity to discern, b) the perception of a thing or person, c) the potential to perceive or understand a truth or fact, and d) the ability to do something in a proper way ("know-how"). Like data and information, knowledge is a matter of scientific inquiry, captured in the subfield of epistemology, the science of what we know and why it is good to know (Plato), how we gain knowledge (John Locke), what restrains and conditions our knowledge (Immanuel Kant), and how knowledge relates to sensory experience (Bertrand Russell).[73] Epistemology is meta-knowledge that systematizes what we know, how we know, and what we sense through knowing. Creating artificial intelligence is the digital equivalent to epistemology, albeit with practical applications. The programming of AI requires a solid understanding of the ways knowledge is gained, to what purposes it is gained, and what applications it serves. In the near future, computing power, storage capacity, and programming expertise will allow us to design an artificial mind similar to a human's. In a growing number of areas—from e-commerce to medical diagnostics—AI is already indispensable. What has yet to be achieved by machine minds is the performing of critical inquiry and the use of emotional intelligence, both of which are crucial aspects of knowledge. Critical inquiry weighs

---

72    Blom, *To Have and to Hold*, 86 and 82.

73    Matthias Steup and Ram Neta, "Epistemology," in *The Stanford Encyclopedia of Philosophy* (Summer 2020 Edition), ed. by Edward N. Zalta, https://plato.stanford.edu/archives/sum2020/entries/epistemology/.

the pros and cons and applies multiple perspectives beyond mathematical logic before arriving at a conclusion. Emotional intelligence is needed to understand the motivation behind human actions and reactions. With the ability to inquire critically and to evaluate emotionally, machine intelligence will shift from being a set of logical algorithmic operations to a state of cognition, defined as the "action or faculty of knowing," and also, a state of self-awareness.[74] In such a state, the *amassing* and *production* of data will give way to *collecting* proper— that is, the intentional selection of like objects and the reassignment of meaning to such objects through their relationship to other objects in a collection. In other words, knowledge is a precondition of collecting, and collecting, in turn, increases knowledge. Without knowledge, an algorithm remains a mathematical operation, whereas knowledge generates intention and determines the meaning an object is assigned. While artificial intelligence might one day reach a state of cognition, self-learning algorithms process the information we have thus far produced in such a way that the steps from humans programming computers to computers programming themselves, from humans writing computer code to computers actively learning, from machine intelligence to machine consciousness increasingly push ethical boundaries. As soon as machines achieve knowledge and begin collecting for their own purposes—intentionally, selectively, and systematically— humans may be relegated to the status of mere observers.

## Preservation and Destruction

Traditionally, collecting was not only a matter of status, science, and education, but also, and often predominantly, of preservation. Preservation, derived from Old French and Medieval Latin, means to "keep something safe." Museums may have been safe houses for objects, but their collections were in part the result of destroying cultural sites and profiting from looting. The Louvre in Paris opened its doors in 1793 to display France's superior culture and later exhibited the "trophies" of Napoleon's victories over European nations. In the decades following the Louvre's opening, Jean-François Champollion, the renowned decoder of hieroglyphics and director of the Egyptian collection at the museum, assembled a rich array of 9,000 pieces in only five years, from monumental statues to reliefs, tombstones, and small fragments. Although much of the collection came from Napoleon's expedition to Egypt, many of Champollion's acquisitions were pieces from other collections such as those owned by Henry Salt, the British Consul of Egypt, or by Edme-Antoine Auguste Durand, a

---

74 "Cognition," *Oxford English Dictionary*, www.oed.com.

"collector-adventurer."[75] If artifacts were not directly "collected" through looting, then they were collected indirectly through traders, who made a fortune with stolen items, and, more importantly, through the exercise of colonial power. Colonial authorities often claimed sole possession of and jurisdiction over the cultural heritage in territories they occupied. Local authorities in Egypt were not able to establish cultural heritage laws until 1835 with a "Decree Banning the Unauthorized Removal of Antiquities of the Country."[76] Even today, though looting and smuggling have long since been banned, they remain rampant, and lead "to the loss of information about the source of antiquities" and of what antiquities reveal about past cultures.[77] Such is the relation of collecting and destroying that one cannot be separated from the other. Until 2000, most of the cultural objects offered at auction at Sotheby's and Christie's in London did not include provenance information. After heirs of valuable artworks—or sometimes national governments—began filing claims to have their property restored to them, museums began to demand information about artifacts' provenance. Most renowned collecting institutions, however, do not return artworks to their rightful owners or repatriate entire sections of their collections to a country voluntarily, which they justify with reference to complicated sale histories (even if looting often marks the beginning of such histories) or because they maintain that the objects would be best "kept safe" where they are—that is, preserved in a fashion that is deemed appropriate by the museum. After museums applied a Western concept of art and culture in a colonial setting for centuries, one way of reconciling property, provenance, and ethical issues would be to share preservation technology so that the artworks' countries of origin would be able to apply the highest standards of preservation once artworks are restored to them.

Western museums are eager to prove their undoubtedly impressive preservation expertise, for example through new digital technologies such as 3D scanning and printing. 3D scanners provide a precise numerical "cast" that can be stored and retrieved as needed. Should an object be reported lost or stolen, the digital file of an object would then allow a reproduction. In some cases, 3D models have been created from 2D photographs such as the Triumphal Arch of Palmyra (see Erin L. Thompson in this volume), a one-third scale replica that was conceived as a response

---

75   Sharon Waxman, *Loot: The Battle over the Stolen Treasures of the Ancient World* (New York: Times Books, 2008), 69–70.

76   International Council of Museums, "Red List of Egyptian Cultural Objects at Risk" (Paris, 2011), https://icom.museum/en/resources/red-lists/.

77   Erin L. Thompson, *Possession: The Curious History of Private Collectors from Antiquity to the Present* (New Haven and London: Yale University Press, 2016), 157.

to the destruction by terrorists of the ancient Palmyra site in Syria in 2015. The replica was unveiled in London and then shown almost exclusively in Western cities, with Dubai being the only exception. Aside from colonial undertones in this enterprise, digital technology poses its own ethical and philosophical challenges. Should 3D scanners and printers "produce" (not reproduce) objects that are more complete than what we have in museums, such as a copy of Alexandros of Antioch's famed *Venus de Milo* statue (originally made between 130 and 100 BCE) *with arms?* Can a 3D "image" ever replace the damaged "original"? And from the perspective of media theory, what would be the original: the destroyed object, the 3D print, the code that transmits the sequence for electronic impulses, or the impulses themselves?

3D printing makes the invisible visible—those elements of an object that were lost over time—but it also hides a past that is ingrained only in memory, patina, and environment, and, in many cases, a past that is irretrievably lost. Archaeology is a race against such loss. Faced with the possibility of utter destruction, private organizations, and governments, guided by archaeologists, deploy the most up-to-date technology to protect cultural and natural goods. At times, "apocalyptic collections"—a type of collection that is meant to save what is most valuable for cultural preservation for centuries or even millennia to come—originate from deep-seated fears of utter destruction. The conservationist Cary Fowler and the Consultative Group on International Agricultural Research (CGIAR) were behind the idea of building the Svalbard Global Seed Vault on the Arctic Island of Spitsbergen, Norway: "The purpose of the Vault is to store duplicates (backups) of seed samples from the world's crop collections." The proprietors deem the vault an "ultimate insurance policy for the world's food supply" and claim that "it will secure, for centuries, millions of seeds representing every important crop variety available in the world today. It is the final back up."[78] The vault serves as an analog equivalent of data storage with every sample of seeds providing DNA that could either be sequenced and artificially reproduced or directly used. Climate change sparked the idea of the vault's construction, and Spitsbergen was an ideal location because of rock and permafrost that would shield seed samples permanently from warm temperatures without much energy use. Despite these efforts, climate change may ultimately destroy the seed collection if no special measures are taken. Newspapers reported in May of 2017 that due to unusually heavy rain and the melting of permafrost, water had entered through the entrance area of the vault.

Another example of an apocalyptic collection is southwestern Germany's Barbarastollen. A former mine that extracted silver and other

---

78 Svalbard Global Seed Vault, mission statement of Crop Trust, www.croptrust.org/our-work/svalbard-global-seed-vault/.

ores, it stored its first metal container of microfilm in 1975. At the height of the Cold War, the West German government decided it was time to protect the treasures of German culture against total destruction and to copy all that was deemed valuable for future generations.[79] Among those treasures are, for example, manuscripts of the most renowned German writers and composers such as Johann Wolfgang Goethe and Johann Sebastian Bach, a document of Charlemagne in favor of Saint Emmeram's Abbey from 794, the crowning documents of Otto the Great from 936, the Papal *Bulla Aurea* (1356), the building plans of the Cologne Cathedral, and—not to judge history through censorship—Adolf Hitler's letter of appointment to the position of Reichskanzler from January 30, 1933. In 2009, over 900,000,000 pictures were captured on 29,400 kilometers of microfilm. In 2010, a new synthetic film technology was introduced that is more durable and allows the pictures to be made in color. Ironically, it was not until 2016 that the German Constitution (*Grundgesetz*) found its way into the archive, namely as the one billionth copy that was created for the Barbarastollen collection (along with 30,000 pages of photographed documents that chronicle its creation). The preservation of so many invaluable documents suggests that German culture needs to be protected above all else, as if the German people are already doomed to nuclear annihilation. Maybe because of the comprehensiveness of the collection, the Barbarastollen is the only site in Germany that is protected by the Hague Convention for the Protection of Cultural Property in the Event of Armed Conflict, a treaty signed in 1954 and ratified as of 2018 by 133 nations. The Nazi book burnings, banning of so-called "degenerate art," and plundering of artworks in occupied nations were a driving force behind the Hague Convention, which now, in turn, protects the copies, or more precisely: information about German cultural heritage. Concealed deep within the mountain, the Barbarastollen project rests upon paradoxes that propelled its realization: to protect the German cultural heritage and ensure its survival, to preserve historically relevant goods, to pass on traditions, and to document a society's rich legacy. These reasons suppose a future in which survivors not only exist but that they also have an interest in a culture and political structure capable of bringing about its own destruction, that is, if they can decipher the documents at all. It remains doubtful that anyone in the future would even know how to use the hardware required to access the microfilm on which the documents are stored, let alone convert them to a more accessible, as of yet unknown, form of media.

---

79    Accordingly, the Barbarastollen falls under the jurisdiction of the Bundesamt für Bevölkerungsschutz und Katastrophenhilfe (Federal Office of Civil Protection and Disaster Assistance), www.bbk.bund.de/DE/Home/home_node.html. East Germany had a similar project located in the town of Ferch, southwest of Berlin.

In apocalyptic collections, deeply rooted optimism meets depressing fatalism. The assumption that future generations will be thrilled to learn about their forbears—even though, in the most negative scenario, those forbears' decisions will have wrecked an entire planet, killed hundreds of thousands of species and billions of people, exposed the remaining survivors to great harm, and did not consider the ethical consequences of their actions—may seem naïve and explicable only by our descendants' desire to find out what led to the dystopian environment we condemned them to live in. Instead of fighting global warming and banning nuclear arms to protect people, animals, and plants, we use resources to preserve cultural goods. Undoubtedly, such projects of preservation are projections of hope and attempts to prolong our lives symbolically through collections of our own cultural production. Considering how little we know about cultures from 5,000 years in the past, it would be hard to imagine that the type of analog media in use at the Barbarastollen would be functional in hundreds or maybe thousands of years. Or any analog media for that matter. Even worse, there is less guarantee that the Internet and the cloud, with their seemingly infinite storage capacity and, hence, duplicability of data, will still be functional. The question of functionality and slow dilapidation begins with the smallest of units, data itself.[80]

Although occasional loss of data is a common phenomenon, often due to improper use of software, computer malfunction, or spotty Internet connection, data corruption is owed to the ravages of time. Data corruption may lead to system failure, thus eradicating the hardware along with what is stored on it (on the topic of hardware preservation see Jessica Walthew in this book). Cloud servers are not free from data corruption and the potential of system failure. Data corruption, even if not caused intentionally by malware, can happen at any point during a data transfer—from data input to data processing, storage, and transmission—and can inhibit end-to-end data integrity. Although modern systems are prepared to replace and repair corrupt data to guarantee the soundness of code, *undetected* data corruption, caused by corrosion, loose cables, vibration, loud noises, power outages, and, in wireless transmission, environmental

---

80   Less pessimistic and in fact enthusiastic about the future, albeit no less guided by the idea of future destruction, was the Westinghouse Time Capsule, created in 1939 for the World Fair Exhibition in New York and built by the Westinghouse Electric and Manufacturing Company. World War II and the consecutive building of the first nuclear bombs provided examples of destruction not long after the Westinghouse Time Capsule was buried. The capsule was built in the shape of a rocket and includes a collection of cultural goods along with 35 objects that were deemed typical for contemporary life. The Westinghouse Time Capsule was determined to be opened 5,000 years after it was sealed, i.e., in the year 6939. See Johannes Endres, "Heterotopian Multilingualism: The Westinghouse Time Capsule (1939)," *Critical Multilingualism Studies* 5, no. 3 (2017): 149–67.

influences such as thunderstorms and cosmic radiation may lead to permanent data loss. Not surprisingly, data companies have been reluctant to release information on loss through data corruption. No company wants to be accused of operating hardware that permits the breakdown of computer code. Hence, studies that deal with the long-term preservation of data are dated and reliable numbers hard to get. David S. H. Rosenthal, analyzing the studies at hand and adding his own observations, comments on the problem of multifactorial data loss and summarizes in 2010:

> Our inability to compute how many backup copies we need to achieve a reliability target is something we're just going to have to live with. In practice, we aren't going to have enough backup copies, and stuff will get lost or damaged . . . Unfortunately, in the real world, failures are inevitable. As systems scale up, failures become more frequent. Even throwing money at the problem can only reduce the incidence of failures, not exclude them entirely.[81]

With growing storage capacity and computing speed, the likelihood of system failures and data loss increases as well. While corruption of code is less prominent in popular discourse, hacking into databases with malign intent is more spectacular and, therefore, embedded in the public mind. Hacks into private accounts on Facebook, Equifax, Twitter, various large banks, and government institutions damaged the reputation of corporations as well as the state, led to high ransom payments, and harmed individuals whose identities were stolen and in many cases used to fraudulently extract money from private accounts.[82] If anything that can be quantified is translated into numbers and anything that can be translated into numbers is computed, then any data that is computable may, at least by common technological standards, vanish at any time.

Data loss is the nemesis of collecting. What was intentionally assembled, ordered, and preserved is at the same time exposed to utter destruction. Many traumatic events in the past testify to the quintessential catastrophe for any collection: libraries have burned so often throughout history—from the Xianyang Palace and State Archives in Qin China in 260 BCE to the Herzogin Anna Amalia Library in Weimar, Germany in 2004—that Georges Didi-Huberman considers "omissions" and "gaps" to be the essence of any archive.[83] It is the absence of libraries and archi-

---

81 David S. H. Rosenthal, "Keeping Bits Safe: How Hard Can It Be," *acmqueue* 8, no. 10 (October 1, 2010), https://queue.acm.org/detail.cfm?id=1866298.

82 The topic of stolen data and data security would require a lengthy discussion.

83 Georges Didi-Huberman, "Das Archiv brennt," in Georges Didi-Huberman and Knut Ebeling, *Das Archiv brennt* (Berlin: Kadmos, 2018), 7–32, here 7.

val collections, or of parts thereof, that tell us stories of armed conflicts, revolutions, religious fanaticism, oppression, mental disorders, and accidents, in other words: acts of intentional or coincidental destruction that record human actions along with the origins and collecting practices that led to libraries' or archives' formation.

If we apply Didi-Huberman's hypothesis to a digital environment, we arrive at the conclusion that system failure and data loss are so widespread an experience that they are an essential part of digital storage. Aside from its ephemerality due to rapid technological advancements in digital media—Paul Virilio warned as early as in 1980 in his *Ésthetique de la disparition* (1980) that reliance on digital technology would lead to the permanent loss of cultural memory[84]—data is at any given moment potentially vulnerable to conditions that account for its obliteration.[85] The possibility of obliteration was, in fact, the main inspiration for what became the Internet. The foundation of the Advanced Research Project Agency (ARPA) in 1958 was one of President Dwight D. Eisenhower's responses to the Sputnik shock, Russia's first successful launch of an outer space mission in 1957. Through its Information Processing Techniques Office, ARPA developed a decentralized communications structure that would enable it to operate in case of a nuclear strike. The ARPANET connected its first remote computers in 1969 and its Network Control Program was implemented by 1970, using its own information coding and decoding protocol (TCI/IP) and infrastructure. The entire network was fully operational by 1975, now under the slightly, but significantly, altered name Defense Advanced Research Project Agency (DARPA), stressing its military origins and purposes. In a next step, universities received funding to build and run supercomputer centers and in return were granted access to the defense communication network in 1981, expanding it as a tool of science.

Scientists produce knowledge. However, knowledge is inextricably linked to two extremes: it can serve the advancement of humanity, or it can promote its destruction. Developing technology to secure strategic advantages over real or perceived enemies—whether it be through weapons, communication, or intelligence—is one of the great incentives for boosting science and the production of knowledge. What secret operatives call "intelligence" is referred to as "information" in the scientific community, with "intelligence" being a mental capacity to comprehend

---

84　Cultural "value," Virilio implies, is measured by its slowness, i.e., its ability to sustain and develop an impact over a long period of time—the very concept of canonization—as opposed to the speed of information flow today.

85　Wendy Hui Kyong Chun, *Updating to Remain the Same: Habitual New Media* (Cambridge, MA: MIT Press, 2016) reflects upon the permanent need to update software as well as to replicate copies to maintain a standard of operation.

and analyze information critically to turn it into knowledge. The Central Intelligence Agency (CIA), for example, *collects* "intelligence" and has "analysts" evaluate troves of gathered material to maintain the upper hand over foes. "Scientia potentia est"—knowledge is power—is a proverb that is often associated with Francis Bacon's *Meditationes Sacrae* (1597), but more likely attributable to Thomas Hobbes's *Leviathan* in his revised Latin version of 1668, where "science" is one of several attributes of power next to "reputation," "prudence," "nobility," "eloquence," and "forme." All of these "virtues" (as Hobbes calls them) ultimately serve to secure power in one hand: "The Greatest of humane Powers, is that which is compounded of the Powers of most men, united by consent, in one person, Naturall, or civill, that has the use of all their Powers depending on his will."[86]

Today, power is concentrated in the hands of corporations through the amassing of data. Once the "collecting" of information is outsourced to private corporations such as Google, Facebook, and Palantir Technologies—an elusive data analysis company, specializing in, among other areas, counterterrorism and information warfare—governments can draw upon these companies' expertise to spy on their customers and even to expand their own surveillance programs. Surveillance is a feature of power, as it concentrates knowledge in the hands of those who surveil. As a result, corporate (data) collectors use their financial and technological advantage to generate profits from knowledge they gained through surveillance, while individual collectors—those who use the Internet to find and acquire physical collectibles or the growing number of those who collect digital objects such as NFTs—knowingly and unknowingly contribute to companies' vast trove of information. What is destroyed in the process of "data collection" is the privacy of individuals, a framework for a fair economic distribution of wealth, and lastly the resources of our planet through increasing amounts of energy consumption that goes into the operation of server farms to process the flow of information. This flow is possible due to a technology that was created to resist destruction and to retaliate in nuclear warfare, and that now serves the accumulation of wealth by corporate collectors in an economic state of surveillance capitalism. In this lucrative ecosystem, the volatility of digital objects stands out. Simultaneously experiential and fleeting, digital objects manifest in

---

86 Thomas Hobbes, *Leviathan: The Matter, Forme, and Power of a Common-Wealth Ecclesiastical and Civill* (no location, Floating Press, 2009), 123. The transformation of knowledge into power goes back to Sun Tzu, *The Art of War*, trans. Lionel Giles (New York: Open Road Media, 2014), 23: "If you know the enemy and know yourself, you need not fear the result of a hundred battles. If you know yourself but not the enemy, for every victory gained you will also suffer a defeat. If you know neither the enemy nor yourself, you will succumb in every battle."

different aggregate states and are prone to dilapidation: as phenomena on a screen, code, electric impulses, and, ultimately, "gaps" in archives due to data corruption. To preserve the inventory of digital objects and to select and acquire new ones is the job of collecting institutions such as museums and archives; to "collect" and monetize data of their users is the declared goal of Internet companies. The following articles in this book introduce different techniques, problems, and theories of collecting in the digital age.

# 1: Collecting: Defining the Subject

*Johannes Endres*

## The Time Capsule as a Case in Point

ON THE 23RD OF SEPTEMBER 1938, the first ever so-called time capsule was buried at the site of the New York World's Fair, which was set to open in April 1939. To this day, it remains one of the most ambitious projects of its kind. Should the creators of the capsule have it their way, the cylindrically shaped, metal container, 7.5 feet tall and 8.75 inches in diameter, will not be unearthed until the year 6939 CE.[1] The Westinghouse Time Capsule will then present its receiver from the far future with a tangible impression of the "achievements" of Western civilization on the eve of World War II. This, at least, is the scenario as imagined in the *Book of Record*, copies of which were deposited in the capsule and also distributed widely, including, in 3,649 copies, to lamaseries in Tibet, Shinto shrines in Japan, and Buddhist temples in India, and to 2,000 libraries, museums and universities across the world.[2] Like the time capsule, the *Book of Record* was conceived by the Westinghouse Electric Company, in collaboration with a group of scientists, engineers, and advertising experts.[3] The capsule's content was selected by way of a public idea contest under the direction of the vice president of the company; it provides a colorful display: from small items of daily use, such as a can opener, safety pin, and toothbrush, to samples of textiles and other materials, to all manner of seeds, banknotes, and other trifles, to texts and images on microfilm and contemporary newsreels. Framed by

---

1 George Edward Pendray, *The Story of the Westinghouse Time Capsule* (East Pittsburgh, PA: Westinghouse Electric & Manufacturing Company, 1939); Johannes Endres, "Hetérotopian Multilingualism: The Westinghouse Time Capsule (1939)," *Critical Multilingualism Studies: An Interdisciplinary Journal* 5, no. 2 (2017): 149–67; Nick Yablon: *Remembrance of Things Present: The Invention of the Time Capsule* (Chicago: University of Chicago Press, 2019).

2 Pendray, *The Story*, 11–12.

3 *The Book of Record of the Time Capsule of Cupaloy Deemed Capable of Resisting the Effects of Time for Five Thousand Years, Preserving an Account of Universal Achievements, Embedded in the Grounds of the New York World's Fair 1939* (New York: Westinghouse Electric & Manufacturing Company, 1938).

the capsule, such seemingly random everyday objects form a potentially meaningful snapshot of the beginnings of the consumer age.

That after 5,000 years the capsule's "message" might no longer be intelligible is something its creators took into account. They equipped it with a "Rosetta stone," a linguistic apparatus intended to help reconstruct the information inside the capsule by way of a reconstruction of the language in which it is couched. In addition to the capsule itself, the *intelligibility* of its content is therefore perishable too, and hence requires protection from the various threats of loss and forgetting. Collecting has in this sense always been at once a "structure of objective devotion" and an "epistemological practice,"[4] a practice that the collector can nevertheless only control to a certain degree. Instead, collections, like other cultural technologies, operate in a future space that is both open and precarious. To manage this "openness to the future" is,[5] in fact, the very challenge faced by all collecting, be it the stockpiling of food, the accumulation of capital, the compilation of art, memorabilia, or collector's items, the storage of knowledge and information, or the kind of collections gathered in time capsules—activities that, in different yet also similar ways, entail the "selective, active, and longitudinal acquisition, possession, and disposition of an inter-related set of differentiated objects."[6] As a result, collections

---

4    Michael Cahn, "Das Schwanken zwischen Abfall und Wert: Zur kulturellen Hermeneutik des Sammlers," *Merkur* 45, no. 8 (1991): 674–90, here 676 and 679.

5    Alois Hahn, "Soziologie des Sammlers (unter besonderer Berücksichtigung der Institution des Museums)," in *Konstruktionen des Selbst, der Welt und der Geschichte: Aufsätze zur Kultursoziologie* (Frankfurt am Main: Suhrkamp, 2000), 440–62, here 442.

6    Russell W. Belk, Melanie Wallendorf, John F. Sherry, Jr., and Morris B. Holbrook, "Collecting in a Consumer Culture," in *Highways and Buyways: Naturalistic Research from the Consumer Behaviour Odyssey*, ed. Russell Belk (Provo, UT: Association for Consumer Research, 1991), 178–215, here 180. The definition seems to exclude money or food storage from the scope of collecting. Hence, Belk et al. point out: "If the predominant value of an object or idea for the person possessing it is intrinsic, i.e., if it is valued primarily for use, or purpose, or aesthetically pleasing quality, or the value inherent in the object or accruing to it by whatever circumstance of custom, training or habit, it is not a collection." While that is a valid point by itself, it does not exclude intrinsically valuable objects from the group of collectibles. For even the whole of a collection of valuable items is worth more than the sum of its parts, something Marx theorized as the "Mehrwert" (*surplus value*) of capital, as opposed to the "use value" represented by its buying power. The same could be shown for stockpiling, which engenders economic, cultural, and emotional assets greater than the sum of the items collected—a fact immediately visible from images of stored food that reveal an infrastructure of repositories, inventory lists, channels of trade etc. that amount to more than just the material value of their content— or for databases, which

can be more or less future-proof, that is, sustainable and successful. They are, in other words, "time capsules" in their own right, whose target date is not always predetermined, but whose contents and structure always connect present, future, and past in ways that are, in equal measure, intricate, fallible, and open to interpretation.[7] So are the letters by Robert Millikan, Albert Einstein, and Thomas Mann that are stored inside the Westinghouse Time Capsule and which, in the spirit of the Rosetta-stone principle that guides the overall project, are authored in different languages: Millikan's and Mann's letters in English, Einstein's letter in German. If, when, and to what end they will reach their recipients, the "Brothers of the future," must for now remain uncertain.[8]

## Collecting, Broadly Conceived

To "collect" means to "gather together in one place or group," usually with the goal of creating a collection of sorts.[9] Collecting is object-centered, while not restricted to physical objects at all. Usages of "to collect" that don't refer to the collecting of something, but refer back to the one who collects, as in to "collect oneself," can be ignored for the purposes of this article. The intransitive use of the word—which does not demand an object and addresses the act of collecting as such—is, however, at the very center of my argument.

The English verb "to collect" has been common at least since the early 1400s and can be found in connection with a widely spread subject area that concerns anything from everyday items (including means of subsistence) to money, texts, and ideas. The application to religious and charitable collections is neither uncommon nor peripheral, but counts among the oldest usages of the word and word family. A "collection" is thus a "group of objects viewed as a whole," including metaphorical usages that extend to non-physical objects, such as thoughts and knowledge, as well

---

lack the discreetness of "differentiated objects" proper, but that through the linkage that connects their parts to each other are differentiated from other objects which are not part of the collection. The problem at stake here is not so much one of differentiation or usefulness or intrinsic value, but of scarcity (of which more below).

7 This fundamentally precarious status of collections is usually underestimated in positivistic research on collecting, but also in the wide-spread discourse on collections as "semiophores" (sign vehicles) with a mostly stable referent; on the latter point see Krzysztof Pomian, *Collectors and Curiosities: Paris and Venice 1500–1800*, trans. Elizabeth Wiles-Porter (Cambridge: Polity Press, 1990).

8 *Book of Record*, 47.

9 For the following, see *Oxford English Dictionary (OED)* (Oxford: Oxford University Press, 2021) (https://www.oed.com); *Online Etymology Dictionary* (https://www.etymonline.com).

as to collective nouns, such as "works" or "materials." The use of "collecting" and "collection" in combination with artworks or artifacts that are collected in museums, archives, or private collections, on the other hand, is a restriction of the wider scope of collecting that not only is historically later but also tends to obscure the similarities between the different forms of collecting.

As I will argue in the following, collecting comes into view as a "comprehensive phenomenon"[10] only if one does not confine it from the outset to particular motivations, occasions, objects, or historical manifestations. While scientific and artistic collections and collections of memorabilia seem to be the most frequent and prominent types of collections, there clearly are others, including collections of objects that are not "things" in a proper sense. For literally "anything" can be collected, from "material objects" to "real occurrences of a certain kind," such as amorous affairs and comet observations, to "items and events from symbolical realities," such as literary motifs and plots, and much else.[11] The same goes for technically reproducible mass commodities like the ones stored in the Westinghouse Time Capsule, and the collecting of virtual objects in and of the digital age. Indeed, collecting appears as a category and activity sufficiently broad to incorporate highly diverse and historically contingent forms of cultural practice. Even the etymological relationship of "collecting" to Latin "collegere" ("gleaning") and "legere" ("reading")[12] only seems to indicate that the semantic scope of more rudimentary survival techniques (such as gleaning crops) must at some point have been transferred metaphorically to more refined and specific cultural performances (such as the gleaning of information). To that effect, collecting is based on a "primal urge"[13] in the general sense that there could be no cultural history of collecting if there were no biological disposition to sustain it.

The diverse forms of collecting are linked by a number of characteristics. First of all, collecting is a *secondary* cultural technique, since for something to be collected it has to exist in the first place. At the same

---

10   Manfred Sommer, "Sammeln," in *Handbuch materielle Kultur: Bedeutungen, Konzepte, Disziplinen*, ed. Stefanie Samida, Manfred K. H. Eggert, and Hans Peter Hahn (Stuttgart: Metzler, 2014), 109–17, here 109–10.

11   Jochen Brüning, "Wissenschaft und Sammlung," *Bild, Schrift, Zahl*, ed. Sybille Krämer and Horst Bredekamp (Munich: Wilhelm Fink, 2003), 87–113, here 90.

12   Cahn, "Das Schwanken," 683; Nikolaus Wegmann, "Im Reich der Philologie: Vom Sammeln und Urteilen," in *Konkurrenten in der Fakultät: Kultur, Wissen und Universität um 1900*, ed. Christoph König and Eberhard Lämmert (Frankfurt am Main: Fischer Taschenbuch Verlag, 1999): 260–72, here 264.

13   Aleida Assmann, "Sammeln, Sammlungen, Sammler," in *Erleben, Erleiden, Erfahren*, ed. Kay Junge, Daniel Suber, and Gerold Gerber (Bielefeld: Transcript Verlag, 2008): 345–53, here 345.

time, it is a *productive* enterprise for which it is true "that the whole is greater than the sum of its parts."[14] The latter point distinguishes collecting from the sheer aggregation of stuff, a process which, by itself, lacks the specific "surplus" that collecting as an active and intentional practice provides.[15] Thus collecting also entails an act of *revaluation*, in that it ascribes a new value to an object that overwrites a previous one, for instance as an article of daily use. The same goes for the Bible inside the Westinghouse Time Capsule; it no longer serves a purpose as a religious text but functions as a historical testament of the existence of such a text. Some have therefore suggested that the items of a collection are not things, but "displays" and *representations*.[16] As such, they are "representational" with regard to other objects or ideas, to which they relate as parts of a whole, links of a series, or samples of a type; it is from this relationship then that they derive a new value assignment.[17] Similarly, the safety pin inside the Westinghouse Time Capsule is a specimen of the usefulness from which it also appears to have been removed. So too are books in a library removed from the economic cycle of book production and distribution, serving, to quote Walter Benjamin, as "copies" ("Exemplare") of all books of the same title and content.[18]

However, Walter Benjamin's observation that a collector or a collection "detaches ("heraushebt") the object from its functional relations"[19] is beside the point, since collections and their objects are functionally determined, too. In fact, there is no such thing as "disinterested" collecting.[20] Suggestions to the contrary seem to ascribe (presumed) characteristics of collections of artworks or curiosities to the practice of collecting

---

14   Brüning, "Wissenschaft und Sammlung," 97; see also Belk et al., "Collecting in a Consumer Culture," 180.

15   Assmann, "Sammeln, Sammlungen, Sammler," 349; Nikolaus Wegmann, *Bücherlabyrinthe: Suchen und Finden im alexandrinischen Zeitalter* (Cologne, Weimar, and Vienna: Böhlau Verlag, 2000), 191 and 194; Christoph Zeller, "From Object to Information: The End of Collecting in the Digital Age," *Arcadia* 50, no. 2 (2015): 389–409, here 403.

16   Hahn, "Soziologie des Sammlers," 449.

17   Walter Nelson Durost, *Children's Collecting Activity Related to Social Factors* (New York: Bureau of Publications/Teacher College, Columbia University, 1932), 10.

18   Walter Benjamin, "Unpacking My Library: A Talk about Book Collecting," in *Illuminations*, ed. Hannah Arendt, trans. Harry Zohn (New York: Schocken Books, 1969), 59–67, here 61.

19   Walter Benjamin, *The Arcades Project*, trans. Howard Eiland and Kevin McLaughlin, prepared on the basis of the German volume edited by Rolf Tiedemann (Cambridge, MA: The Belknap Press of Harvard University Press, 2002), 857.

20   The notion of "disinterested" collecting is quite common; see, for instance, Benjamin, *Arcades Project*, 857; Hahn, "Soziologie des Sammlers," 448.

in general. This does justice neither to the phenomenological diversity of collecting, nor to collections of artworks, curiosities, and other artifacts in particular. For even the latter are shaped by purposes, directly or indirectly, in that they tend to serve as means of individual or collective identity formation, edification and education, entertainment and distraction, commemoration and exchange. That means that all collecting carries some sort of *economic* significance and deals with related issues of ownership, availability, and regulation. The Westinghouse Time Capsule underlines this fact through its utilitarian heteronomy of serving as an instance of practical philanthropy, a public attraction, and a promotional event at once. In other words, collections are concerned with a *de-contextualization* that goes hand in hand with a *re-contextualization* in a different functional and spatial context. To think of collections as dream worlds and utopias, as psychological research often does,[21] misses a crucial point: every collection, even of supposed ego-substitutes and *ersatz* fictions, is embedded in the actual world, and be it through traces of usage that are real enough to be turned into marketable commodities, like user profiles on the Internet.

That everything *can* be collected does not, of course, imply that everything *is* a collection. On the contrary, collecting is not only selective and active, in that it is based on the "intervention" of a collector,[22] but also *intentional*, even if the intention might become intelligible only in hindsight.[23] But collecting entails more than simply amassing things in one location; the items of a collection also need to be connected with each other by way of an organizing principle, or as Niklas Luhmann would have it, a "disorder with a non-arbitrary structure,"[24] that is indicative of the type of collection to which they belong. Such a "connectivity scheme"[25] establishes a *syntagmatic* principle of combination in addition to a *paradigmatic* principle of selection. While the latter, the paradigmatic principle of selection, regulates which objects go into the collection, the former, the syntagmatic principle of combination, controls their

21  Jean Baudrillard, *The System of Objects*, trans. James Benedict (London: Verso, 1996), 85–106; Werner Muensterberger, *Collecting: An Unruly Passion* in *Psychological Perspectives* (Princeton, NJ: Princeton University Press, 1994).

22  Wegmann, *Bücherlabyrinthe*, 191.

23  Mieke Bal, "Telling Objects: A Narrative Perspective on Collecting," in *The Cultures of Collecting*, ed. John Elsner and Roger Cardinal (London: Reaktion Books, 1994), 97–115, here 101–2; Manfred Sommer, *Sammeln: Ein philosophischer Versuch* (Frankfurt am Main: Suhrkamp, 2018), 77–78.

24  Niklas Luhmann, "Kommunikation mit Zettelkästen: Ein Erfahrungsbericht," in *Öffentliche Meinung und sozialer Wandel: Opinion and Social Change; Für Elisabeth Noelle-Neumann*, ed. Horst Baier (Opladen: Westdeutscher Verlag, 1981), 222–28, here 225.

25  Wegmann, *Bücherlabyrinthe*, 193.

connectedness within it. This double mechanism has frequently been described in relation to other models of organization and control. That textual metaphors play a prominent role in such descriptions is not a coincidence. Just as words of a language that refer to the world beyond language derive meaning from their simultaneous relationship to other words of that language, so does the meaningfulness of a collection depend on both the objects of which it is comprised and the manifold relations of these objects to one another. In the same way, books in a library refer to the outside world *and* to other books, pictures in a museum to real-world subjects *and* to other pictures of the world, and even collected capital to the things it can buy *and* to the internal value structure that underlies the monetary system. The list of contents of the Westinghouse Time Capsule exhibits such a coordinate system on a very basic yet sensible level: it not only lists the items inside the capsule but also divides them into five subject groups.[26]

Collecting thus always requires, at a minimum, a *dual* operation: comparing the objects of the collection with those that are not part of the collection, and comparing them to other objects within the collection itself. In doing so, two different determinations have to be made: certain objects have to be found *alike*, while others have to be found *unalike*. For a collection to make sense, these determinations have to be decoded again, consciously or unconsciously, by its user (who can be the collector or someone else); by no means do collections just "speak" for themselves. Collections are therefore also "overstructured" in that they play out on two different structural levels, a degree of cohesion that distinguishes them from their environments, without assuming an "extraterritorial" position outside of the former: collections are this-worldly, even if their objects are not. Using a Foucauldian term, they could therefore be called "heterotopias," places "outside all places, although they are actually localizable."[27] Once collections lose their distinctiveness, though, they blend in with their environments, as is the case with digital collections and their expansive search routines, in which collecting reaches its *conceptual* boundaries by way of their *practical* over-extension.[28]

This typical overstructuredness, or markedness, or "topophilia"[29] of collections, be they analogue or digital, is not an end in itself; nor are such features typical expressions of some sort of Western rationalism that can

---

26   Pendray, *The Story*, 25–41.

27   Michel Foucault, "Different Spaces," in *Aesthetics, Method, and Epistemology*, trans. Rodney Livingstone, ed. Michael W. Jennings, Howard Eiland, and Gary Smith (New York: New Press, 1998), 175–85, here 178.

28   Zeller, "From Object to Information," 400.

29   Gaston Bachelard, *The Poetics of Space*, trans. Maria Jolas, with a new foreword by John R. Stilgoe (Boston: Beacon, 1994), xxxv.

be easily criticized. Quite the opposite: collections are so unstable, violable, and improbable that without any solidifying measures they would be doomed to fail.[30] Collecting is thus not simply a process through which the collection is gradually assembled; collections also demand constant curation and care. That is still true for the digital age and for digital databases, which rely on updating routines, and it is already true for the collecting of means of subsistence and the logistic apparatus of time capsules, which both have to be protected against physical destruction and information loss. In the case of the Westinghouse Time Capsule such upkeep is achieved through an extensive chain of tradition, consisting of people who translate the *Book of Record* into currently spoken languages, and institutions and organizations, like libraries and the Internet, that inscribe the capsule's whereabouts into a collective memory, and through the collection's material preservation, for which the Westinghouse Electric Company took advantage of technological innovations of its time.

The internal structuring and the expiration date of collections differ, however, in terms of their respective density and extent:[31] from syntactically rather discrete or loosely coupled "lists" like those that organize digital databases, which are more or less arbitrarily (re)configurable; to the shelving systems of libraries and the architecture underlying museum displays, which are less flexible; to encyclopedic collections of *all* specimens of one type or of *all* information relevant to one topic, which can only be expanded under certain specific conditions; and, finally, to time capsules, which are so hermetic (that is, syntactically dense) that they appear intolerant to all changes and additions whatsoever. While the Westinghouse Time Capsule, due to its high syntactical density, can count on a duration of 5,000 years, the life cycle of a list of Google search results amounts to just a few seconds or less. However, it is not the case that collections are inherently interminable or fragmentary;[32] on the contrary, collecting seems to raise a claim for completeness and closure that contradicts the average experience of a world usually resisting such expectations.

---

30  Nikolaus Wegmann, "Im Labyrinth: Über die (Un-)Möglichkeit der Bibliothek als Qualitätsmedium," *Bibliothek Forschung und Praxis* 42, no. 2 (2018): 1–9, here 2.

31  For a differentiation of "syntactically dense" vs. "discrete" see Nelson Goodman, *Languages of Art: An Approach to a Theory of Symbols* (Indianapolis: Hackett Publishing Company, 1988), 127–76.

32  See, however, the unanimous and ubiquitous claims by Baudrillard, *The System of Objects*; Cahn, "Das Schwanken."

# Collecting and Scarcity

The lack of specificity that characterizes collecting as a concept and practice overall is, on the other hand, met by "object-specific techniques of tracing down, preparing, and preserving"[33] that vary from collectible to collectible, so much so that they can hardly be compiled here in a comprehensive fashion (not even in the loosely coupled format of a list). The institutional history of collecting since the early modern period has doubtlessly been dominated by the cabinet of curiosities, the art collection, the museum, the library, the archive, and—since 1996—the Internet. Contrary to what the sprawl of these institutions suggests, the history of collecting is not simply one of increasing globalization: from the originally "European tradition"[34] of the cabinet of curiosities and the modern, bourgeois museum, to the basically worldwide phenomenon of the Internet. Instead, collecting—both as an anthropological disposition and media technology—is embedded into local traditions of cultural techniques and communication practices as well as their historical evolution, on which collecting still depends. As such, collecting is not some kind of "super form" from which its history consequentially unfolds as one of a continuous accumulation of knowledge and power (as Foucault's concept of an "archaeology of knowledge" has it).[35] However, the varied manifestations of collecting indicate that wealthier societies and individuals collect more. One needs to be able to afford collecting, whether it is crop for the year to come, or information, or money; in each case, a sacrifice has to be made, and a need postponed. Besides, wealthier societies and individuals have at their disposal more objects, signs and media that can be collected, not to mention higher life expectancy; one must live long enough to compile a longitudinal collection that is later still cared about.

The fact that nowadays increasing numbers of people are able to use the Internet also makes collecting, including its potential objects and technologies, accessible to more and more people. Such a process begins with modern public museums (which collect at the expense of others), city libraries (that cater to an urban readership), and co-operative banks (that do not lend money to everyone). Collecting therefore is, and always has been, only as elitist or egalitarian, as hegemonic or non-hegemonic, as exclusive or inclusive as the societies in which collecting is done.

Collecting is also not a necessary consequence of plenitude. It is not what exists in abundance, nor what is old, new, beautiful, or original, that makes for a collection, but only what is *scarce*. Boom times of collecting

---

33 Brüning, "Wissenschaft und Sammlung," 90.

34 Susan M. Pearce, *On Collecting: An Investigation into Collecting in the European Tradition* (London: Routledge, 1995).

35 Michel Foucault, *The Archaeology of Knowledge and the Discourse on Language*, trans. A. M. Sheridan Smith (New York: Pantheon Books, 1972).

are thus also times of scarcity. "Scarce" is not the same as "rare." Scarcity applies to an "intermediate state between possession and deprivation ("Haben und Nicht-Haben")"[36] and follows from a "tension" that is marked by the intensity of a desire on the one hand and the quantity of a good on the other.[37] The collecting of supplies, artworks, or rare books are evident cases in point, but the same applies to means of production and reproduction such as artificial resources, capital, or genes, and even to codes and algorithms that generate information—while the databases that such codes and algorithm produce and reproduce might end up in the public domain and become widely accessible. Consequently, the scope of collecting has to be extended from "rare objects"[38] to just about anything that is, or appears to be, scarce, including technologically reproducible items, like the safety pin in the Westinghouse Time Capsule, which, in the context of the collection of that capsule, is equipped with an artificial semblance of scarcity, as well as to digital objects such as digital music, digital books, and digital cars that through an attached market price are rendered scarce on purpose.[39] That means that collecting is not only "conservative,"[40] but also a sustainability strategy, which makes sure that scarcity does not itself become scarce and the complexity of the world does not become too great.[41]

Collecting's focus on scarcity also implies that the age of technical reproducibility, contrary to Benjamin's famous suggestion, is *not* the "antithesis" of collecting.[42] Or else digital copies of art works would have put an end to the museum as an institution, which they have not; they have only pushed for its extension onto the Internet and contributed to

---

36    Georg Simmel, *The Philosophy of Money*. Third enlarged edition, ed. David Frisby, trans. Tom Bottomore and David Frisby (London: Routledge, 2004), 73.

37    Alois Hahn, "Soziologische Aspekte der Knappheit," *Kölner Zeitschrift für Soziologie und Sozialpsychologie* (1987): 119–32, here 120; see also Niklas Luhmann, "Knappheit, Geld und die bürgerliche Gesellschaft," *Jahrbuch für Sozialwissenschaft* 23, no. 2 (1972): 186–210.

38    Russell Belk, "Ownership and Collecting," in *The Oxford Handbook of Hoarding and Acquiring*, ed. Randy O. Frost and Gail Steketee (Oxford: Oxford University Press, 2014), 33–42, here 35.

39    Rebecca D. Watkins, Abigail Sellen, and Siân E. Lindley, 2015, "Digital Collections and Digital Collecting Practices," *Proceedings of the 33rd Annual ACM Conference on Human Factors in Computing Systems—CHI '15* (2015), 3423–32.

40    Sommer, "Sammeln," 115.

41    On the "scarceness of scarcity" in economic systems that are based on production and reproduction see Hahn, "Soziologische Aspekte," 130–31.

42    Walter Benjamin, *The Work of Art in the Age of Its Technological Reproducibility, and Other Writings on Media*, ed. Michael W. Jennings, Brigid Doherty, and Thomas Y. Levin, trans. Edmund Jephcott et al. (Cambridge, MA: The Belknap Press of Harvard University Press, 2008), 40.

a "disappearance" of material exhibits in some cases.[43] Neither is it true
that throwaway societies divert anything and everything to the proverbial
garbage pile of disdain and forgetting, which functions as the "reversion
of the archive."[44] Rather, as a cultural and media technology, collecting
appears flexible enough to adjust to its various economic, societal, political, and technological environments in past and present. "Dispersion"
or "distraction" therefore cannot be said to be the opposite of collecting, as Benjamin has it when speaking of collecting's "struggle against
dispersion."[45] They are, in fact, prerequisites of collecting: were things
"already . . . very close to each other, they could no longer be collected."[46]
The same goes for the act of forgetting, which is not necessarily at odds
with the kind of remembrance that collecting is also after. As the example
of the Westinghouse Time Capsule underlines, the selection criteria effective in collecting go hand in hand with a censoring of the past and how
it is being remembered. Collecting is thus not only concerned with the
accumulative practices of storing, compiling, and copying, but also with
more complex questions of canonizing that concern the privileging of
certain objects, memories, and information over others.[47]

Scholarship on collecting has further suggested that collecting should
be differentiated from both hoarding and fetishism. Hoarding lacks the
selective and active component that is typical for collecting, while fetishism lacks its reflectiveness and self-understanding;[48] yet some research also
regards collecting and fetishism as the same.[49] In the end, the difference,

---

43   Steven Conn, "Do Museums Still Need Objects?," in *Do Museums Still
Need Objects?* (Philadelphia: University of Pennsylvania Press, 2010), 20–57. This
phenomenon, however, has been anticipated since at least Walter Lippmann's article "The Museum of the Future," *Atlantic* 182, no. 4 (October 1948): 70–72.

44   Assmann, "Sammeln," 349.

45   Benjamin, *Arcades Project*, 211; Benjamin, *Work of Art*, 40.

46   Sommer, "Sammeln," 110.

47   Christoph Neubert, "Speichern," *Historisches Wörterbuch des Mediengebrauchs*, ed. Heiko Christians, vol. 1 (Cologne: Böhlau, 2014), 535–55; Petra
McGillen, "Kompilieren," *Historisches Wörterbuch des Mediengebrauchs*, vol. 1
(Cologne: Böhlau, 2014), 352–68; Aleida Assmann, *Cultural Memory and Western Civilization: Functions, Media, Archives* (Cambridge: Cambridge University
Press, 2011), 119–36, on the distinction between memory as "storage" and
"function."

48   Belk et al., "Collecting in a Consumer Culture"; *Die Hortung: Eine Philos-
ophie des Sammelns*, ed. Andreas Urs Sommer, Dagmar Winter, and Miguel Skirl
(Düsseldorf: Parerga, 2000); Hartmut Böhme, "Fetisch und Idol: Die Temporali-
tät von Erinnerungsformen in Goethes *Wilhelm Meister*, *Faust* und *Der Sammler
und die Seinigen*," in *Goethe und die Verzeitlichung der Natur*, ed. Peter Matussek
(Munich: C. H. Beck, 1998), 178–202.

49   Baudrillard, *The System of Objects*; Muensterberger, *Collecting*; Bal, "Telling Objects."

if any, between collecting on the one hand, and hoarding and fetishism on the other, might come down to their different levels of social approval. The frequently made distinction between collecting *proper*—of art, books, and objects of pastime—and *improper* forms of collecting—of thoughts and ideas, commodities, and apparently worthless objects—is hardly a helpful one.[50] Mieke Bal's suggestion of a third category, "anticollecting"—of objects that have no relation to each other—is not compelling either,[51] unless one wants to conceive of the heterogeneity and seeming randomness of information in databases and on the Internet as such. While the boundlessness of digital collections might support such a claim, it is contradicted by the very logic of collecting, whose objects are always already connected through a system of horizontal relationships within the collection itself that gives it cohesion by separating it from the environment from which said objects have been taken (like the cohesion given to a collection of everyday items that no longer just reference the world but also those other items with whom they form the collection).

## Storage-Based versus Retrieval-Based Collecting

Compared with the structural order in place in every collection, which has been discussed at least since Walter Nelson Durost's groundbreaking study on *Children's Collecting* from the 1930s, the cultural know-how required to create and use collections has received much less attention. It is instead assumed that such know-how just exists: "What collecting is, we all know. And everyone knows how to do it."[52] Obviously, not everyone knows how to set up a *Zettelkasten* (lit., "slip box"), let alone a library. Neither does everyone know how to effectively use the Internet, despite the fact that it is customarily taken as self-explanatory. But as microcosmic (that is, ambitious) time capsules like the Westinghouse Time Capsule demonstrate, collecting very much requires so-called "paratexts,"[53] such as the *Book of Record*, that, similar to an "instruction manual,"[54] provide information on how collections work. In the case of collections and collecting practices with a shorter life span and a shorter chain of tradition, such know-how can be acquired through less explicit practices of instruction and learning, first and foremost by imitation. But that does not

---

50  See, for instance, Sommer, *Sammeln: Ein philosophischer Versuch.*
51  Bal, "Telling Objects," 111.
52  Sommer, *Sammeln: Ein philosophischer Versuch,* 7.
53  Johannes Endres, "Zeitkapsel und Paratext," in *Verborgen, unsichtbar, unlesbar—zur Problematik restringierter Schriftpräsenz,* ed. Tobias Frese, Wilfried E. Keil, and Kristina Krüger (Berlin: de Gruyter, 2014), 214–32.
54  Wegmann, *Bücherlabyrinthe,* 193.

change the fact that established routines of usage are always in existence, and are usually far from self-evident regardless of the collection at stake.

That applies even to the Internet and to digital databases like the *Internet Archive* (www.archive.org), which in 2010 was the world's largest database, with 150 billion pages and a monthly growth rate of 20 terabytes ($200^{12}$ bytes).[55] However, the dramatically shortened life cycle of collections, information, and interfaces in the digital age hardly leaves time or room for a culture of "paratexts." Now as ever, though, collecting also means to "prepare for" an action that can happen "only afterwards—and as a result of an additional operation," following that of collecting itself.[56] The question of how to use a collection can therefore not be answered by the collection as such, but has to be addressed separately, an undertaking hardly performed in relation to "new" media.

But is digital collecting still collecting at all? Does it still fit a definition of collecting even as general as Russell Belk's, according to which collecting is "the selective, active, and longitudinal acquisition, possession, and disposition of an inter-related set of differentiated objects (material things, ideas, beings, or experiences) that contribute to and derive meaning from the entity (the collection) that this set is perceived to constitute"?[57] More often than not, this question has been answered negatively.[58] And indeed, the seemingly universal accessibility of data, the replacement of actual by virtual objects, and the introduction of new forms of ownership (an aspect crucial to the history of collecting) has called the nature and meaningfulness of collecting into question. Definitions of traditional forms of collecting that suggest that collecting is an "operation that, in direct contact with a concrete and real phenomenon, establishes a pattern of interconnection,"[59] cannot but go amiss when applied to digital collecting and the information age. That has to do not only with the introduction of new technologies but also with the fact that digital collecting inverts a practice that formerly characterized collecting throughout its history.

Typically, collecting represents the *invisible*—memories, meanings, affective relationships, values—through the *visible*—the objects of a collection; such a focus on visibility is also the reason why theories of collecting tend to overestimate the physicality of its objects. In contrast, in

---

55   Jannis Kallinikos, Aleksi Aaltonen, and Attila Marton, "A Theory of Digital Objects," *First Monday: Peer-Reviewed Journal of the Internet* 15, no. 6 (June 2010); https://doi.org/10.5210/fm.v15i6.3033.

56   Wegmann, "Im Reich der Philologie," 264–65.

57   Belk et al., "Collecting in a Consumer Culture," 180.

58   Lev Manovich, "The Database," in *The Language of New Media* (Cambridge, MA: MIT Press, 2001), 218–43; Kallinikos et al., "A Theory of Digital Objects"; Zeller, "From Object to Information."

59   Wegmann, *Bücherlabyrinthe*, 192.

digital collections, the *invisible*—codes and algorithms—renders the content of the collection—information and data—*visible*. What is collected are no longer texts, as in the so-called "Gutenberg Age," but hypertexts and metadata that a machine reads in the background and from which what the users see is permanently recreated.[60] In this way, traditional *storage*-based collecting, that was used to collect images, texts, and objects, has been replaced by a *retrieval*-based collecting that, following a Noah's-ark principle, only collects the means needed to continuously reproduce such images, texts, or objects. Such retrieval-based collecting not only saves space and time, making collecting cheaper; it also redefines the scarcity problem characteristic to collecting: the objects of collections are no longer scarce themselves, and in fact have multiplied to the extent of a gigantic information flood,[61] scarce are now the memories, meanings, affects, and values that are associated with the content of a collection—and that are not simply inherent to it. The replacement of storage-based collecting by retrieval collecting has thus also replaced the purpose of collecting—the memories, meanings, affects, and values that constitute its human quality—by the technical process of collecting itself. The future of collecting will therefore have to be concerned with producing or regaining meaningful user strategies without which collecting is going to lose its most crucial asset: the human being.

# Research

Research on collecting has grown immeasurably, due not least to the rediscovery of Walter Benjamin and his now-famous *Rede über das Sammeln* (Talk about Book Collecting) from 1931.[62] That research extends to almost every conceivable aspect of collecting: its history, present, and future. Its scope has been further extended by more specific contributions addressing collecting's most prominent manifestations: cabinets of curiosities, museums, libraries, archives, private collections, time capsules, garbage piles, databases, the Internet, and so on. Some of these contributions deserve to be mentioned separately, such as Horst Bredekamp's

---

60  Gerhard Lauer, "Die zwei Schriften des Hypertexts: Über den Zusammenhang von Schrift, Bedeutung und neuen Medien," in *Regeln der Bedeutung: Zur Theorie der Bedeutung literarischer Texte*, ed. Fotis Jannidis (Berlin: de Gruyter, 2003), 527–55; Kallinikos et al., "A Theory of Digital Objects"; Yuk Hui, "What is a Digital Object?," *Metaphilosophy* 43, no. 4 (2012): 380–95.

61  James Gleick, *The Information: A History, a Theory, a Flood* (New York: Vintage Books, 2011).

62  This is not the place to give a comprehensive account of Benjamin's thoughts on collecting, among which is also his essay *Eduard Fuchs, der Sammler und der Historiker* from 1937 ("Eduard Fuchs: Collector and Historian," *New German Critique*, 5 (Spring, 1975): 27–58.)

now-classical study on the history of the cabinet of curiosities and the prehistory of the modern museum;[63] Anke te Heesen and E. C. Spary's collected volume on epistemological functions of collecting;[64] Nikolaus Wegmann's study on routines of "searching and finding" in the age of the library;[65] Umberto Eco's encyclopedic kaleidoscope of cultural and art historical aspects of "lists" and their use;[66] Susan Pearce's reconsideration of collecting as a typically European cultural practice;[67] Russell Belk's research on collecting in modern and postmodern consumer societies;[68] Werner Muensterberger's psychological typology of the "collector";[69] Philipp Blom's illustrative account of private collections and their emotional history;[70] and finally Lev Manovich's and Marcus Burkhardt's various publications on collecting as a digital technology.[71]

Particularly among English-speaking scholars, the works of Russell Belk have established a critical standard that subsequent research should not neglect. Belk follows a "naturalistic" approach in that he understands collecting as a "specialized form of consumer behaviour," which he sees in line with behavioral patterns regulating capitalist economies and their fixation on commodities.[72] He has also come up with likely the most comprehensive definition of collecting, already cited above. Manfred Sommer has, on the other hand, presented a phenomenological study of collecting as a cultural practice. In his "philosophical attempt" on the subject, Sommer tries to get to the "things themselves," in the sense of Edmund Husserl, yet restricts the concept of collecting in a way that is diametrically opposed to Belk's approach and the one followed here: "There is

---

63   Horst Bredekamp, *The Lure of Antique and the Cult of the Machine: The Kunstkammer and the Evolution of Nature, Art and Technology*, trans. Allison Brown (Princeton, NJ: Markus Wiener, 1995; first published in German, 1993).

64   *Sammeln als Wissen: Das Sammeln und seine wissenschaftsgeschichtliche Bedeutung*, ed. Anke te Heesen and E. C. Spary, 2nd ed. (Göttingen: Wallstein, 2001).

65   Wegmann, *Bücherlabyrinthe*.

66   Umberto Eco, *The Infinity of Lists: An Illustrated Essay; From Homer to Joyce*, trans. Alastair McEwen (London: MacLehose, 2012; first published in Italian, 2009).

67   Pearce, *On Collecting*.

68   See, among others, Russell W. Belk, *Collecting in a Consumer Society* (London: Routledge, 1995).

69   Muensterberger, *Collecting*.

70   Philipp Blom, *To Have and to Hold: An Intimate History of Collectors and Collecting* (Woodstock, NY: Overlook, 2003).

71   Manovich, "The Database"; Marcus Burkhardt, *Digitale Datenbanken: Eine Medientheorie im Zeitalter von Big Data* (Bielefeld: Transcript, 2015).

72   Belk et al., "Collecting in a Consumer Culture," 180.

only *one* form of collecting," Sommer states, and that form finds "its purest expression in aesthetic collecting."[73]

For as long as collecting and collectors have received critical attention, there have been critiques of collecting, be they from an either Marxist or consumer-critical perspective,[74] a deconstructive perspective,[75] the perspective of an institutional history of collecting,[76] a postcolonial perspective,[77] or, more generally, a perspective of cultural criticism.[78] Currently, questions of a (presumed or actual) crisis of collecting play an important role, which revolve particularly around collecting's future possibilities in the age of information, computing, and digitization.[79] Such questions, as well as questions concerning collecting and artificial intelligence, are likely to shape the discourse for some time to come.

There is also a constantly growing number of publications from literary studies that engage with collecting *in, of* and *as* fiction.[80] A literary text that is of paradigmatic importance is Goethe's *Der Sammler und die Seinigen* (The Collector and His Circle, 1799). Despite its rather specific focus—on a fictive cabinet of curiosities and its history—Goethe's text deserves attention on a general level. It unfolds as a collection of (fictional) letters and thus reflects its subject matter, collecting, through the very form, a collected correspondence, in which it is represented. The scholarship on collecting, too, frequently attempts to imitate such self-reflectivity, by emphasizing the relevance of collecting as both a subject and the form of its presentation, as is the case with one or two "collected volumes" on collecting. In Goethe's text, however, the corresponding levels of content and form do not just reinforce each other, in the sense that the "collective" nature of knowledge informs the knowledge of collecting and vice versa. Additionally, the multiple voices in the epistolary

---

73   Sommer, *Sammeln: Ein philosophischer Versuch*, 47.

74   Baudrillard, *The System of Objects.*

75   Michel Foucault, *The Order of Things: An Archaeology of the Human Sciences* (New York: Vintage Books, 1994; first published in French, 1966), 125–65.

76   Elazar Barkan, "Collecting Cultures: Crimes and Criticism," *American Literary History* 10, no. 4 (1998): 753–70.

77   Roy MacLeod, "Postcolonialism and Museum Knowledge: Revisiting the Museums of the Pacific," *Pacific Science* 52, no. 4 (1998): 308–18.

78   James Clifford, "On Collecting Art and Culture," in *The Predicament of Culture: Twentieth-Century Ethnography, Literature, and Art* (Cambridge, MA: Harvard University Press, 1988), 215–51.

79   Boris Groys, *Logic of the Collection* (Cambridge, MA: MIT Press, 2021; first published in German, 1997); Watkins et al., "Digital Collections"; Zeller, "From Object to Information."

80   As an exemplary case, see the copious volume *Sprachen des Sammelns: Literatur als Medium und Reflexionsform des Sammelns*, ed. Sarah Schmidt (Paderborn: Wilhelm Fink, 2016).

exchange also negotiate between the different views of collecting and eventually dissect the claim that all collecting makes: "for that property a certain collection has, that it pulls close what is dispersed and somehow dissolves and annihilates, through the might of the plenty, even the affection of an owner towards some single treasure."[81]

As Goethe seems to have known, collecting not only assembles what is scattered; it also distracts those who indulge in it. In this way, its mechanisms work in opposite directions, staving off hasty conclusions about what is and what is not collecting. Collecting's appeal, it appears, rests as much on the pettiness, bigotry, obsessiveness, and shortcomings for which it has been criticized and ridiculed, as it lives on the affection, curiosity, sophistication, and sociality with which it has been, and continues to be, undertaken.

---

81 *Goethes Werke,* ed. under the patronage of the Grand Duchess Sophie von Sachsen (Weimar: Hermann Böhlaus Nachfolger, 1896), 1:47, 121–207, here 140–41 (my translation).

# Part I.

# Spaces of Collecting

# 2: Collector as Curator: Collecting in the Post-Internet Age

*Boris Groys*

THERE ARE MANY THEORIES about why people collect art. But whatever subjective reason or desire motivates an individual collector, their collection invariably becomes an object of public scrutiny. Art is a public affair—and sooner or later every collection becomes presented to the public view. And in the public space, every collection becomes an exhibition, and every collector becomes a curator. Some collectors try to avoid this moment of turning a collection into an exhibition. Other collectors build private museums or donate their collections to public museums but at the same time try to secure that their collections will not be dispersed and, thus, continue to demonstrate the personal tastes of and choices by their collectors/curators. Private collectors and curators are also often subjected to a similar critique: they are accused of being selective and imposing their personal taste on the general public. The history of collections and exhibitions is the history of struggle against selectivity and for more inclusivity. However, today this struggle seems to have reached its endpoint and lost its relevance. The reason for this development is the emergence of the Internet.

The Internet has no curators. Here everyone can produce texts and images—and make them accessible to the whole world. As a result, the Internet offers the technology that makes art production and distribution relatively cheap and easily available for an individual. Potentially everyone can use a photo or video camera to produce images, a text-processing program to add commentaries, and the Internet to distribute the results on a global scale—avoiding any kind of censorship or selection process. At first glance the Internet seems to be the end of all selectivity. The relationship between the space of museum or private collections and the Internet is, as a rule, imagined as a relationship between the global, unified space of the Internet and the "limited" space of the museum and, for that matter, the limited space of the whole art system.

In practice, however, the Internet leads not to the emergence of a universal public space but to the tribalization of the public. The Internet is an extremely narcissistic medium—it is a mirror of our specific interests and desires. It does not show us what we do not want to see. In the context of the Internet we also communicate only with people who share our interests and attitudes—be they political or aesthetic. It follows that the non-selective character of the Internet is an illusion. The factual functioning of the Internet is based on the non-explicit rules of selection according to which users select only what they already know or are familiar with. Some search engines are able to comb the entire Internet. But these programs, too, have particular goals and are controlled by big corporations and not by individual users. For these individual users the Internet is the opposite of, say, an urban space where we must permanently see what we do not necessarily want to see. In many cases we try to ignore these unwanted images and impressions, in other cases they provoke our interest—but in any case, they expand our field of experience.

The same can be said about the museum. The curatorial choices let us see what we would not choose to see, what is even unknown to us. Being a public institution, the museum, if it is properly functioning, tries to transcend the fragmentation of the public space and create a universal space of representation that the Internet is incapable of creating. Museum exhibitions are interesting and relevant when they select their contents from different segments of the Internet and social networks. The same can be said about private collections and individual exhibitions. In other words, in the post-Internet age an "interesting" collection or exhibition brings together images, signs, and documentations describing artistic actions from different Internet milieus—as in the past "interesting" collections and exhibitions connected art objects from different parts of the world. This operation of collecting that moves things from their original contexts to a new, artificial space of the collection was often criticized as undermining the originality and, thus, the actual meaning of the artworks that can manifest only in the original contexts in which they were created. Let us consider some prominent examples of such a critique.

In his essay *Das Kunstwerk im Zeitalter seiner technischen Reproduzierbarkeit* (1939, The Work of Art in the Age of Mechanical Reproduction), Walter Benjamin famously defines the "exhibition value" of the artwork as an effect of the reproducibility of art.[1] Both, reproduction and exhibition, are operations that remove the artwork from its historical place—from its "here and now"—and send it on a way of global circulation. Benjamin believes that as a result of these operations the artwork loses its "cult value," its function in ritual and tradition, and, hence, its aura. Here "aura" is understood as inscription of the artwork into its original historical context. The reproduced or exhibited artwork loses its

---

1    Walter Benjamin, *The Work of Art in the Age of Mechanical Reproduction*, in *Illuminations: Essays and Reflections*, ed. Hannah Arendt, trans. Harry Zohn (New York: Schocken Books, 1968), 217–51, here 224–25

aura because it is taken out of the world of living experience to which it originally belonged. Each copy refers to the original but does not truly present it. The same can be said about the exhibited artwork: it refers to its original context and aura but, actually, prevents the exhibition visitor from experiencing this aura. Being liberated, isolated from its original environment, the artwork remains "materially" self-identical but loses its historical place and, consequently, its truth. Here art, understood as the production of "visible" artworks that can be exhibited and reproduced, manifests a deep insufficiency: according to Benjamin the most important dimension of the artwork—its relationship to its original context—remains invisible and, as a result, irreproducible and non-exhibitable.

It seems that Martin Heidegger takes an opposite view in his essay *Der Ursprung des Kunstwerkes* (The Origin of the Work of Art, 1935–36), written around the same time. Heidegger writes that we originally experience all things as tools that we use to achieve certain practical goals.[2] Insofar as we only use such tools, we overlook their own "thingness" and the way in which we use them. According to Heidegger, art is the medium of truth because it discloses the world in which we exist—precisely by allowing us to contemplate the things that we use but overlook. Here it seems that the work of art reflects its world and makes it visible.[3] However, Heidegger also believes that the artwork loses its ability to disclose the world when this artwork, in turn, is used by the art institutions as a mere tool itself—when art is collected, transported, exhibited, and so on. Although using a different vocabulary, Heidegger's claim is no different from Benjamin's: the artwork is "true" only if it keeps a relationship to the world which this artwork originally possesses—and it loses its "truth" when removed from this original context with the goal of being collected and/or exhibited. Heidegger describes a difference that reminds us of Benjamin's difference between "cult value" and "exhibition value." He writes: "When a work is brought into a collection or placed in an exhibition, we say also that it is 'set up.' But this setting up differs essentially from setting up as erecting a building, raising a statue, presenting a tragedy at a holy festival."[4] In other words, Heidegger differentiates between an artwork that is inscribed into a certain historical and/or ritual space and time and an artwork that is merely "exhibited" at a particular location but could be removed at any given moment—and therefore is contextless, worldless.

---

2   Martin Heidegger, *On the Origin of the Work of Art*, in Heidegger, *Basic Writings*, trans. David Farrell Krell (New York: HarperCollins, 2008), 143–212, here 158–59.

3   Heidegger, *Origin*, 162–63.

4   Heidegger, *Origin*, 169.

But why can only the immediate, local context of the artwork—its specific "here and now"—be depicted? Why is it impossible to determine its place in the global world? Is the "world image" ("Weltbild"), as Heidegger will call it later (see below) possible? At the beginning of his *Vorlesungen über die Ästhetik* (Lectures on Aesthetics, 1835–38, posthumously), Gotthold Wilhelm Friedrich Hegel states that the time of "Bilddenken" ("picture-thinking") is over and in its relationship to its highest goal, which is to present the truth, art is a thing of the past.[5] Already in his *Phänomenologie des Geistes* (Phenomenology of Spirit, 1806–7), Hegel insists on a critique of "picture-thinking." To the ancient Greeks, the gods presented themselves as statues, as images. But Christianity taught us to distrust images, proclaiming God to be invisible. However, Hegel does not believe that art cannot present the truth as an image because the truth is hidden behind the surface of the visible, sensible world. Hegel does not share Immanuel Kant's understanding of truth as a transcendent "Ding an sich" ("thing in itself"). Rather, he believes that truth resides in "der an- und fürsichseiende Geist" ("the spirit that is in and for itself").[6] This means that we are not outside but inside the truth. And, being inside the truth, we cannot see it—we can only move within it following the movement of truth itself by submitting our own thinking to the rules of dialectical logic. Our social life is regulated by a system of laws. Our relationship to nature is defined by science. We can understand law and science, we can think them—but they do not show themselves as images. By producing art, however, we present our own thinking in the context of the external, sensible world. But our thinking is presented there in an "entäußerten" ("alienated") form.[7]

Compared with Hegel, the position of Heidegger is much more complicated. He believes that the production of "world images" ("Weltbilder") is not an ancient but precisely a modern phenomenon.[8] At the same time, according to Heidegger, this production is based on an ontological fallacy: Man imagines himself to be a subject, while to him the world presents itself as an object, an image.[9] This illusion is not accidental—it is based on the specific "positioning" ("*Stellung*") of man in the modern world. This positioning is defined not so much by modern science, as Hegel once believed it to be, but rather, following Heidegger, by modern technology. Modern technology creates the framing, or

---

5    G. W. F. Hegel, *Vorlesungen über die Ästhetik I*, in *Werke in 20 Bänden*, vol. 13 (Frankfurt am Main: Suhrkamp, 1970), 25.

6    G. W. F. Hegel, *Phenomenology of Spirit*, trans. A. V. Miller (Oxford: Oxford University Press, 1977), 325.

7    Hegel, *Ästhetik*, 28.

8    Martin Heidegger, *Die Zeit der Weltbilder*, in *Holzwege* (Frankfurt am Main: Vittorio Klostermann, 1977), 75–113, here 85.

9    Heidegger, *Weltbilder*, 87–88.

"apparatus" ("Gestell"), that allows man to position himself as a subject vis-a-vis the world.[10] As Heidegger says, this "apparatus" remains concealed from us—precisely because it opens the world to our gaze. Now, Heidegger speaks about "Gestell" as "producing and presenting (*Her- und Dar-stellend*)" and mentions in this context "erecting a statue in the temple precinct."[11] The problem of the "Gestell" begins to be related to the "exhibition" ("Ausstellung")—understood not as a pure act of presenting but as presenting of presenting, as revelation of the "Gestell." This means that the exhibition presents not only an image to our gaze but also demonstrates the technology of presenting, the inner "apparatus" and structure of the "Gestell," the mode in which our gaze is determined, oriented, and manipulated by modern technology. Indeed, when we visit an exhibition, we do not only look at the exhibited images and objects but also reflect on the spatial and temporal relationships among them, their hierarchies, the curatorial choices, and strategies that produced the exhibition, and so on. The exhibition exhibits itself—before it exhibits anything else. And by so doing, the exhibition exhibits the "Gestell," the modern technology that let us see the world as the "world image" ("Weltbild"), to have a "worldview" ("Weltanschauung"). To conclude: the "worldview" is a technologically created illusion—but the world "exhibition" shows precisely how this illusion is produced and presented. In this way, the "exhibition" ("Ausstellung") is able to reveal our "Gestell," our true positioning in the world.

The history of modern world fairs, or "world exhibitions," started as early as 1851 at London's famed Crystal Palace—an impressive iron-and-glass structure that was built solely for the purpose of a four-and-a-half-month-long exhibition from May to October. In the art context, the great museums like the Louvre (Paris), the Hermitage (St. Petersburg), or the Metropolitan Museum of Art (New York), as well as exhibitions like the *Documenta* in Kassel or numerous Biennials, had and still have a claim to present art of the entire world. Here the individual items are removed from their original contexts—and put into the artificial context of a collection in which the images and objects meet what could never have met "historically" in "real life." In the context of these collections we can see, for example, the Egyptian gods besides Mexican or Inca gods that would never have met in their respective universes—in combination with the utopian dreams of the avant-garde that were never realized in "real life." These removals from the original contexts and positionings in new contexts implicate the applications of violence, including economic and direct military intervention. That is why art collections and exhibitions

---

10  Heidegger, *Weltbilder*, 87–88.
11  Martin Heidegger, *The Question Concerning Technology*, in *Basic Writings*, 307–41, here 324–25.

display orders, laws, and trade practices that regulate our world as well as ruptures to which these orders are subjected—wars, revolutions, crimes. These orders cannot be "seen" but they can be and are manifested in the organization of the exhibition—in the way in which art "frames." As visitors we are not outside but inside this frame. We are exhibited through the exhibition—to ourselves and to others. That is why the exhibition is not an object but an event. The aura of an artwork does not simply get lost when this artwork is removed from its original, local context. Every artwork becomes re-contextualized and attains a new "here and now" in the event of an exhibition—and in the history of exhibitions in general. That is why an exhibition cannot be reproduced—one can reproduce only an image or an object that is placed in front of a "subject." But the exhibition can be reenacted, restaged. In this respect, the exhibition is similar to the theatrical *mise en scène*—but with one important difference: in the case of the exhibition visitors do not remain in front of the stage but enter the stage, become participants in the exhibition-event. This basic characteristic of the exhibition, including an exhibition of a collection, is relevant also for the Internet age.

The artworks that are specifically produced for the Internet take, as a rule, a character of documentary realism. On the Internet artists mostly combine photographs, videos, and texts—in other words, they function as freelance journalists. They use the means of production and distribution that are prescribed by the Internet to be compatible with its protocols—protocols that are generally used for the spreading of information. In this sense, artists lose their traditional role of "form shapers." Instead, they become content providers: they document contents that are not covered by mainstream media. And they cover these contents in a somewhat "subjective," personalized way from a perspective that the mainstream media does not take. This content can be an already existing situation that is strange in itself or, on the contrary, too trivial to be taken up by standard journalism. It can be a documentation of forgotten or publicly repressed historical events. But it can also be a situation that was produced by the artists themselves—actions, performances, and processes initiated in an aesthetic framework and then documented by their creators. And it can be completely "fictitious"—here the process of creating fiction becomes part of that which is documented. The cumulative effect of these strategies is not far from nineteenth-century realism when artists combined conventional means of representation with personalized choices of contents along with "subjective" interpretations.

In this sense, the Internet offers a solution to the old conflict between art and mass media. As early as during the nineteenth century mass media became the primary source of information, including information about art. Individual artists could not compete with these media. Instead, they increasingly became topics covered by the media.

That means they became more and more the content, whereas the media functioned as providers of this content. This process started with artists and poets of Romanticism and intensified itself during the period of the historical avant-garde movements at the beginning of the twentieth century—for example, in the case of Italian Futurism or early Dada. The primary way to receive information about avant-garde art events was to read about them in the press—and maybe to look at the drawings or photographs that illustrated the press coverage. For the artist, the shift in perspective was significant, because within art production content did lose its dominant role over time. This process culminated in abstract art. In abstract art, artists consider the form of their artworks to be their content. The function of providing content in a traditional sense was now fulfilled by journalism and art history. This condition was deeply unsatisfying for the artists. The ascent of electronic media and the emergence of the Internet changed this condition by allowing artists to become the providers of their own contents once again. Online, artists cover their own activities—and are liberated from selection and censorship imposed on them by the mass media. Art in the digital age, hence, is identical with journalism—both of which become individualized, personalized with regard to their content even if both of them remain standardized in their form. The theoreticians of twentieth-century formalism, for example Roman Jakobson, believed that the artistic use of the means of communication entails the suspension and even annulment of information, of content—in the art context, the content is completely absorbed by the form. Yet in the context of the Internet, the form remains identical for all the messages—and thus the content becomes immunized from its absorption by the form. The Internet reestablishes on the technological level the conventions of content presentation that dominated in the nineteenth century. Avant-garde artists protested against these conventions because they believed them to be purely arbitrary and merely culturally determined. But in the context of the Internet such a revolt against these conventions no longer makes any sense because they are inscribed into information technology itself.

Accordingly, art is presented on the Internet as a specific kind of activity: as documentation of a work process that takes place in the real, offline world. More importantly, on the Internet art operates in the same space as military planning, tourism, capital flows, and so on: Google shows, among other things, that there are no walls in the space of the Internet. The user of the Internet does not switch from the everyday use of things to their contemplation—the Internet users use information about art in the same way in which they use information about all other things in the world. It seems as if we all became an infinite museum's or gallery's staff—art being documented explicitly as taking place in the unified space of profane activities. Of course, during recent decades art museums and galleries began to exhibit art documentation of performances, artistic interventions, or long-time artistic projects alongside traditional artworks. But this neighborhood is highly problematic. Artworks are art—they immediately present themselves as art. So they can be admired, emotionally experienced, analyzed, and so on. But the art documentation is not art: it merely refers to an art event, or exhibition, or installation, or project that we assume has really taken place. The art documentation refers to art, but it is not art. That is why the art documentation can be reformatted, rewritten, extended, shortened, and so on. One can subject art documentation to all such operations that are forbidden in the case of an artwork because such operations would change the form of the artwork itself. The form of the artwork is still institutionally backed because only the form guarantees the reproducibility and identity of any specific artwork. On the contrary, documentation can be changed at will, because its identity and reproducibility is guaranteed by its "real," external referent and not by its form. But even if the emergence of art documentation precedes the emergence of the Internet as an art medium, only with the introduction of the Internet has art documentation obtained its legitimate place in the framework of art.

As said, contemporary art exhibitions use the Internet in the same way in which they previously used locally produced art. These exhibitions remove the particular documentation from their original Internet sites and combine them in a way that contradicts the usual Internet topology. Here again, the removal of the documentation from its original site reveals the hidden "apparatus" ("Gestell") of the Internet. The exhibition makes its own framing visible—and, consequently, it also makes visible the Internet topology itself. Every exhibition practice is selective, including the art exhibition practice. But this selection is also—or at least should be—an anti-selection that is transgressive and, most importantly, explicit through exclusion. The curatorial selection is relevant precisely when it crosses local borders, be it geographical borders or the borders of particular Internet groups and chat rooms. Here we encounter a seemingly paradoxical phenomenon of universalist selection. The selection is universalist not when it is all-inclusive. The selection becomes universalist when it reveals the universal practice of framing, the universal "Gestell" that defines and directs our gaze. And the only way to reveal this "Gestell" is to remove and relocate the images and objects of our world, in other words: to make an exhibition.

The application of exhibition practices with respect to Internet art documentation confronts the art system with new challenges: the Internet documentation should not be merely relocated but also reformatted. The collector of the art documentation becomes its curator. Collecting art documentation not only locates them in a real, offline space but also gives them a certain form. The new orientation toward meaning and communication does not imply that art became somehow immaterial, that its materiality lost its relevance, or that its medium dissolved into its message. The contrary is the case. Every artwork is material—and can only be material. Language itself is material through and through—as a combination of acoustic and visual signs. The transmission of information on the Internet is also a material process—using electricity as its medium and the Internet's hardware as its material tool. An equivalence, or at least a parallelism, can be seen between word and image, between the order of words and the order of things, the grammar of language and the grammar of visual space. Every documentation that is circulating on the Internet can be presented by an installation using different media inside the exhibition space. But while the individual artwork can be reproduced, the exhibition-event can only be documented. Such a documentation if posted online begins to circulate on the Internet. As a result, the exchange between museum and Internet takes on the character of exchange between documentation and installation: what was an installation inside an art exhibition space becomes a documentation on the Internet—and vice versa.

Meanwhile, the goal of the art exhibition practice remains the same—to create a "world exhibition" by combining traditional art objects and different art documentations in one and the same exhibition space. Our time is characterized by a new tension between the global and the local. This tension originates in the way in which global markets operate: some products are distributed only locally, some of them globally. The same can be said about the global art market that is dominated by auction houses like Sotheby's and Christie's and big international galleries. The new online exhibitions are transgressive also in relationship to this global sector of the art trade. International exhibitions like the *Documenta* and some Biennales show art that is not globally traded but has an international and historical significance—manifesting in and reflecting on the contemporary age. In this respect these exhibitions continue a tradition of the "great" museums of the past.

These traditional universalist museums received institutional support through the national state that tried to unite its population as well as through the imperial state's ambitions to integrate non-Western cultures. Today the creation of the same kind of universal museum would require the patronage of the universal state. However, such a universal, global state does not exist. This is why we could say that today's art system plays a role in the symbolic substitution of such a universal state by favoring private and public collections as well as temporary exhibitions that claim to present the universalism of global art and culture—that means art and culture of the non-existent, utopian global state. Our time is characterized by a lack of balance between political and economic powers, between public institutions and commercial practices. Our economy operates on the global level, whereas our politics operates on the local level. It is at this juncture that art collecting and curating play a crucial political role by at least partially compensating for the lack of global public space and global politics.

# 3: Should Libraries Still Be Charged with Collecting in a Digital Environment?

*Michael Knoche*

L IBRARIES HAVE BEEN building and cultivating collections of trustworthy print publications to fulfill their function as reliable storage facilities for centuries. The scope and selectivity of the collection were always criteria for the library's rank. Collection development has typically been regarded as the noblest task of the academic librarian. Today, digital publications are ubiquitously available. Funding agencies consider the continued collection of printed materials by libraries to be problematic, because there is no guarantee that there will be a future demand for them. From this perspective, it seems reasonable for libraries to care only about information and texts in electronic/digital format as currently needed by their users. In this essay I argue that library collections, which are a combination of printed books, other media, and digital resources, still add great value to research. Every single library, however, can fulfill its task only within a network of other libraries.

There is no other institution for which the question of collecting is so existentially important as it is for libraries. Government archives receive their material more or less automatically through the administrative activity of the institution to which they belong. The reason for most museums' existence is similar: to add original objects to their holdings and to develop them into unique collections. For them, digital media are only the means to an end, to improve users' access to those objects. Academic libraries predominately deal with non-unique objects that are accessible from many different places. Thus it remains completely open as to whether or not libraries should develop their own collections for the future. At any given moment in the here and now, thousands of decisions for or against collections are being made that will be pivotal for the future of libraries, their function, and appearance.

## Collecting in Anticipation of Demand versus Just-in-Time-Delivery

Funding agencies complain the loudest about the alleged "waste" of money by libraries. Financial experts accuse libraries of purchasing sources for an uncertain demand without being able to promise that they will ever be read. They ask if libraries could not acquire just the publications that are currently necessary for teaching and research purposes. Financial officers and chief accountants emphasize the efficiency of a just-in-time purchase and delivery system in the industrial sector and claim that these methods should suffice equally well for libraries.

Another example of abandoning the old paradigm of collecting in anticipation of a diminished demand is the decision by the Deutsche Forschungsgemeinschaft (German Research Foundation) in 2012 to give up the principle of special collecting fields and instead favor specialized information services. Within the former system of special collecting fields, forty-four libraries were commissioned to comprehensively acquire scientifically relevant literature for one of the 120 collecting fields. All participating libraries had agreed to make their special holdings available across the country and beyond. This way, collections of analog and digital media in each and every scientific field evolved that are simultaneously broad and deep: a universal collection, distributed throughout the country.

The decision to end this program in 2012 was controversial among German librarians. Although representatives of the German Research Foundation repeatedly emphasized that the change in priorities was merely a correction of their funding policies and was not to be understood as a statement about the development of library collections, their message was clear: the development of comprehensive collections in the sense of a reservoir was no longer supported.[1] Consequently, a new program was adopted that is intended to support new information services "under special consideration of the research interests in the respective specialist communities," or "Fachinformationsdienste."[2] As a result, the focus in funding shifted from collecting to information services.

---

1    Christoph Kümmel and Peter Strohschneider, "Ende der Sammlung? Die Umstrukturierung der Sondersammelgebiete der Deutschen Forschungsgemeinschaft," *Zeitschrift für Bibliothekswesen und Bibliographie* 61 (2014): 120–29, here 126. Critical of this is Rolf Griebel, "Ein folgenreicher Paradigmenwechsel: Die Ablösung der Sondersammelgebiete durch die Fachinformationsdienste für die Wissenschaft," *Zeitschrift für Bibliothekswesen und Bibliographie* 61 (2014): 138–57. See also Kizer Walker, "Re-envisioning Distributed Collections in German Research Libraries: a view from the U.S.A.," *Bibliothek Forschung und Praxis* 39 (2015): 7–12.

2    Deutsche Forschungsgemeinschaft, "Fachinformationsdienste: DFG stärkt Dienstleistungen der Bibliotheken für die Wissenschaft," *Pressemitteilung* 54 (December 20, 2013), www.dfg.de/service/presse/pressemitteilungen/2013/pressemitteilung_nr_54/index.html. See also Anne Lipp, Sigrun Eckelmann, Johannes Fournier, Katja Hartig, Angela Holzer, Christoph Kümmel, Franziska Regner, and Stefan Winkler-Nees, "Die digitale Transformation weiter gestalten: Das Positionspapier der Deutschen Forschungsgemeinschaft zu einer innovativen

If one is willing to forgo collection development in anticipation of demand in libraries, librarians would condone the procurement of virtual material and say farewell to printed literature. Only electronic publications can be provided immediately, that is, upon demand. The acquisition of books, however, would be too time consuming and costly in comparison. Would such a transformation—one that is in fact already in place and produces data on its own—be feasible and desirable?

In certain scientific fields, an e-only policy is not only feasible but more critical when research results evolve on the basis of or in competition to other comparative research projects: in the experimental, simulation-capable and observational forms of research (that is, in most natural and social sciences, technical disciplines, and medicine), the maximum speed and precision of information are of the utmost importance. Research results in these fields are almost entirely digitally accessible and see a high level of distribution. Libraries serve in such cases as distributing institutions and intersections of scientifically produced knowledge.

Nevertheless, one question remains open: If libraries no longer offer collections according to the abundance paradigm, then researchers must know exactly what they are looking for. It would be a misconception to assume that researchers only consult a library when certain publications are needed. Libraries work like the finest search engines, enabling users to discover much more than what they thought they were looking for.[3] Surely, searches in the World Wide Web result in productive findings, but library collections open up access beyond search algorithms with their often-clumsy pathways of knowledge in an uncurated environment.

To put it another way, scholars often enter a library—and this is true for all disciplines—with the same expectation as readers paging through the newspaper. They cannot say in advance what exactly is of interest to them. They browse headlines and select an article from the content provided, sometimes here, sometimes there. The newspaper offers a wealth of information, from which perhaps only every twentieth article is read attentively. Similarly, researchers and scholars examine new acquisitions at a library or journals on display in order to find out what topics are new or are currently being discussed in their respective fields. Like a newspaper, a library collection can provide information and inspiration—assuming it is rich, inviting, and accessible, and stimulates discovery.[4] The lack of a

---

Informationsinfrastruktur," *Zeitschrift für Bibliothekswesen und Bibliographie* 59 (2012): 291–300.

3    Ross Atkinson, "Six Key Challenges for the Future of Collection Development," *Library Resources & Technical Services* 50 (2006): 244–51, here 247.

4    Richard Landwehrmeyer, "Ich brauche ihre Bibliothek gar nicht: Reminiszenzen eines ausgedienten Erwerbungsbibliothekars," in *Der Ort der Bücher: Festschrift für Joachim Stoltzenburg zum 75. Geburtstag,* ed. Uwe Jochum (Konstanz: Universitätsverlag, 1996), 205–224, here 217.

reservoir of publications that reflects the latest state of knowledge in a particular field would also have serious implications for interdisciplinary cooperation. How can researchers become familiar with neighboring disciplines if there is no curated pre-selection, and online publications have to be supplied each time anew and in their entirety?

How does this serendipity-principle work in a traditional library? Let us take as example a book that deals with literature and art in Germany around 1970. The librarian would place the physical book on the shelf either under art history or literary theory. Any librarian would be well-advised to include a catalog reference—or tag—that brings attention to the field of philosophy, so that a Nietzsche scholar interested in Nietzsche's views on art would also be able to find the book. This researcher will then undoubtedly discover a discussion from around 1970, in which Nietzsche's aesthetics were an important point of reference. Between the book's shelving and subject indexing, the library establishes connections between publications.

A collection's abundance challenges the library visitor to make multiple decisions as to what contexts are meaningful for their area of interest. They may find a book on the same shelf, for example, that treats their problem from a completely different perspective, or they may discover something unexpected while searching the catalog. Confronted with not one but many answers to questions that did not exist before the bibliographical search had begun, the user finds a string of connections, made by the librarian, to this publication. Collections maintained by librarians, therefore, are far more than just the sum of their individual publications. Nikolaus Wegmann calls this phenomenon the "labyrinthine character of the library" that embodies its true strength.[5]

## Collecting in the Humanities

Within the humanities, a strict e-only policy would not only be undesirable; it would not even be feasible. In 2017 a total of 72,000 printed books were released in Germany alone.[6] Only roughly a third of the subscriptions to magazines and journals, for example, of the Bayerische Staatsbibliothek—one of the most e-friendly libraries in Germany—are available in digital format.[7] For example, there is no digital version of the journals that are crucial for the field of musicology such as "Die

---

5 Nikolaus Wegmann, "Im Labyrinth," *Bibliothek Forschung und Praxis* 42 (2018): 370–78.

6 *Buch und Buchhandel in Zahlen 2018* (Frankfurt am Main: MVB, 2018). Only printed books are counted completely; e-books and print-on-demand publications are not sufficiently covered.

7 Griebel, "Paradigmenwechsel," 152.

Musikforschung," "Acta musicologica," or "Musiktheorie." Moreover, the majority of publications of the twentieth century still under copyright are available only in print; a very small percentage have been published online by Google Books; however, they are incomplete and illegal according to German law. Only as of the year 2000 did a significant number of legal (that is, publisher-licensed) e-book editions begin to become available in addition to the printed versions. The humanities cannot do without the substantial portion of literature that is still exclusively available in printed form. The historian Martin Schulze Wessel pleads to this effect in a widely acclaimed article:

> Literaturbeschaffung hat langfristige Folgen: Was nicht gekauft wird, ist künftig nicht vorhanden und lässt sich nur selten nachträglich erwerben. Die . . . Geschichtswissenschaften . . . leben vom Paradigmenwechsel; was heute bedeutsam erscheint, kann morgen irrelevant werden. Der Politikgeschichte der fünfziger Jahre wäre das Sammeln von Quellen und Literatur, die für sozialgeschichtliche Fragestellungen wichtig ist, nebensächlich erschienen; die Sozialgeschichte der sechziger Jahre hätte alltagsgeschichtliche Fragen bei der Literaturbeschaffung ignoriert, und alle zusammen hätten sich kaum für den Erwerb von Büchern und Zeitschriften zur Frauen- und Gendergeschichte eingesetzt. Welche Themen künftig relevant sein werden, wissen wir nicht.

> [The acquisition of literature has long-term consequences: What isn't purchased now will not be available in the future and can rarely be acquired later. Studies in the field of history rely on paradigm shifts: what seems important today may become irrelevant tomorrow. Political history would have deemed the collecting of primary sources and literature that became important for questions relevant to social history insignificant; the subfield of social history of the 1960s would have ignored questions pertinent to everyday lives and neglected relevant book acquisitions; and none of them would have invested in the acquisition of books and magazines about the history of women and gender. We cannot know which subject matter will be relevant in the future.][8]

According to Schulze Wessel, who eloquently presents the position of the German Association of Historians, the consequence of abandoning future-oriented collecting practices would be the loss of entire research objects for the humanities. For this reason, he maintains that research-oriented libraries should continue to develop collections on a broad scale.

---

8    Martin Schulze Wessel, "Sammeln für die Interessen von morgen." *Frankfurter Allgemeine Zeitung*, April 8, 2015, N4.

These collections would be a combination of printed books, various other media, and digital resources alike.

Books, like all other media, must be shown in a catalog system that is not only an inventory list but also treats them according to the principles of Linked Open Data and consequently standardizes them. Linked Open Data means that bibliographic data must be released without restriction under open licenses for further processing and linking. The principle of standardization requires, for example, that the name of an author will be listed in all its variations. This is easy to handle when libraries participate in the collaborative production of standard data. In addition to millions of personal names, for example, the German Gemeinsame Normdatei (Comprehensive Standard File) now also contains geographical names, conference titles, work titles, and so on, with all its variations—for an unambiguous assignment of a person or thing. If the same rules are applied internationally, the standards files can also be exchanged via an identification number on a large scale.[9]

Beyond matters of organizing book and media collections, the broader question of what libraries collect and how they may form a network is of the essence. There are two aspects that justify the continued existence of individual library collections: the selection of sources worthy of storage and the establishment of relationships between collections. The idea of a "digital world library" that contains virtually everything that has ever been published is as utopian as it is horrifying. We would be confronted with a gigantic heap of disorganized and hence useless information not unlike what the Internet already produces. Collecting and indexing is such a complex and intellectual achievement that it cannot be organized centrally for humanity as such or even for a single nation.

Thus far, I used the notion of "collecting" in the pragmatic sense of a librarian, that is, by referring to the acquisition of publications that may be selected and added to the book collection by following certain criteria. Librarians establish a large reservoir of materials in order to meet a known demand and to somehow foresee the needs of future researchers.[10] I would like to address three questions in particular, followed by considerations pertinent to each of these questions: First, Historical library collections often include specific sub-collections, such as special collections or private estates. How can these sub-collections be made productive

---

9 Thomas Mann, "The Research Library as Place: On the Essential Importance of Collections of Books Shelved in Subject-Classified Arrangements," in *The Library as Place: History, Community, and Culture*, ed. John E. Buschman and Gloria J. Leckie (Westport, CT: Libraries Unlimited, 2007), 191–206.

10 Peter Strohschneider, "Faszinationskraft der Dinge: Über Sammlung, Forschung und Universität," *Denkströme: Journal der Sächsischen Akademie der Wissenschaften* 8 (2012): 9–26.

for research purposes? Second, Is it possible to assign digital data that is stored on library servers in the form of attributes of a collection itself (that is, not on the level of metadata similar to those in library catalogs)? Third, What does the future of collecting in libraries look like?

## 1. Collections within Collections

Some of the oldest European libraries already include autonomous sub-collections that are often merged with library collections and catalogs today. In the early modern period, for example, very few books were acquired by regular purchases from bookstores. Instead, it was typical to integrate entire estates, special collections, or private libraries into public libraries. "Like a set of matryoshka stacking dolls, a library houses a number of collections nested inside each other," as Wulf D. von Lucius puts it.[11] Only in a few cases, such as medieval autographs or incunabula, were the libraries able to answer questions about the historical context from which individual books originated and then place them within a library collection accordingly—when it came to particularly valuable objects, it was considered standard knowledge and widely shared among librarians. Librarians were, however, usually unable to answer questions about the sources of the majority of their holdings. For centuries, librarians were primarily engaged in presenting their holdings according to factual parameters and not provenance. To give just one example: as the director of the Weimar library, Johann Wolfgang Goethe had the private book estate of Duchess Anna Amalia divided up according to preexisting subject areas. As a result, the Duchess's collection was incorporated into the massive library holdings.

Nevertheless, the cultural-historical context of each library's holdings became a more established area of self-reflection and even research. Consequently, Jürgen Weber recognizes a rediscovery of sub-collections within libraries.[12] Provenance data is now frequently available as part of electronic catalogs. The next step would be to make the affiliations of widely strewn objects to their original sub-collections apparent. There are currently some very promising approaches to describing these collections,

---

11 Wulf D. von Lucius, "Bücher sind mehr als ihre Inhalte: Gedanken über Bücher, ihre Materialität, ihre künstlerische Gestaltung, ihre Besitzgeschichte und den sammlerischen Kontext." *Libernensis: Zeitschrift der Universitätsbibliothek Bern* 1 (2008): 6–13.

12 Jürgen Weber, "Sammlungsspezifische Erschließung: Die Wiederentdeckung der Sammlungen in den Bibliotheken," *Bibliotheksdienst* 43 (2009): 1162–78. See also Ulrich Johannes Schneider, "Bücher als Herausforderungen der Wissensgeschichte," in *Frühneuzeitliche Bibliotheken als Zentren des europäischen Kulturtransfers*, ed. Claudia Brinker von der Heyde and Annakatrin Inder (Stuttgart: S. Hirzel, 2014), 263–71.

but there are not yet any generally recognized and comprehensively applied regulations. One approach comprises the collection data set that the Herzogin Anna Amalia Bibliothek has been using for several years. It follows the Dublin-Core-Standard and includes information about contents, legal status, use, collector, heritage, and the relationship to other sub-collections. Figures 3.1 and 3.2 show two examples of such collection descriptions from the OPAC (Online Public Access Catalog) of the Herzogin Anna Amalia Library, Weimar.

Figure 3.1. Collection data set for Goethe's private library.
All 6,000 titles can be accessed from this page.

Figure 3.2. Collection data set for Goethe's book loans from
the Ducal Library.

## 2. What Are the Benefits of a Library that Makes Its Affiliated Collection Information Transparent?

First, collections connect certain objects with a particular historical context and location. As collections are developed according to specific criteria, they represent a cultural-historical body that can be investigated by researchers in regard to their genesis and their significance. Second, thematic collections usually consist of a series of similar objects (for example, eighteenth-century English novels). The density of materials enables the differentiation between typical and atypical objects, allowing for comparative studies. Third, collections separate objects from the outside world by means of selection and thus help to better manage the overwhelming diversity of printed materials and media that is published every year.

Here is an example to illustrate why knowledge about the affiliations of objects within a collection is of great benefit. Having been published by the thousands, a Reclam booklet with four missing pages made its way from Friedrich Nietzsche's private library to the Herzogin Anna Amalia Library. This booklet is significant for a variety of reasons. Nietzsche purchased the narrative poem "The Prisoner of the Caucasus" by Aleksandr Pushkin from 1875 and marked up the text while reading it. This specific booklet not only offers Pushkin researchers insights into Pushkin's reception in Germany, but it also offers the Nietzsche researcher, to no lesser degree, insights into Nietzsche's interest in Pushkin. At the same time researchers interested in the process of reading per se gain an understanding of an individual reading practice, namely Nietzsche's method of reading with a pencil in hand, while book historians may retrieve information about the production methods and durability of inexpensive book editions and their circulation and use. But the booklet also simply offers the literature lover the opportunity to read Pushkin's poem and the Nietzsche admirer a chance to hold a work in their hand that was once in the possession of the philosopher himself.

For good reasons, this specific case could be considered what Susan Leigh Star calls a "boundary object."[13] Such objects can be meaningful in various contexts and be interpreted differently by various individuals. Just imagine the loss of information had the Herzogin Anna Amalia Bibliothek not highlighted the provenance of this otherwise quite unspectacular little book in its catalog. Otherwise library patrons might have questioned why the library had kept such a defective and cheaply produced copy of Pushkin's poem in its collection.

---

13   Susan Leigh Star and James Griesemer. "Institutional Ecology, 'Translations' and Boundary Objects: Amateurs and Professionals in Berkeley's Museum of Vertebrate Zoology, 1907–39," *Social Studies of Science* 19 (1989): 387–420. See also Susan Leigh Star et. al., *Grenzobjekte und Medienforschung*, ed. Sebastian Gießmann and Nadine Taha (Bielefeld: Transcript 2017).

In short: libraries have recognized that collections may increase the dimension of significance of individual objects by providing additional information pertaining to their provenance and history of acquisition. This contextual information not only enriches the library's holdings but offers library patrons a plethora of ways to interpret and "read" books.

This raises the question of the status of libraries' electronic resources and whether they can be considered part of their holdings. Libraries enjoy showing how many electronic resources can be found in their catalogs. But strictly speaking, the many licensed e-books, journals and data banks cannot be included in their collections. Libraries do not purchase electronic media but can only offer their users access to them for a limited period of time. Collections, on the other hand, require a permanent location and must be in the possession of an owner. As seen above, collections of physical objects can be seen as "polycentric," that is, they do not serve a single purpose but can be approached from different directions and with diverse intentions.[14]

This limitation does not hinder libraries from simultaneously establishing digital collections in hopes of fulfilling the very same requirements. These collections consist of copies of real objects, such as digitized old prints or files that were digitally produced, such as movies. Research data that was generated during the course of scientific study plays an increasingly important role, too. In the humanities, research data may include personal letters by an author that a researcher has transcribed for their project, to name just one example of the use of additional electronically reproduced material. Digital text editions along with their sources and research data make up another growing subfield of digitized material that could constitute its own collection over a period of time. The added value of such library collections beyond their accessibility through the Internet lies in the fact that libraries create a networked research space in which the various digital resources are intelligently linked, quality assurance and long-term availability are guaranteed, links remain stable, and the provenance of information is transparent.[15]

The fact that objects in digital collections are easily copied and coexist in other contexts does not speak against collecting them. In principle, this also holds true for books. It is more important for the library to guarantee the authenticity of its objects. This can only be achieved by granting

---

14   The term "polycentric" is used by Ross Atkinson, "The Conditions of Collection Development," in *Collection Management: A New Treatise*, ed. Charles B. Osburn and Ross Atkinson, vols. 1–2 (Greenwich, CT: JAI, 1991), 26–48.

15   Cf. Thomas Stäcker, "Von Alexandria lernen: Die Forschungsbibliothek als Ort digitaler Philologie," in *Frauen—Bücher—Höfe: Wissen und Sammeln vor 1800/Women—Books—Courts: Knowledge and Collecting before 1800; Essays in Honor of Jill Bepler*, ed. Volker Bauer, Elizabeth Harding, Gerhild Scholz Williams, and Mara R. Wade (Wiesbaden: Harrassowitz, 2018), 93–103.

libraries curatorial control and ownership over the data that they collect and provide. Following best practices with the greater public in mind, libraries are the institutions that possess the necessary expertise and neutrality and are independent and trustworthy enough to take responsibility for the integrity of the data and the stability of the knowledge they gather.

It must be stated that the term "collection" cannot be limited exclusively to real objects. Electronic files can also grow into collections.[16] Nowadays there are libraries that almost exclusively acquire electronic resources. If they focus on the humanities, however, I believe that they should continue to invest in printed materials. Such libraries will continue to be hybrid collections for a long time to come.

## 3. The Future of Collecting in Libraries

Libraries that remain committed to their mandate to collect and are willing to continue to expand both their analog and digital holdings are confronted with tremendous logistical challenges. At the same time, expenditures grow while budgetary restrictions limit financial latitude.[17] Such libraries can only fulfill their mandate for the benefit of research if they begin to focus on special types of objects or collecting practices, if they have not already done so. All library tasks from collection development to bibliography, physical storage, storage of digital data, and the transfer of information, to name a few, can only be organized in concerted cooperation that includes internal and other research networks at the city, regional, and national levels, but ideally at an international level as well.

An example might illustrate the necessity of this cooperation: In order to cover one collection field—let's say: the history of Hungary—e-books, data banks, and other electronic resources need to be purchased along with printed literature. As they can usually only be licensed for a limited time, it must be determined how libraries intend to organize long-term access (hosting via Portico or Clockss would be two, albeit in my opinion insufficient, options). They must also store the available documents on Open Access and make them accessible. In addition, all media require qualified metadata that is discoverable in catalogs and search engines. Furthermore, there should be fast interlibrary exchanges so that printed material may quickly reach the hands of as many readers as possible. This example demonstrates that even for a seemingly small collection field the task of collecting and the assurance of all its adjacent responsibilities is

---

16  Cf. Andreas Degkwitz, "Digitale Sammlungen: Visionen eines Neubeginns," *Bibliothek Forschung und Praxis* 38 (2014): 411–14.

17  *Die Zukunft des Sammelns an wissenschaftlichen Bibliotheken*, ed. Michael Knoche (Wiesbaden: Harrassowitz, 2017).

enormous. This is why collecting must be divided into sub-tasks, which can then be solved by different cooperation partners. Each individual library may then decide whether it will "intensively" collect and archive its objects accordingly, or whether it will only collect, but not archive, or whether it will only offer access to digital publications.

Each library's acquisition activity can be understood as part of a network.[18] Consequently, libraries collect by utilizing the intelligent division of responsibilities. Collecting, then, can be seen as a "collective" enterprise and libraries as actors within a wide network that best functions as a system.[19]

---

18 Considerations for a system-wide collection concept are already well advanced in the United States. Cf. Lorcan Dempsey, Brian Lavoie, and Constance Malpas, *Understanding the Collective Collection: Towards a System-wide Perspective on Library Print Collections* (Dublin, OH: OCLC Research, 2013).

19 Michael Knoche, *Die Idee der Bibliothek und ihre Zukunft* (Göttingen: Wallstein, 2018); see also *Stärkung des Systems wissenschaftlicher Bibliotheken in Deutschland:. Ein Impulspapier des Ausschusses für Wissenschaftliche Bibliotheken und Informationssysteme der Deutschen Forschungsgemeinschaft Bonn*, Mai 22, 2018, www.dfg.de/download/pdf/foerderung/programme/lis/180522_awbi_impulspapier.pdf.

# 4: Museums and Collecting as/and Media in the Digital Age

## Peter M. McIsaac

IN THIS ESSAY I EXAMINE select museum responses to new media in order to develop ways of thinking about the changing contours of institutionalized collecting in the digital age. My approach is grounded in a conception of the museum as a discrete medial form whose operations have been and will remain crucial in shaping important aspects of collecting as a social practice and form of cultural memory. As I think of them, museums operate by means of key processes, practices, and competencies involved in organizing, classifying, assigning meaning, and remembering objects, both materially in space and in interaction with medial forms prevailing at particular historical moments. Conceived this way, museum processes and competencies are not the sole purview of museums as we have come to know them, nor have they been in the past. As an analysis of select historical junctures of medial rupture and institutional change shows, these processes and competencies have at times been shared with, or shaped by, other discrete media, institutions, and actors beyond current configurations of museums as they are known today. In addition to illuminating why museums are unlikely the victim of media substitution outright, an analysis of such a juncture raises the expectation that museums can and will experience reconfigurations relative to other entities with which they share their key processes.

I will present my argument in three parts. First, I will briefly delineate my conception of the museum as medium, with an eye toward linking museal processes with long-standing functions museums have had in arbitrating the world and organizing knowledge about it. As the analysis in part 2 will make clear, these functions remain connected with collecting through several historical junctures, in ways related to memory and knowledge production that can be expected to persist into the digital age in significant ways. To demonstrate this, the analysis will mark shifts in what Paula Findlen has described in terms of a *dispositif*[1] manifested by

---

1    Paula Findlen, "The Museum: Its Classical Etymology and Renaissance Genealogy," *Journal of the History of Collections* 1, no. 1 (January 1989): 59–78,

various forms of media of memory and learning from the Renaissance to the present. Here I will focus on two points: first the intertwined and privileged roles collecting and earlier conceptions of the "museum" have had in generating the value and meaning of objects. And second, how collections-based practices helped develop cognitive capacities to cope with the increasing amount of knowledge created by forms of new media that today is called "information overload." In part 3, I deploy these terms in the digital age, in order to examine how museums' *dispositif* for the digital age is taking shape, precisely with respect to flows of information, data, and metadata, and the place of museum environments in the digital age. As I will argue, museums are being transformed all along the line by digital technologies, yet as I will try to show in examining two cases of museal embrace of technological transformation (the Imperial War Museum North and the Cleveland Museum of Art), their emerging contours provide visitors with opportunities to resituate digital flows with respect to embodied existence and cognition.

## Museums as Medium

My approach to the question of museums and collecting in the digital age involves conceiving of museums in terms of what I have elsewhere called the "museum function."[2] In this conception, the museum function of a particular age or period can be thought of in terms of particular processes and practices that include collecting, inventorying, storing and preserving, and processing and displaying objects, and what in today's terms might be called relevant data and metadata. On the one hand, such an approach aims to mobilize a commonplace of much museum studies scholarship, often presented as etymologies of the word "museum" reaching back to the Ancient Greek usage, that there is a stable set of human-object relations in Western cultures designed to respond to ongoing human needs.[3] Yet these etymologies and other approaches have also clearly shown that practices of collecting, inventorying, storing, and displaying can vary widely from period to period, such that particular configurations may not draw the boundaries between their respective containers, institutions, and practices, and those with access in immediately recognizable ways.

---

here 59. Findlen uses the phrase "epistemological structure" to describe what I, following Foucault, am calling a *dispositif.*

2    Peter McIsaac, *Museum of the Mind: German Modernity and the Dynamics of Collecting* (University Park, PA: Penn State University Press, 2007), 12–14.

3    Jeffrey Abt, "The Origins of the Public Museum," in *A Companion to Museum Studies*, ed. Sharon Macdonald (Malden, MA: Blackwell, 2010), 115–34, here 116–23; and Findlen, 59–61.

Such an approach relying on object- and information-based practices has affinities with conceptions of the museum recently advanced by a number of scholars working in media and technology studies. As media theorist Wolfgang Ernst has repeatedly stressed, the "museum" deserves to be regarded as operating as a key element in a society's epistemological grid, which, as Ernst explicitly notes, can vary widely in terms of its particular dispositions of things and relationships to ways of preserving and knowing the world.[4] Ernst's approach, which generates insights by denying the museum the capacity to operate as a technical medium and observing differences between "media proper," that is, technical and new media, is helpful for foregrounding museums' unique and privileged connections to objects and people.[5] As Ernst has explained in a recent interview with Michelle Henning, museums' involvement with material objects puts them in the position of holding things that resist being fully subsumed by digitization.[6] With the increasing penetration of digital technologies into ever-greater aspects of today's world, museums can thus become ever more important as realms distinct from the digital and virtual, for reasons that also implicate people as embodied beings. As Ernst points out, museums do nothing with information without human beings as processors, setting them apart from technologies that can operate without a human dimension.[7]

Yet in denying the museum the capacity to operate as, or even be informed by, technical media *tout court*, Ernst's perspective is limited for thinking about ways that museums may prove capable of incorporating digital technologies, even as they remain crucial for defining the place of objects in/and physical space in relation to emerging notions of past, present, and future. With this concern, my approach has more in common with the work of Ross Parry and Andrew Sawyer, whose notion of the museum as an "adaptive medium" seeks, as does mine, to grasp museum configurations in terms of historical and technological contingencies that simultaneously allow for interpenetrations and exchanges between traditionally museal and technological realms.[8] Connections also exist to the

---

4    Wolfgang Ernst, "Archi(ve)textures of Museology," in *Museums and Memory*, ed. Susan A. Crane (Stanford, CA: Stanford University Press, 2000), 17–34, here 17–18.

5    Michelle Henning, "Museums and Media Archaeology: An Interview with Wolfgang Ernst," in *The International Handbooks of Museum Studies: Museum Media*, vol. 3, ed. Michelle Henning (New York: Wiley, 2015), 3–22, here 4–7.

6    Henning, "Museums," 4–5.

7    Henning, "Museums," 7.

8    Ross Parry and Andrew Sawyer, "Space and the Machine: Adaptive Museums, Pervasive Technology and the New Gallery Environment," in *Reshaping Museum Space: Architecture, Design, Exhibitions*, ed. Suzanne MacLeod (New York: Routledge, 2005), 39–53, here 39–40.

media archaeological approach of Andrew Hoskins and Amy Holdsworth, for whom the (over)abundance of digital media is a particular concern with regard to museums that were originally designed to thrive in environments of content-scarcity and a high degree of control over the way material objects set past, present, and future into relation.[9] The idea that museums might respond to the end of scarcity with a careful employment of digital and other new media in order to "reveal and interrogate the fissures, the unintended, and the gaps" in the flow of digital media and counter the "digital crushing of historical distance," offers a valuable way of articulating what digitally equipped museums can contribute to a world awash in digital flows.[10] Where my approach seeks to go beyond those of Parry and Sawyer or Hoskins and Holdsworth—which focus narrowly on museum architectures and curatorial perspectives, respectively—is to provide a medially conceived, historically grounded, and visitor-oriented account of how the encounters of museums and the digital can be thought to affect collecting and human cognition going forward.

Before going on, it is worth noting that one thing all these approaches suggest, looking to the past and to the future, is that theories of media substitution are unproductive for thinking about possible interplay between museums and digital media. That is to say, the idea that museums will outright perish with, or be subsumed by, the advent of digital technologies might well deserve consideration for what it reveals about our current cultural anxieties, but it does not get very far with respect to explaining the ability of museums to reconfigure in relation to prevailing forms of technology and media. In this regard, it is important to recall that digital and new media have been strongly implicated in the expansion of museum paradigms into everyday culture.[11] As the changing meanings of curation—including the rise of the verb "to curate" in more than one language—for instance indicate, ever-widening aspects of culture, particularly in its digital forms, are subject to processes of musealization.[12] As Hans Ulrich Obrist argues, such developments are by no means coincidental, in the sense both that they represent the latest stage in developments reaching back centuries, and that they are anchored in the

---

9    Andrew Hoskins and Amy Holdsworth, "Media Archaeology of/in the Museum," in *The International Handbooks of Museum Studies: Museum Media*, vol. 3, ed. Michelle Henning (New York: Wiley, 2015), 23–41, here 23–25.

10    Hoskins and Holdsworth, "Media Archaeology," 28.

11    Andreas Huyssen, *Twilight Memories: Marking Time in a Culture of Amnesia* (New York: Routledge, 1995), 14–18; and Mark W. Rectanus, *Culture Incorporated: Museums, Artists, and Corporate Sponsorships* (Minneapolis: University of Minnesota Press, 2002), 216–25.

12    Terry Smith, *Thinking Contemporary Curating* (New York: Independent Curators International, 2012), 17–19.

changing forms and functions of exhibition as cultural practice.[13] Rather than something coincidental, the attachment to museum terminology as a means of articulating the impacts of digital technologies is a strong indication that museum-based practices represent key touchpoints in both comprehending and shaping the emerging contours of digital culture.

## Museum Operations as Means of Shaping Medial and Cultural Competencies

Whatever forms these transformations and exchanges between the digital and museal ultimately end up taking, what I want to highlight as I move into part 2 is the notion that in the digital age, key cultural competencies are being shared or negotiated among more than one medial or institutional entity involved in collecting. Such a condition is in many ways nothing unusual in historical terms, insofar as the relationships and hand-offs between entities involved in collecting and prevailing media have in fact varied a great deal. As scholars have tended to agree with regard to the Renaissance and early modern era, for instance, written and physical collections were, unlike today, in many ways permeable in how they shaped and mediated human-object relations and were functionally interchangeable. In the early modern era, an appropriate book could have been called a museum as much as physical arrays of objects, which could in turn also contain books and libraries. Significant about this situation for my purposes is that arrays of objects in books and space could both address the functional needs collecting practices were pressed to fulfill. As Paula Findlen puts it, "the humanistic notion of collecting as a textual strategy and the social demands of prestige and display fulfilled by a collection, *musaeum* was an epistemological structure which encompassed a variety of ideas, images and institutions that were central to late Renaissance culture."[14] The fact that texts could carry the designation of museum does nothing to diminish the fact that object-based collections and displays remained crucial for Renaissance scholars and intellectuals to understand and enact, mentally and physically, the operations that went into grasping the world and what was known about it.

The early modern example is significant not merely because it demonstrates the point that more than a variety of media might be implicated in collections' ability to produce socially useful meaning and value. Rather, the *dispositif* Findlen locates in the Renaissance and early modern period developed in response to "the empirical explosion of materials that a wider dissemination of ancient texts, increased travel, voyages of discovery, and more systematic forms of communication and exchange had

---

13   Hans Ulrich Obrist, *Kuratieren!* (Munich: C. H. Beck, 2014), 35–39.
14   Paula Findlen, "The Museum," 59.

produced."[15] As scholars such as Ann Blair have also recently recognized, the media and materials of libraries, *Wunderkammern* (cabinets of wonder), and memory theaters functioned not merely as means of knowing the world, but in terms of information management systems developed to cope with challenges Blair likens to today's "information overload" and "information management."[16]

Such conditions surface not just in the bibliographic and archival systems in Blair's study but also in early modern works such as Tommaso Campanella's utopian dialogue *La città del Sole* (written in 1602, published 1623 in Latin under the title *Civitas Solis: Idea republicae philosophicae*, translated into English as *City of the Sun*). A text that figures prominently in Andrew McClellan's recent account of the origins of core ideals and functions in today's museums,[17] *City of the Sun* presents a vision of an ideal society whose perfection is grounded in the use of massive exhibitions covering the insides and outsides of all but one of its seven city walls to represent the natural and human-made state of the world.[18] As such, the Solarian city emerges as a kind of *Wunderkammer* laid out over the course of an entire city, promoting encyclopedic, ordered knowledge of the entire world and everything in it. As the traveler who purports to have seen the City of the Sun claims, the collections-based presentation of the world's knowledge not only enables children to absorb all that is known in easy fashion;[19] the methods of museum-based learning prove crucial for the city's elites to maintain the command of all aspects of knowledge that enables them to act as wise and humane leaders. Responding to his interlocutor's objection to the idea that any one person could obtain encyclopedic knowledge ("But who can know so much?"), the Genovese sailor reports how the city's residents responded to his own expressed disbelief:

> You must understand that your argument [that it is impossible to know so much; PM] is applicable to your own people rather than to ours because you term a man learned if he knows more than others do about Aristotle's grammar or logic or about some certain author—knowledge which requires only servile memory and which deprives the mind of vitality because it meditates upon books instead

---

15　Paula Findlen, *Possessing Nature: Museums, Collecting, and Scientific Culture in Early Modern Italy* (Berkeley: University of California Press, 1996), 3.

16　Ann M. Blair, *Too Much to Know: Managing Scholarly Information before the Modern Age* (New Haven, CT: Yale University Press, 2010), 1–5 and 169.

17　Andrew McClellan, *The Art Museum from Boullée to Bilbao* (Berkeley: University of California Press, 2008).

18　McClellan, *Art Museum*, 15.

19　Tommaso Campanella, *The City of the Sun: A Poetical Dialogue*, trans. Daniel J. Donno (Berkeley: University of California Press, 1981), 41–43.

of things . . . in our city the sciences may be learned with such facility, as you can see, that more may be gained here in one year than in ten or fifteen among you."[20]

As a method that promotes a mode of learning supposedly ten- to fifteen-times more efficient and rapid than that of books, collections-based learning supports forms of active remembering uniquely capable of understanding and navigating the world in all its respects. Crucial about this model is not merely its being thought capable of managing large amounts of knowledge, but a condition in which knowledge and information are rapidly accelerating due to the explosion of reproducible media (print) and technological innovation. As the Genovese sailor notes toward the end of the dialogue and extensive discussions of how the city's exhibitory structure undergirds their entire society:

> Genovese: Oh, if you only knew what they deduce . . . from our present century, which has produced more history in a hundred years than the whole world did in the preceding four thousand! More books have been written in the last century than in the previous five thousand years. And what they say about our stupendous inventions—the compass, the printing press, the harquebus—mighty signs of the imminent union of the world: . . . there will be a great new monarchy, reformation of laws and arts, new prophets and a general renewal. . . . Know this: that they have discovered the art of flying, the only art the world lacks, and they expect to discover a glass in which to see the hidden stars and a device by which to hear the music of the spheres.[21]

In terms surprisingly like what has been claimed about the explosion of information in our age, the Genoese sailor states two different times just how much human research and innovation and their relation to print media are changing what can be known. As part of a vision that includes political, social, technological, and medial advances on a scale difficult to imagine in seventeenth-century Europe, it could hardly be otherwise that the problem of information overload is presented as resolved. Indeed, the utopia depends on being able to master and exploit that explosion of knowledge. Yet it is precisely because of its inclusion among the key issues to be engaged that *City of the Sun* reveals its awareness of the gravity of the challenges presented by massively expanding knowledge and the expectation, however unreachable, that a society capable of harnessing collections-based processing, storage, and display techniques to master

---

20  Campanella, *City of the Sun*, 45–47.
21  Campanella, *City of the Sun*, 121–23.

crushing flows of information—and newly arising technical inventions—is where that problem could reasonably be solved.

## Museums and New Medial Baselines in the Age of Digital Overload

In moving to the question of museums and collecting in the digital age, it hardly needs to be emphasized that the media, institutions, and practices involved in cultural memory have of course undergone massive expansion in recent decades, with a far greater range of technical media also requiring consideration than has been typical in thinking about collecting and museums before the digital age. Historical attempts to tackle problems similar to information overload show that constellations of old and new media other than those familiar to us are possible, meaning that nothing should be assumed a priori about the ways media and technologies will interact.

Beyond historical considerations, developments in museum response to new media and especially computer technology can help us get a better sense of some of the ways that museums will be shaped by and inevitably express digital values. As Ross Parry has shown in 2007 in his *Recoding the Museum,* these are transformations whose beginnings reach back as much as forty years.[22] As Parry is quick to note, the stories of museums and computing are anything but uniform or straightforward, even if the potential benefits of adopting methods of computerized records management and cataloging, of networked collaboration across institutions, and of providing networked public access to all sorts of museum information, to name but a few, were envisioned as early as the 1960s.[23] But even if that potential remains as yet unrealized, one thing Parry's account makes clear is that digital impacts will be equally as pervasive behind the scenes as they will be in the areas visitors typically think of with respect to museums.

A hallmark of these changes, as a growing number of studies attests, is an ever-increasing centrality of good quality, machine-readable museum data with metadata becoming the concern, in some fashion, of practically everyone who works in museum environments. In the process, museum roles are under ever-growing pressure to change. In one sense, change means with respect to how museum staff carry out their particular roles: in some cases it has been shown that curators—once a role considered relatively insular in many institutions, particularly with respect to digital technology—increasingly benefit from familiarity with standards in

---

22   Ross Parry, *Recording the Museum: Digital Heritage and the Technologies of Change* (New York: Routledge, 2007), 15–31.
23   Parry, *Recording the Museum,* 1–10.

computer-based cataloguing and the quality of data on their objects, how collections are reflected in the museums' web presence, the workings of social media, and in some cases even the online museum shop.[24] A lot depends on how institutions implement information technology. What this means for institutional cultures is something that is still hard to generalize about, but there have been suggestions that considerations of data and metadata might increasingly push museum staff to work in closer contact with departments and positions—and perhaps less hierarchically—than they have in the past.

For these reasons, it seems crucial to acknowledge that even museums that maintain a traditional object-based focus will be affected by values and practices that come with digital culture. And then there are the many reasons for museums to embrace the digital turn in more expansive ways, including the hope that such an embrace might help solve issues not necessarily or only of a digital making. Many museums are under acute pressure to expand their audiences, to prove themselves more inclusive, and to increase use of their collections, much of which feeds back on questions of revenue in a variety of ways. Seen this way, traditional museums' ability to persist might be thought to depend on increasing their perceived relevance, meaning that audiences care enough about what museums offer that they survive to transmit what they have into the future. In particular, museums will need to find ways of connecting with and supporting visitors' perceptual and cultural needs.

There are paradoxes and tensions that arise on the path to museums leveraging the digital to enhance their traditional object- and space-based richness, even if it has been recognized that their material legacies are perhaps their most potent and most important retort to digital culture and its purported blind spots.[25] But to say something about the directions this has been taking, I want to turn to two cases, Manchester's Imperial War Museum North and the Cleveland Museum of Art, that represent

---

24 Murtha Baca, Erin Coburn, and Sally Hubbard, "Metadata and Museum Information," in *Museum Informatics: People, Information, and Technology in Museums*, ed. Paul F. Marty and Katherine Burton Jones (New York: Routledge, 2008), 107–27, here 110–11; Gabriela Zoller and Katie DeMarsh, "For the Record: Museum Cataloging from a Library and Information Science Perspective," *Art Documentation: Journal of the Art Libraries Society of North America* 32, no. 1 (2013): 54–70, here 56–60; Elena Villaespesa, "Diving into the Museum's Social Media Stream: Analysis of the Visitor Experience in 140 Characters," in *Museums and the Web 2013: The Annual Conference of Museums and the Web, April 17–20, 2013, Portland, OR*, https://mw2013.museumsandtheweb.com/paper/diving-into-the-museums-social-media-stream/; R. J. Wilson, "Digital Heritage: Behind the Scenes of the Museum Website," *Museum Management and Curatorship* 26, no. 4 (2011): 373–89, here 375–77.

25 Henning, *International Handbooks*, 4–5.

moments where museums, in adopting computer-based technologies, can be seen to be making digital technologies a key baseline in shaping how museums relate past, present, and future in line with the contours of a post-scarcity, digital world.

The first museum I will consider is the Imperial War Museum North, a case that has gotten some scholarly attention for the way the digital informs its operations on a deep level. The Imperial War Museum North was designed by Daniel Libeskind. The museum's complex architectural forms, as Libeskind tells it, are meant to represent the world torn apart by the ravages of war.[26] That such intricate designs are unthinkable without computer-based tools might seem apparent enough, but as Ross Parry and Andrew Sawyer point out, there are points in that architecture where the contours of interior walls were constrained and shaped by considerations of the Imperial War Museum's key exhibition concept, called *The Big Picture Show*. Consisting of a variety of videos projected onto all the museum's surfaces (and objects and visitors), *The Big Picture Show* is an integral element of the museum's permanent display, taking place each hour in ways that make it inescapable. Loud, immersive, and pervasive, it forces embodied response no matter where one is in the gallery.

In Andrew Hoskins and Amy Holdsworth's interpretation, *The Big Picture Show* represents the museum's attempt to showcase the museum's audiovisual collections of photography, art, archival footage, oral history, and testimony, yet it is deployed in such a way as to respond to the problem that in the digital age, approaches to museum display based on artifactual scarcity (the museum's command of original objects and artifacts) seem hopelessly feeble.[27] As a post-scarcity counter-strategy, the Imperial War Museum North deploys a time-limited cinematic installation, creating a moment of medial mediation set to work in the distinct spatial environment of the museum punctuated by singular physical artifacts. Conceptually, its experientially unique qualities are designed to position the museum to intervene in digital processes and force a new meeting of past, present, and future, looking to turn back what digital theorist Peter Lunenfeld has referred to as a warping of cultural memory resulting from an increasingly dominant "blended presentness" of digitally mediated media.[28]

Important about *The Big Picture Show* is the conceptual insight into the need to render presentations of past material digitally in order for

26 Studio Libeskind, "Imperial War Museum North: Manchester, United Kingdom, 2001," https://libeskind.com/work/imperial-war-museum-north/.

27 Hoskins and Holdsworth, "Media Archeology," 23–25.

28 Peter Lunenfeld, *The Secret War Between Downloading and Uploading: Tales of the Computer as Culture Machine* (Cambridge, MA: MIT Press, 2011), 45–46, also quoted by Hoskins and Holdsworth, "Media Archeology," 24.

them to become experiential elements of the museum environment. Part of this strategy involves a presentation of historical film and images ordered in such a way as to delineate media of the past vis-à-vis media of the present in ways that enable visitors to integrate the museum's physical artifacts into new forms of embodied experience they will also carry with them upon leaving the museum. Key to this strategy is its scale and full-body immersiveness, with images projected at sizes many times larger than life on all available surfaces, whose coordinated positioning requires computer-aided design, and accompanied by voiceovers so loud as to drown out all other sound. But if these presentations manage to imprint themselves on visitors, and shape their sensorial experience, they do this whether or not visitors necessarily desire or know what to do with it. Indeed, little in the exhibit design works to entice connections between the material of *The Big Picture Shows* and the physical installation, in part due to the low levels of light that accompany the projections. And while *The Big Picture Shows* create an experience shared by all visitors, the overwhelming volume of the presentations prevents exchanges between visitors during the presentation, cutting off the potential for social exchange and connection that theorists such as Nina Simon have deemed highly desirable.[29] Such moments might be enhanced with display techniques designed to transform the museum's physical artifacts into what Nina Simon calls "social objects," a form of performativity that taps visitor involvement to allow the museum to reach its full potential equipping visitors to take museum lessons into their post-museum lives.[30]

The Cleveland Museum of Art (CMA) takes the idea that digital framing can provide experiential baselines for visitors in ways that enable greater involvement of visitor desires and decision-making.[31] The center of this participatory strategy is called Artlens. A revision of the CMA's original foray into digitally informed displays known as Gallery One,[32] Artlens was reconceptualized in order to take advantage of newer technologies and learn from shortcomings in the original designs. Key about its approach is that the CMA has tended to find mass digitization of its

29   Nina Simon, *The Participatory Museum* (Santa Cruz: Museum 2.0, 2010), 25–29.

30   Simon, *Participatory Museum*, 125–33.

31   Caroline Goeser, "Blending Art, Technology and Interpretation: Cleveland Museum of Art's Gallery One and Artlens," *Art Museum Teaching* (April 15, 2013), https://artmuseumteaching.com/2013/04/15/blending-art-technology-interpretation-cleveland-museum-of-arts-gallery-one-artlens/.

32   Jane Alexander, Jake Barton, and Caroline Goeser, "Transforming the Art Museum Experience: Gallery One," in *Museums and the Web 2013: The Annual Conference of Museums and the Web, April 17–20, 2013, Portland, OR*, https://mw2013.museumsandtheweb.com/paper/transforming-the-art-museum-experience-gallery-one-2/.

collections on its own insufficient in positioning the museum with respect to digital culture. The CMA has twice declined to participate in Google Art and Culture, a mass digitization project based on Google's collaboration with museums around the world with the aim of creating a kind of universal virtual museum with much greater reach than any one individual museum.[33] At the same time, the CMA does not seem to overly fear the idea that the existence of digital reproductions will outright supplant originals per se. They have recently given Creative Commons Access to over 30,000 objects via an API (Halperin), and they also promote the downloading of museum objects into their app to be revisited after a museum visit. Rather, Cleveland puts stock in exploring how the museum environment can deploy digital techniques so that visitors can gain better orientation in the digital age, seeking to help focus attention, discover, and develop meaningful relationships to artifacts and their relevance going forward.

Artlens is a complex combination of technologies, but some of its most fascinating elements are deployed in what CMA calls *Artlens exhibition*, a dedicated space with a rotating set of traditional art works combined with digital interactives that promote explorations via embodied engagement with particular works. Important about these interactives is that they require simple gestures that are intuitive and easy to learn, in any case with no need to touch a screen or device. Interactives and objects are designed in such a way that there are multiple paths to and from objects and/or interactives, encouraging serendipity and flexibility. Whatever way visitors end up getting involved with interactives, however, activities work to ensure regular returns to objects, or "look up" experiences, that seek to keep digital technologies a lesser priority than encounters with objects. Importantly, returns to objects often take place in the *Artlens exhibition*, yet a variety of features also prompt visitors to find similar kinds of work throughout the museum, supported by a location-sensitive app that collects information from the visitors' interactions as well as finds from the Artlens wall. The Artlens wall is a custom-made, 40-foot-long multi-touch digital representation of 4,000–4,500 pieces of art held by the museum designed to promote exploration and serendipity. It serves up works less for inspection on the wall, than to help visitors to discover a subset of material likely to be relevant to them, working in sync with tools designed to help visitors take objects into their world in a double sense: primarily in the sensual realm of the museum, but also in digital form for later rediscovery and exploration, with the app storing digital copies. More than merely being easy to access, these objects are linked together through a series of embodied experiences generated by

---

33   Nancy Proctor, "The Google Art Project: A New Generation of Museums on the Web?," *Curator: The Museum Journal* 54, no. 2 (2011): 215–21.

the visitor, whose singular sensory and memory traces provide the base-line for future exploration in digital and non-digital ways.

As I hope to have shown, each of these cases might be thought to pursue an agenda in which the museum seeks to provide an environment outside the normal crush of the digital, where not just respite from the "always on" might be found, but where bodily response might be trained to improve or enhance engagement with material artifacts and potentially also images themselves. In this sense, museums are beginning to develop tools for handling information overload, paradoxically, in ways informed by the collecting, organizational, and display capacities of digital formats. These capacities are becoming integral elements in that process, such that the possibilities of collecting going forward will be shaped by the hand-offs between the regimes of old and new media.

# Part II.

# Recollection

# 5: Quality Storage: Collecting as a Technique of Reading

*Nikolaus Wegmann*

T HE INVENTION OF the "Great Books" curriculum nearly one hundred years ago in the United States has been almost forgotten. According to this curriculum, all of Western culture is condensed into a collection of specially selected literature that ranges, for example, from Homer to Hemingway. Nowadays, this nostalgic book utopia looks like a dated Sunday School where allegedly Western values, norms, and traditions replace religion. Nonetheless, without reassurance of a meaningful past, there is only an overrated form of presentism. But how is this past accessible in a way that the significant not only is separated from the less significant but above all retains its quality for the here and now. Simply glorifying the past by recommending the works of "great" authors as a timeless treasure will not be sufficient. The following argument is not focused on the treasure itself, understood as the norms, values, and esthetic preferences of a past era. Rather, light is shed on the "Great Book" as a specific media format as a cultural technology that is widely practiced but little understood in its operational logic. In plain language, as a historian of media practices I am interested in advanced forms of book-reading as a way to collect and store cultural heritage.

## 1

We do not know exactly what quality storage could mean. Something that would provide our society with a type of storage that collects ideas and objects that have been important, even irreplaceable, in the past and should still be accessible today. What would be required to create an all-inclusive storage of such extent? In a Western society that is characterized by accelerating technologies, there is an easy solution for everything. Just believe in the militant technological optimism of Silicon Valley and push a button: *To save everything, click here!*[1] Storage is always within reach, just

---

1   Evgeny Morozov, *To Save Everything, Click Here: The Folly of Technological Solutionism* (New York: PublicAffairs, 2013).

click and it is done. Anywhere and anytime. Neither expertise, nor practice is needed. Effortlessly and instantly. Even the problem of selection is solved thanks to the low cost of storage. Do not bother to select, just save it all. No special skills required.

To go beyond such oversimplified approaches, one must first understand "quality storage" as a challenging problem. Because wherever specific demands are made regarding the quality of storage, things proceed differently. Just think of the so-called Barbarastollen in a forest near Freiburg in Germany, a suspended section of a former ore mine deep under the earth. This 700-meter-long tunnel is the central depository for the Federal Republic of Germany's archived photographic documents of great cultural significance. Everything is copied on 35-millimeter polyester film, totaling more than 28,000 km.[2] The perishability of the films means they will last approximately 500 years. Only then would they have to be recopied. The construction of this storage bunker goes back to the 1960s, when Germany was a front state during the Cold War. But it became public only in the 1989 with the fall of the Iron Curtain.

What is preserved, what is collected at the Barbarastollen? Photographs of "irreplaceable cultural heritage"[3] as the legal definition attests—with over a billion collected documents.[4] Microfilms are stored in 1,500 stainless-steel air- and water-tight containers. But all numbers are out-of-date because the filming of this material is still underway. Is this the solution to the problem of all-inclusive storage? The project certainly has few imitators. Only the Netherlands and the Vatican have comparable projects. After all, there are objections against such enterprises beyond financial considerations.

First, this form of long-term storage is ultimately *inaccessible*. The only access intended by its creators is reserved for the survivors of catastrophic wars or natural disasters. Only if the originals are destroyed do the backups become significant. It is an open question as to how this

---

2    By 2009, 28,000 km of documented material was stored on microfilm. Today's total is not yet made public; see Bundesamt für Katastrophenschutz und Bevölkerungshilfe, "Neue Ordnung im Barbarastollen," Meldungen (July 20, 2009), https://web.archive.org/web/20150118143018/http://www.bbk.bund.de/SharedDocs/Kurzmeldungen/BBK/DE/2009/20071530_Bergungsort_Ordnungssystem.html.

3    Entry   Barbarastollen:   https://de.wikipedia.org/wiki/Barbarastollen. Elaborate research on this large-scale national storage project is a desideratum for cultural studies.

4    In the year 2016, on the national holiday Day of German Unity, a filmed copy of the original basic law including all related files was brought down into the storage facility, marking the new addition in a promotionally effective act as the billionth document. Online: https://www.fluter.de/historische-dokumente-deutschlands-im-barbarastollen.

post-catastrophic access is supposed to function. This much is certain: access is guided by a strong belief in the power of an antiquated device, a rather unimpressive apparatus: a magnifying glass. A magnifying glass assures access to the stored past as the instrument typically used in microfilm reading devices because the film requires no other decoding. Second, because storage space is not an issue, there is only *weak selectivity*. Storage is to include (to quote from the official mission statement) "everything of specific significance to German history and culture."[5] But if "everything" is to be included, any access to such a *monstrous quantity* must become problematic. Finally, to store the entirety of German cultural heritage in one location is to subject it to great risk, as a single precise attack could result in total loss. The legendary fire of the Library of Alexandria could be repeated.[6] But the past is not just a legend. Just think of the Bosnian War of 1992, when the Serbians intentionally targeted Sarajevo's National Library in order to extinguish the collected cultural heritage of the Bosnians and the Croats.

# 2

The next case study has its roots in the Cold War as well. And here, too, the problem of quality storage is viewed from the perspective of catastrophes. But the solution this time is not a feat of engineers. Instead it has to do with readers, precisely the authority that the Barbarastollen has locked out. What kind of readers are we talking about?

By "readers" I refer to an extremely committed group of bibliophiles or "book-lovers" who are active in a sociopolitical context in which the possession and reading of books—as it was the case East of the Iron Curtain—are prohibited and disobedience is harshly punished. In this and similar contexts, books are haunted because according to state propaganda, they promote antisocial behavior—criticism, diverse opinions, and conflict. They are toxic to a community in which the powerful keep everyone and everything under control. The counteragent is a kind of fire department in reverse, which does not put out fires but puts every individual book all the way up to entire libraries to the torch. Only the bibliophiles resist; the vast majority of people have replaced reading with enormous, wall-sized televisions, showing whatever supports the regime.

As concretely visible paper objects, books cannot be hidden from the "firemen" by these dissidents, typically intellectuals, professors, librarians,

---

5    Entry Barbarastollen: https://de.wikipedia.org/wiki/Barbarastollen.

6    The fall of the Great Library is a storied event adding mythical depth to its history. The one-time destructive fire might be the more dramatic story compared to a slow decline over time.

collectors, and similarly book-oriented "species." In addition, books can be memorized to a certain degree and thus kept from their destruction. *Fixed in memory*, significant books survive. The manual for this personalized or human storage technology is a fictional story, a dystopia as presented by Ray Bradbury in 1953. The title reveals a catastrophe that is already present everywhere: *Fahrenheit 451. The temperature at which book paper catches fire and burns.*[7]

There cannot be many such bibliophile readers. Reading—whether under real or fictional totalitarian regimes—requires an enormous willingness to accept personal risks. Furthermore, memorizing a *very long* text is not an easy task. Prose cannot be compared to epics whose rhymes made it possible for ancient cultures to pass them on from generation to generation. Moreover, any text once memorized is at risk of being forgotten. For how long can a biological memory be securely stored? And how can one check the memory for correctness if the original paper format no longer exists?

*Fahrenheit 451* provides no answers. Technology does not become a topic of its own. The main line of this book is a parable of book burning as a proof of an authoritarian and anti-human society. What it provides is a brief statement that shows how books, when memorized by many individuals, exist *in multitudes*. In fact, any reader can only learn one entire book by heart. They can escape isolation only through the occasional gathering of "book-lovers." Such gatherings would be contest-like disputes or exchanges in which memorized books are cited back and forth, without fixed rules or an explicit goal. However, there seem to be no commentaries for these books based on a memorizer's own interpretation. The danger would be too great that an interpretative or hermeneutic approach would imperil the exact wording of the text. The precious text from the past would dissolve into random variations, with no possibility of controlling the deviations and returning to the original wording or text. At the end of *Fahrenheit 451*, the city from which the dissidents have fled is destroyed by a nuclear attack. The regime comes to an end—and the survivors will return to start anew on the basis of a book culture that had been nearly erased were it not for the memorizing efforts of some individuals. Whether this would work even in a fictional setting remains unclear. There is no sequel to *Fahrenheit 451*.

Let us revisit the case for "quality storage." We have discussed two examples thus far, one that exists in the real world and one that presents itself in the literary imagination. They serve as a heuristic aid to figure out how a convincing form of cultural storage may keep the past alive. The

---

7   Ray Bradbury, *Fahrenheit 451*, first edition 1953; the book's tagline explains the title: "Fahrenheit 451–the temperature at which book paper catches fire, and burns . . ."

bunker solution relies on technological devices to preserve an "irreplace-able cultural heritage" that is carefully closed and remains inaccessible until doomsday has passed. Once it is discovered by the survivors of a catastrophe, the content would be the same. Gold remains gold. But what if after a thousand years the 1,500 treasure chests in the Barbarastollen have become a tomb of a forgotten culture doomed to remain unknown and indecipherable? When the graverobbers are not interested in the obscure plastic inside the barrels but in the sparkling stainless steel of the containers themselves? Even *Fahrenheit 451* shows a crucial flaw when it comes to storing culture: a book learned by heart but only mechanically recited without meaning or understanding will not keep the past alive: its words are dead on arrival.

# 3

I would like to offer another case study. What you see in figure 4.1 is well known to those who are familiar with the tradition of canonical literature and often on display in libraries. The very first of such a books series was published 1901 in 51 volumes under the title *Harvard Classics*. What is shown in the photograph is an example of the *Great Books of the Western World*, a series originally published in the United States in 1952 by *Encyclopædia Britannica* to present the *Great Books* in a visually impressive 54-volume set. The original editors had several criteria for adding a book to this collection: The book must be relevant to contemporary culture and not only be "important" in its historical context; and it must be a

Figure 4.1: Great Books of the Western World. 60 vol.
set. Britannica Edition (https://www.amazon.com/
Great-Books-Western-World-Britannica/dp/B01H9DBNHY).

part of "the great conversation about the great ideas,"[8] that is, a book has to match at least 25 of the 102 great ideas as identified by the editors.[9] The books were not chosen on the basis of ethnic and cultural inclusiveness, historical influence, or the editors' agreement with the views that were expressed by the authors.

Contrary to the many, and very understandable, objections to the selection criteria, I would like to make a case for this method. What we see is a visual representation of an almost timeless, and thanks to large editions, *affordable and large-scale storage technology.* In the German-speaking world it is called: "Das Gute Buch," in English, as indicated above, the "Great Book." More than, as held for centuries in European history, the "one and only" Bible, a series of "Great Books" is an amorphous body of texts. Sets like the *Encyclopædia Britannica's Great Books of the Western World* are an attractive offer for its readers, at least in a time when such a set is cherished as an investment in personal education or *Bildung*—and as a very visible proof of the owner's cultivation of the mind.

Today, "quality storage" bound in fine leather has become unfashionable. Remove the bindings and the golden letters: Would the "Great Book" as in the *Harvard Classics* series still be considered a "great book"? Sociologists have quick answers. "Great books" represent the norms, values, and cultural preferences of the white middle class. That is all very true. I am more interested in the form itself, however, which leads to the question as to why all these valuables can only be accessed through an exhausting operation such as reading, especially the reading of voluminous books which have already been read over and over again by other individuals (or oneself)? Questions of value are in truth unspecific in the case of the "Great Book," in spite of a rhetoric of significance. Only the book, the medium, is great. And yet these books are certainly not without significance. According to common belief they simply *have to be read.*

Let us turn to "common sense" for help and look into the widely accepted source like the *Encyclopædia Britannica.* Not only is there an entire sub-section, five volumes, that covers "Great Books," but there is also a "Gateway to the Great Books." In this section we find references to the valuable *contents* of "Great Books." Arriving at the selection of "Great

---

8    Great Books of the Western World, Wikipedia, https://en.wikipedia.org/wiki/Great_Books_of_the_Western_World.

9    These 102 ideas, ranging from Angel to World are the final result of an extensive distilling process based on writings that have "passed the test of time." Mortimer Adler, the driving force behind this large-scale enterprise, elaborated his findings in 102 individual essays. Mortimer Adler, *The Great Ideas: A Lexicon of Western Thought* (New York: Scribner Classics, 1999).

Books" as well as a glimpse of their content allegedly requires deep thinking, eternal wisdom, and universal values, categories that endure over time seemingly through the sheer power of their inherent qualities. In this case, a storage technology of its own seems to be unnecessary. A well-bound book of acid-free paper is all that is needed.

But the *Encyclopædia Britannica* goes into greater detail about something else, namely the correct way to deal with books. And this neither refers to devotion nor to philosophical hermeneutics, but focuses directly on an easily overlooked technical process involved. At the center stands a fundamental teaching of how to approach a canonical text, namely through "the art of reading the book."[10] This "art" can be reduced to one basic rule, a rule which does not refer to values and norms at all: "*'Great books' are readable again and again, with renewed pleasure and added profit.*"[11] "*It might almost be said, that a book which is not worth rereading one or more times is not really worth reading carefully in the first place.*"[12] Clearly, the difference between a book and a "Great Book" is decided by the criterion of rereading. Only a "Great Book" deserves to be reread, because it gets better over time and thus gains that authority we attribute to a significant cultural achievement.

Can we also analyze this temporal anomaly that is included in the act of rereading? Are we forced to simply admire and praise the "Great Book" because it was labeled as such by higher authorities? Metaphysics does not help to explain how we arrived at the "Great Book" as a form of "quality storage." We have to go back to the process of rereading as the singular operation through which the "Great Book" emerges. Despite the *Encyclopædia Britannica*'s case for the "Great Book" as an inventory of values, or a catechism of fixed questions and answers, rereading is the only operation that generates cultural "treasures" that withstand the grind of time. Rather, the "Great Book" is born out of an operation that each and every book requires: *re-reading*.

How exactly does rereading generate/create the "Great Book"? What actually happens during this operation? Let us follow the general truth the *Encyclopædia Britannica* is passing on: As a *temporal* operation, rereading is the decisive source for the extended life span of a "Great Book." But then, time cannot be tamed or stopped. Instead, the opposite—to follow Niklas Luhmann—is the case.[13] Time can bind, perhaps

---

10   Robert Hutchings, Mortimer Adler, editors in chief, *Gateway to the Great Books. Encyclopedia Britannica* (Chicago: Encyclopædia Britannica, 1963), 19.

11   Robert Hutchings, Mortimer Adler, *Gateway*, 16.

12   Robert Hutchings, Mortimer Adler, *Gateway*, 18.

13   More on this simple and—therefore?—powerful concept of historical semantics: Niklas Luhmann, *Die neuzeitlichen Wissenschaften und die Phänomenologie* (Vienna: Picus, 1996), 56 and 58–59.

two (or more) events; in this case, two or more readings. Without the intervention of rereading, events like single readings would all but guarantee the disappearance of the "Great Books." It is precisely this act of joining through repetition that forms the core of rereading. In each case it transforms individual readings into a fixed form of iteration, and it is precisely through the emerging succession of connected readings that duration emerges.

Once set in motion, rereading produces additional effects that have objective and social implications. One of these effects is the enhanced credibility that a reader connects with the "Great Book." This, again, requires a close look at the mechanics of rereading. Every new reading says something not only entirely different from a previous reading—otherwise there would be no reason for the repetition of the process. At the same time, it does not simply reproduce what was said before, because the process would be futile if there were not an element of variation. What is designated in this way is never totally different from what has been said before nor is it a dogmatic—and boring—repetition. Rather, both variety and redundancy are in place at the same time, thus strengthening certainty and credibility. That which is meaningful today was also meaningful in the past and will presumably continue to be meaningful in the future. Why should the chain of rereadings that has already held for so long stop at some point?

Through rereading the "Great Book" we acquire a surplus because a subsequent reading does not simply generate the same results over and over again. Ultimately, the operation always occurs in a situation that is *different* from the first. A second reading includes the first reading. And when the first reading is included, the second reading also captures what and how the first reading was executed and, thus, necessarily deviates. Nonetheless, this deviation retains much of the identity of the text that was read the first time. The text to be repeated reveals itself through the repetition as the same and, hence, illuminates the new context of the second reading and produces new meaningful references and understandings.

If rereading creates permanence, the "Great Book" necessarily produces a surplus of meaning. And this is a quality that not only includes the past and the present, but also the future. From an uninterrupted succession of rereadings we can expect the disclosure of hitherto undetected meanings *ad infinitum*.

Once the "Great Book" is explicated as a technical medium, it appears as a phenomenon autonomous of external causalities. This very special book operates as a self-creating circuit, as a recursive loop, in which that what is created becomes itself the creator. It is an autopoietic technology, a system capable of reproducing and maintaining itself.

# 4

Granted, this technical explication of rereading is elaborate—especially since the *practice of rereading* does not need detailed knowledge at all. As the crucial infrastructure for a collection, or canon of "Great Books," it remains largely invisible, that is, as long as this infrastructure does what it is supposed to do, namely, to *generate* "greatness" of a Western Canon of books. The infamous "canon wars," battles over what is supposed to be part of a canon and if canons should not be abandoned altogether, missed this functional aspect. Instead, the controversy is all about the *list*, the right selection of books and authors, one side arguing in favor for the timeless embodiments of Western experiences or values, the other demanding a revision based on priorities shared by a generation of scholars pursuing race-, gender-, and cultural-studies pertaining to high schools and colleges.

In the 1980s and 1990s, higher education was consumed by the canon wars. Participants could not agree on authors that ought to be taught and researched. Lost in these battles over *what* should be read or taught, was the question of *how* books from the past have been read and thus stored and formed the cultural memory of our society. But this is exactly the course one must take, however, to see what is currently being taught and practiced in schools.

Timeless existence is a beautiful illusion, and that holds true not only for cultural products. Precisely therein lies the actual point of weakness, according to my technological assessment presented here. What happens when the elaborate skill of rereading is no longer taught and practiced as the load-bearing infrastructure of the Western Canon? When it is replaced by other forms of reading? Currently, developments hint at the direction of how future techniques of generating a canon may look like.

The state of reading is changing. Reading in schools is no longer practiced mainly as a "Gateway to Great Books." There is now a new, so-called *smart* alternative. The growing success of this new approach is based on an old promise: once we are able to observe how the actual reading process unfolds, we can actively intervene and thus improve reading skills dramatically. Precisely this level of surveillance is now offered in the form of software bundles, used in the classroom as "learning apps" that claim to *monitor the actual reading* of the student. No more guessing of who read what and certainly no more problems with grading.

The two dominant apps in the field are distributed and sold under telling brand-names: *Accelerated Reading* and *Scholastic Reading Counts!*[14] "Accelerated" courses are the ones that really or only count, like in

---

14 One of the telling websites making advertisements for the company: http://mediaroom.scholastic.com/node/126.

accelerated math, the early version of an Advanced Placement class, a college-level course taken in high school. Advanced Placement courses save time and money in the process of finding and being admitted to college. *Scholastic reading counts!*—with exclamation mark—directly addresses the anxieties of skeptical parents who focus on college admission and costs and have yet to be convinced of the usefulness of technology to achieve the best outcomes for their children and their wallets. Scholarly reading sounds like quality reading—and this app supports only what truly counts.

What can these apps do? What do readers gain from their use? Such apps transform the process of reading books into big data. Computer-based technology assembles data from thousands of readings, corroborated by asking additional questions that are designed to show how much readers can remember. On the basis of this collected data, quizzes are designed to "help" teachers in the classroom. Focused on questions that are based on students' memories of facts instead of thought processes, they, as a result, only allow one correct answer. Through this protocol, teachers will see at a glance whether a student has read a book or not. Comprehension, critical thinking, or more individualized procedures are less of interest. Everything that would undermine the *quantifiable effectiveness* that companies promise in their advertisement has to be ruled out.

None of the corporations' mission statements mentions the books themselves and certainly not their quality. Not only are specific titles missing but the conceptual terms "Great Book" or "canon" are also omitted. Instead, students are explicitly encouraged to pick whatever book they "want." More or less anything can be chosen, thanks to databases that cover over 100,000 books that have already been processed into the aforementioned literary quizzes option for each of the apps. No need for teachers to organize his or her own assessment. Canon or "Great Book" is replaced by an operational concept called *extended range*: "Over 35,000 reading practice quizzes are available on books from over 300 publishers and imprints. Independent of any publishing interests: Accelerated Reading ensures that there are plenty of books to interest every reader available on the programme." The website sums up: allegedly perfect reading "made painless."[15]

Quality storage without "pain," that is one of modern technology's selling points. This painless, quantifiable approach is set *against the old operational ontology of rereading*. Rereading as the most significant way to access the cultural past requires a serious commitment, without any guarantee of instant success. Difficulty, problems of understanding, and so forth, are vital elements of the process—without ever reaching a point of

---

15   All you ever wanted to know about this version of computer aided reading: https://www.renaissance.com/products/practice/accelerated-reader-360/.

completèness. To the contrary: rereading, once set in motion, will always question and rephrase what has been read before.

Rereading as a recursive operation is a skill that must be applied to keep the past alive, and thus continuously alter the canon—understood as an objective version of quality storage. Rereading is a demanding concept, even more so because we cannot outsource it to engineers, memory artists, preceptors, or app designers. After all, the texts themselves have to be read to keep the collection that is stored in our cultural memory alive.

# 6: Phenomenology of Memory in an Age of Big Data

*Clifford B. Anderson*

## Memory and Memoranda

WHAT WOULD IT MEAN to depend on machine-retrieval of past experiences rather than on personal recollection? How might changes in the phenomenology of memory affect archival practices and, by extension, reshape our collective memory of the past? In *Phaedrus* (written around 370 BCE), Plato famously dwelled on the claim that literature is injurious to memory, relating the discussion between Theuth, an Egyptian God, and Thamus, King of Egypt, about the invention of writing:

> The story goes that Thamus said much to Theuth, both for and against each art, which it would take too long to repeat. But when they came to writing, Theuth said, "O King, here is something that, once learned, will make the Egyptians wiser and will improve their memory; I have discovered a potion for memory and for wisdom." Thamus, however, replied, "O most expert Theuth, one man can give birth to the elements of an art, but only another can judge how they benefit or harm those who will use them. And now, since you are the father of writing, your affection for it has made you describe its effects as the opposite of what they really are. In fact, it will introduce forgetfulness into the soul of those who learn it; they will not practice using their memory because they will put their trust in writing, which is external and depends on signs that belong to others, instead of trying to remember from the inside, completely on their own."[1]

By the end of antiquity, the debate between Thamus and Theuth had been decisively resolved in favor of Theuth. While the written record may not have made us wise, this record and related forms of tangible media have vastly extended our cultural knowledge. As Abby Smith Rumsey

---

1 Plato, *Phaedrus*, trans. Alexander Nehamas and Paul Woodruff (Indianapolis: Hackett, 1995), 79.

remarks in *When We Are No More: How Digital Memory Is Shaping Our Future*, Socrates's "prediction that external memory systems would hurt us as a species completely missed the mark. If we had not turned mind into matter, our biological memory would have been stuck forever in the present, small of scale and leaving little behind when we die."[2] The resolution of the argument also gave birth to the memory institutions of Western culture. Librarians, museum professionals, and archivists have become the primary stewards of cultural memory, rather than bards, oracles, and poets, curating rather than singing about cultural heritage to preserve it for the future.

In the twenty-first century, a new tension is arising between the written record and data-driven inquiry. Big data scientists have become the brash new Theuth of our era. Engineers push forward with the development of hardware to store ever-greater quantities of information, and software developers constantly invent new algorithms to query that data efficiently. The hope is to capture everything and, rather than crafting and curating, to let the data speak for themselves. What effect will big data have on personal and cultural memory? How will these changes affect our memory institutions? And what wise Thamus will warn us against the unintended consequences for our self-knowledge?

## Husserl's Phenomenology of Memory

I pursue a broadly phenomenological approach to the questions at stake in this article. The phenomenological tradition is rife with technical terminology, giving it a reputation for difficulty. The German philosopher Edmund Husserl (1859–1938) aspired to making phenomenology into a rigorous method, as scientific as any of the natural sciences. In what follows, I do not dwell on the rich conceptual apparatus of phenomenology but seek to summarize its application to memory and recollection. My approach to phenomenology owes much to Rudolf Bernet, professor emeritus at the Catholic University of Louvain and former director of the Husserl Archives, who offered a remarkable course on the phenomenology of memory, ranging from Augustine to Freud to Barthes, during the academic year 1991–92.

Husserl presented his phenomenology of memory in a brief work rendered variously in English translation as *The Phenomenology of Internal Time Consciousness* or *The Phenomenology of the Consciousness of Internal Time*.[3] In the opening section, Husserl carries out a phenomenological

---

2    Abby Smith Rumsey, *When We Are No More: How Digital Memory Is Shaping Our Future* (New York: Bloomsbury, 2016), 44–45.

3    This slim book has a complex history of composition. Husserl developed his phenomenology of time in lectures he delivered over a twenty-year period,

suspension of "objective time." By objective time, he means the time of the "chronometer" or "clock time." "Just as the actual thing, the actual world, is not a phenomenological datum, neither is a world time, the real time, the time of nature in the sense of natural science and even in the sense of psychology as the natural science of the psychic."[4] In his later works, Husserl refers to this suspension of belief as the phenomenological *epoché* or "bracketing" of scientific knowledge as well as folk knowledge.[5] He aims not to contribute to an empirical theory of time but to explore our experience of time.[6] Given that physicists like Carlo Rovelli cast doubt on whether time fundamentally exists,[7] Husserl's bracketing of objective time saves him from entangling his analysis in the scientific *théorie du jour*.

After criticizing the philosopher Franz Brentano's concept of time, Husserl begins to unfold his own phenomenological theory. He takes as his datum the experience of listening to a melody. How is it that we perceive the succession of notes? The notes do not follow one another discretely, but become layered together. The notes that we heard a moment ago inform what we are hearing now even as they fade into the past. Husserl describes this presence of the past in the present moment as "retention," explaining: "The tone-now changes into a tone-having-been; the *impressional* consciousness, constantly flowing, passes over into ever new *retentional* consciousness."[8] These are not dim echoes of the tone that sounded in the present, but the retention of the sounding tone

---

spanning the years 1893 (two years after the publication of the first volume of his *Philosophy of Arithmetic* in 1891) to 1917 (while he was writing his *Logical Investigations*, published 1901–2). In 1928 Martin Heidegger published a series of lectures that Husserl had delivered in 1905, along with supplementary materials from other years, as *Vorlesungen zur Phänomenologie des inneren Zeitbewusstseins*. A critical edition with related texts appeared as Volume X of the German *Husserliana* in 1966 and in English translation in 1991. The critical edition preserves the 1928 version of the text, though its editor indicates interpolations from later years into the lecture notes from 1905. In short, Husserl's phenomenology of internal time is difficult to summarize without making high-level decisions about substance and terminology.

4   Edmund Husserl, *On the Phenomenology of the Consciousness of Internal Time*, trans. John Barnett Brough (Dordrecht, Netherlands: Springer, 1991), 4–5.

5   Edmund Husserl, *Ideas Pertaining to a Pure Phenomenology and to a Phenomenological Philosophy*, trans. Frederick Kersten, vol. 1 (The Hague: Springer, 1983), 60 et seqq.

6   Husserl, *On the Phenomenology*, 4–5.

7   Carlo Rovelli, *The Order of Time* (New York: Riverhead Books, 2018).

8   Husserl, *On the Phenomenology*, 31.

shifted from present to past. Or, as Husserl described it, retentions are the "comet tail"[9] or "memory-trail"[10] in our flow of experience.

Husserl termed the counterpart to retention "protention." What we experience in the present, he argued, is not only a function of what we have heard in the immediate past; what we expect to hear in the future shapes our perception as well. When listening to the first movement of Beethoven's *Third Symphony*, for instance, we do not hear one *sforzando* chord after another, but listen with six in mind. The present is not a discrete event, but a function of the imminent future and the immediate past—the now exists within this temporal "fringe."[11]

In §14 of *On the Phenomenology of the Consciousness of Internal Time*, Husserl differentiates two forms of memory, which he termed "primary" and "secondary." The first is the retention of the immediate past that we have described above. The second is recollection, which he argues takes place in distinct forms: a "simple grasping" or "flash," or a reproduction of past experience.[12] Our focus in this section is on reproduction or representation of memory. According to Husserl, secondary memory reproduces a past flow of experience, allowing us to relive a sequence of those former "nows." From a phenomenological perspective, the reproduction of the past is qualitatively distinct from the experience of the past. We do not experience an event again as a living present, but recollect it under the aspect of the past. Husserl describes recollection as having a double intentionality.[13] That is, we direct our consciousness toward a past event that, when summoned from memory, reproduces the intentional stance when we first experienced the event.

Husserl's explication of how we recollect the past brings his implicit curatorial stance to the fore. Recollection permits us freely to modify past experiences, granting us the ability to slow them down or speed them up.[14] On the downside, recollecting also diminishes the vivacity of the event. As Husserl puts it, "the 'clear' (in the first sense [that is, of the original perception of the event]) already stands before me as if seen through a veil, obscurely—and, in fact, more or less obscurely, etc."[15] Problematically, this obscurity provides the opportunity for errors to propagate as we misremember the sequence of events.[16]

Husserl shared Thamos's perspective that memory develops from practice. He provides a recipe for preserving the clarity of the past in

---

9   Husserl., *On the Phenomenology*, 32.
10  See Husserl, *On the Phenomenology*, 389.
11  Husserl, *On the Phenomenology*, 37.
12  Husserl, *On the Phenomenology*, 37.
13  Husserl, *On the Phenomenology*, 55–56.
14  Husserl, *On the Phenomenology*, 49.
15  Husserl, *On the Phenomenology*, 49.
16  Husserl, *On the Phenomenology*, 51.

our recollection. The trick, as he explains it, is to recall an event in secondary memory while the primary memory is still fresh.

> Now the question is whether this evidence pertaining to time consciousness can be preserved in reproduction. This is possible only through a coinciding of the reproductive flow with a retentional flow. If I have a succession of two tones C, D, then while fresh memory lasts, I can repeat this succession, even repeat it adequately in certain respects. I repeat C, D, internally, with the consciousness that C occurred first and then D. And while this repeated succession is "still living," I can proceed in the same way again, and so on. Surely, in this way I can go beyond the original field of evidence.[17]

The fixation of memory by recalling it again and again while the event is still fresh in our mind is a practical suggestion, but this method provides at best a limited means of overcoming the intrinsic obscurity of the past. How frequently can we take the time to review and recall events to fix them in memory? We have limited opportunity to follow Husserl's advice because we typically do not have time to pause, recall, and reflect in our busy lives. When we take the time to go over and over an event so that we will not forget it, we are curating that memory with the hope of adding it to our long-term store of recollections. For the rest of what we experience in our day-to-day existence, we make use of what we recall in the short term and resign ourselves over the long term to consigning those experiences to the obscurity of the past.

Not all memory is curated, of course, and not all recollection arises from conscious effort. As Husserl acknowledged, we also remember events spontaneously and, sometimes, involuntarily. A canonical example of involuntary memory is the episode with the infusion of the madeleine at the opening of Marcel Proust's *In Search of Lost Time* (1913–27).[18] Traumatic events also sear memories into consciousness, which arise involuntarily in connection with external stimuli. Traumatic memories stand diametrically opposed to voluntary, curated recollections. We seek to rid ourselves of these memories, or at least to rob them of their power. If we follow Freud, these traumatic memories can be repressed or even rejected, but their haunting presence cannot be exorcized without psychoanalytic labor and effort. The psychoanalytical practice is about recovering, but also forgetting, or at least reconfiguring and reducing the presence of traumatic memory: a kind of counter-curation of the unconscious.

---

17  Husserl, *On the Phenomenology*, 52.

18  Marcel Proust, *Swann's Way*, trans. Lydia Davis (New York: Viking, 2003), 45.

## Curating Memories

Husserl's recommended exercise for fixing the flow of historical events in memory seems to fall firmly on the side of Thamos: without conscious effort and repetition (like doing "reps" at the gym) our ability to recollect atrophies. An obvious rejoinder to Husserl is that he praises hard work where a simple solution beckons: namely, just write it down—or externalize what we want to recall in the future. From the diaries of Samuel Pepys (1633–1703) to Jan Morris's recent *In My Mind's Eye: A Thought Diary*,[19] keeping logs of daily events fixes these memories for us, preserving an external record so that we do not have to exercise our recollection. In some cases, diarists seek to counteract our natural tendency to curate by forcing themselves either to write a certain amount each day, no matter how little of note actually took place,[20] or by exhaustively describing what happened, but only on particular days.[21]

Writing turns out, of course, to be another form of curation. Like the process of mental repetition, the act of writing takes time and cannot avoid the problems of selectivity and choice implicit in Husserl's theory of memory. In *Ongoingness: The End of a Diary*, Sarah Manguso describes her attempts to capture the entirety of her daily existence in her diary, which eventually approached a million words after twenty-five years of writing.[22] Keeping the diary functioned as a hedge against the passage of time, serving as an act of defiance against the transitoriness of existence. Obviously, writing the diary was a Sisyphean activity as time continues to move forward despite her efforts to translate it into eternity. Among the reasons for forgoing her diary was the recognition that, no matter how much she wrote, more was lost than preserved. "To write a diary is to make a series of choices about what to omit, what to forget. A memorable sandwich, an unmemorable flight of stairs. A memorable bit of conversation surrounded by chatter that no one records."[23] Writing extends our capacity to preserve memories, but simultaneously forces us to acknowledge more consciously the act of curation.

The same limitation applies to other forms of recordation, including photograph and video. The ability to capture scenes from everyday life

---

19  Jan Morris, *In My Mind's Eye: A Thought Diary* (New York: Liveright, 2019).

20  Harry Mathews, *20 Lines a Day*, 2nd ed. (Normal, IL: Dalkey Archive, 1989).

21  Christa Wolf, *One Day a Year: 2001–2011*, trans. Katy Derbyshire (London: Seagull Books, 2017).

22  Sarah Manguso, *Ongoingness: The End of a Diary* (Minneapolis: Graywolf, 2015), 3.

23  Manguso, *Ongoingness*, 6.

so effortlessly can mislead us into imagining that we are moving beyond curation but, of course, the opposite is true. More than writing about events after the fact, the act of taking photographs and videos during events places us in the role of an observer rather than participant. As Doris Grumbach sardonically notes in *Coming into the End Zone: A Memoir*: "Photography. The whole impoverishing act of 'taking' pictures of family, friends, events, places. Like the actor who replaces the character, the photograph replaces what might otherwise have lingered in memory. For some persons, I believe, scenes go directly from the lens to the film without ever entering their minds."[24] Manguso evinces a similar sentiment, going as far as abandoning photography because of its deleterious effects on her memory: "When I was twelve I realized that photographs were ruining my memory. I'd study the photos from an event and gradually forget everything that had happened between shutter openings. I couldn't tolerate so much lost memory, and I didn't want to spectate my life through a viewfinder, so I stopped taking photographs."[25] In defense of photography, the curatorial lens can preserve the essence of a moment that would otherwise become lost in the flow of time. Henri Cartier-Bresson's *The Decisive Moment* is exemplary in this respect;[26] Cartier-Bresson's ability to capture the essence of an event on film shows the power of curation against the background flow of images on Instagram and GoPro videos on *YouTube*.

Modern curators make use of contemporary recording technolo gies to expand the limits of curation and to discover its boundaries. Hans Ulrich Obrist, the director of the *Serpentine Galleries* in London and pre-eminent peripatetic curator of our era, has become famous for his long-running interview sessions with artists, which he records on airplanes, in taxi cabs, and other on-the-move settings. In 2006, he and Rem Koolhaas conducted a twenty-four hour interview marathon at the *Serpentine Galleries*.[27] In *Ways of Curating*, Obrist comments on the purpose of these interviews:

> Conversations are a way of archiving or preserving the past. One of the most important concepts underpinning my conversation practice came from the late historian Eric Hobsbawm, whom I interviewed several times starting in 2006. He spoke about history as a "protest against forgetting." But recollection is a zone of contact between past, present, and future. Memory is not a simple record

---

24  Doris Grumbach, *Coming into the End Zone: A Memoir* (New York: Norton, 1991), 18.

25  Manguso, *Ongoingness*, 35.

26  Henri Cartier-Bresson, *The Decisive Moment* (Göttingen: Steidl, 2015).

27  Rem Koolhaas and Hans U. Obrist, *Serpentine Gallery: 24-Hour Interview Marathon; London* (London: Trolley Books, 2008).

of events but a dynamic process that transforms what it dredges up from its depths, and the conversation has become my way to instigate such a process.[28]

Obrist's insight about the transformative nature of recollection echoes Husserl's phenomenological perspective. Conversing about the past involves that same two-fold intentionality, replaying the flow of the event in recollection as we continue to experience the conversation in time. What we discover when we read these interviews alongside one another is that certain events recur, asserting themselves in different guises. In Obrist's *Everything You Always Wanted to Know about Curating but Were Afraid to Ask*, the editor crosses out these repetitions whenever they occur and strikethrough lines appear repeatedly on the surface of the pages.[29] I imagine the editor retained rather than removed these repetitions because they bring Obrist's curatorial practice to the surface, exhibiting his repertoire of anecdotes and stories—his descriptions of his celebrated "Kitchen Show" in St. Gallen in 1991 being the most obvious example[30]—as they shift and evolve during his career. Obrist straddles the border of curation and aggregation. In his recorded conversations, he pushes curation as far as it takes him without giving up the concept of care and crafting. But a growing movement seeks to break right past these bounds, leaving selectivity and curation behind to get at the unfiltered truth about themselves and their lifeworlds.

## The Quantified Self

After the birth of our son, my wife and I began a spreadsheet of his activities. We logged all his bodily functions, from ingestion to excretion, noting any unusual events. We tracked his weight, temperature, and, when he was sick, his oxygen saturation. We also recorded when he was sleeping or waking. Plenty of apps are available now to record that information and more data, like heart rate and bodily motion, in real time, enabling nervous new parents to produce beautiful charts of their babies' activities. How quaint to think back to parents measuring their children's growth by carving notches on the sides of kitchen doors. We stopped tracking our son's development about a month after his birth. I cannot say what happened to the record of his first days. As the quantified self-movement takes off, parents may become more deliberate about maintaining those logs, bequeathing them as data for their offsprings' self-understanding.

---

28  Hans Ulrich Obrist, *Ways of Curating* (New York: Farrar, Straus & Giroux, 2014), 57.

29  Hans Ulrich Obrist, *Everything You Always Wanted to Know about Curating* * *but Were Afraid to Ask*, ed. April Elizabeth Lamm (Berlin: Sternberg, 2011).

30  Obrist, *Ways of Curating*, 81 et seqq.

Kevin Kelly and Gary Wolf coined the term "quantified self" in 2007 and started a company around the concept, which puts on seminars and conferences to foster self-discovery through self-tracking. In an article titled "Know Thyself: Tracking Every Facet of Life, from Sleep to Mood to Pain," Gary Wolf explains the rationale behind the movement:

> Self-trackers seem eager to contribute to our knowledge about human life. The world is full of potential experiments: people experiencing some change in their lives, going on or off a diet, kicking an old habit, making a vow or a promise, going on vacation, switching from incandescent to fluorescent lighting, getting into a fight. These are potential experiments, not real experiments, because typically no data is collected and no hypotheses are formed. But with the abundance of self-tracking tools now on offer, everyday changes can become the material of careful study.[31]

Wolf notes that self-trackers tend to share their data, enabling the community to build a repository from like-minded enthusiasts. Drawing on a metaphor from Jesse H. Ausubel,[32] an environmental scientist at Rockefeller University, Wolf describes this collective data as a "macroscope," an instrument for looking at large-scale patterns formed by linkages of data.[33]

The academic community is now tracking the self-tracking community. In *Self-Tracking*, Gina Neff and Dawn Nafus provide a concise introduction to the self-tracking movement, focusing on participants in the "Quantitative Self" meet-ups but looking at the broader phenomenon as a whole.[34] And self-tracking has become an enormous business. Neff and Nafus cite a projection that "Over forty-two million fitness trackers a year will be sold by 2019."[35] The movement attracts a diverse lot, from people suffering from chronic conditions to health-nuts to artists. A shared concern is to collect the data they need from the tracking devices they use. In some cases, the devices hand over the data through attractive apps. But other devices restrict access to data, seeking to prevent unauthorized use by non-medical professionals.

---

31  Gary Wolf, "Know Thyself: Tracking Every Facet of Life, from Sleep to Mood to Pain, 24/7/365," *Wired* 17.7 (June 2009), www.wired.com/2009/06/lbnp-knowthyself/.

32  Jesse H. Ausubel, "A Botanical Macroscope," *Proceedings of the National Academy of Sciences* 106, no. 31 (August 2009), doi:10.1073/pnas.0906757106.

33  Wolf, "Know Thyself."

34  Gina Neff and Dawn Nafus, *Self-Tracking* (Cambridge: MIT Press, 2016).

35  Neff and Nafus, *Self-Tracking*, 107, citing a prospectus for an industry report titled *Connected Wearables* by Johan Svanberg of Berg Insight.

Depending on what you wish to measure, self-tracking requires different degrees of intervention in your quotidian existence. A step counter runs essentially in the background, reminding us of its presence when it malfunctions or of its absence by gaps in the data when we forget to bring it along in the morning. Heart-rate monitors, pulse oximeters, and blood glucose meters require greater interventions and need to become part of the everyday routine. A goal of the self-tracking movement is to make these interventions manageable through creative approaches to capturing the data. A good example of creative self-tracking is a photographic food journal. The genre of photographing artfully presented meals is well-established on Instagram. A food journal takes this genre from the domain of aesthetics to data science. As Neff and Nafus note, "A common practice is to take a picture of your food just before eating, which can track qualities like color, freshness, and portion size without having to look up a calorie count."[36] The collection of these images has aesthetic qualities, but the assimilation is indirectly curated, determined by eating habits rather than artistic merit.

The question of data privacy looms large over the quantified self-movement. Participants are cognizant of the potential for misuse, but the building of a macroscope necessitates the sharing of data and, in general, this goal overcomes qualms about personal privacy. As self-trackers share information, they build a broader web of facts about who we are. When the gaps close, will we discover our genuine image in that tangled skein of data?

# The Art of Appraisal

Among the hardest tasks when becoming a professional archivist is getting over the sentiment that you must keep everything. Early career archivists generally err on the side of keeping too much. "What if?" thinking plays a major role in filling up the shelf with boxes of valueless materials. "What if I throw away a form of evidence that future generations come to value?" goes the worry. Archival administrators worry about the opposed problem of running out of space. "What if we fill up our archives with dross and detritus and cannot accession new and notable scholarly collections?"

Archivists call the process of deciding what to keep and what to throw away "appraisal." By that term, they do not mean to put a monetary value on collections. As German archival theorist Hans Booms writes, appraisal is the "constitutive act by which societal data are converted into 'historical

---

36   Neff and Nafus, *Self-Tracking*, 74.

sources.'"[37] When sifting through potential new collections, archivists follow legal and professional guidelines; when appraising personal papers, for instance, archivists generally discard business and medical records and also remove third-party material like student evaluations. But the art of appraisal is not algorithmic. Archivists must exercise judgment. Recently, I was talking with a colleague who was puzzling over the number of drafts of a published book to keep in a collection that contained dozens of manuscripts-in-progress. The archivist opted to retain three or four at different stages of development. Too many? Too few? There is no single right answer.

The act of appraisal provides archivists with social authority. As Hans Booms remarked about governmental archivists, "The person who decides which events in social life are transmitted to us through the record, and, as a result, decides which are preserved to form part of a society's memory and which are not, is thereby making decisions which are important for society."[38] From a Husserlian perspective, we would say that these decisions "sediment" our cultural knowledge.[39] The exercise of this social power can also threaten the legitimacy of the archive. Whose interests are served by what the archivist keeps and what gets tossed away? In his argument against the Marxist archival theorists of the former East Germany, Booms proposed that appraisal be conducted pluralistically, giving voice to the differing spheres of society in the Federal Republic of Germany. Given the fundamental significance of winnowing historical data into the cultural record, the latest trend in archives today is co-curation, that is, inviting the community to make appraisal decisions alongside archivists. What happens when these communities ask archivists to preserve records in media that they would typically jettison as unimportant? As Terry Cook asks in *"We Are What We Keep; We Keep What We Are"*: *Archival Appraisal Past, Present and Future*: "Should we not preserve these voices and sounds by indeed 'democratizing archives' and 'archiving democracy,' through participatory partnerships, with our fellow citizens, determining collaboratively and collectively with them of what society's enduring archival memories should consist?"[40] If self-tracking becomes a major social activity with a large community of practitioners, archivists

---

37 Hans Booms, "Society and the Formation of a Documentary Heritage: Issues in the Appraisal of Archival Sources," trans. Hermina Joldersma and Richard Klumpenhouwer, *Archivaria* 24, no. 0 (January 1987): 69–107, here 76.

38 Booms, "Society," 78.

39 Edmund Husserl, *The Crisis of European Sciences and Transcendental Phenomenology: An Introduction to Phenomenological Philosophy* (Evanston, IL: Northwestern University Press, 1970), 52.

40 Terry Cook, "'We Are What We Keep; We Keep What We Are': Archival Appraisal Past, Present and Future," *Journal of the Society of Archivists* 32, no. 2 (October 2011): 173–89, here 184, doi:10.1080/00379816.2011.619688.

will begin to collect and preserve the lifelogs of members of the quanti-fied self-movement.

## Archiving the Quantified Self

The conversation between archivists and self-trackers has yet to begin, at least to my knowledge. While we created in 2018 a new position at Vanderbilt of Curator of Born-Digital Collections to appraise and acces-sion digital materials, we had email, word processing files, collections of images, and audiovisual files in mind when formulating the role. If pushed, we might consider adding social media postings to our permanent collection. But donors have never approached us about preserving their self-tracking data. In part, that may be because its usefulness to research-ers seems limited. After all, all this data would seem to serve primarily to improve and extend our quality of life. After death, the value of that data plummets. The donor's heirs might want to keep self-tracking data for the sake of personalized medicine, assuming that physicians could fruit-fully assimilate that information into their electronic medical records.[41] But would researchers care to know, for instance, Salmon Rushdie's aver-age resting heart rate when writing the *Satanic Verses* (1988)?

In the not-too-distant future, the community of self-trackers may see more value in preserving their data beyond the natural span of life. In "Predicting Me: The Route of Digital Immortality," Paul Smart notes that self-tracking data may provide the key to reconstituting individuals after death:

> From this perspective, the aim of digital recording technologies is not so much to monitor information that is distinct from that con-fronting the biological brain; rather, the aim is to use digital record-ing technologies as a substitute for biological sensors, recreating the kind of information streams that characterize the sensorium of the biological individual. In this respect, there seems to be ample cause for optimism.[42]

The challenge of collecting self-tracking data is not the scale—though archivists would undoubtedly need to step up their big data expertise—but the concept. The goal of self-trackers is to discover themselves in the ordinary, not the exceptional. Would the outcome of digital immortality

---

41  See Neff and Nafus, *Self-Tracking*, 153 et seqq.

42  Paul R. Smart, "Predicting Me: The Route to Digital Immortality?," in *The Mind-Technology Problem: Investigating Minds, Selves and 21st Century Artifacts*, ed. Robert W. Clowes, Klaus Gärtner, and Inês Hipólito (Berlin: Springer, in press), 14.

be what its proponents expect? Speculative fiction gives us reason for doubt. In "Be Right Back," a 2013 episode of the television show *Black Mirror*, a grieving women takes a chance on a commercial offer "to resurrect" her husband by building a chatbot and then a humanoid robot from the traces of her deceased spouse's social media postings.[43] The spouse initially derives comfort from the familiarity of the android, but inevitably becomes disappointed with its saccharine and predictable conversation. While the android manifests the external behavioral traits of her former husband, extrapolating new responses appropriately from her spouse data, the android is incapable of surprising her. The spark that made her spouse a person—we might say, his *soul*—does not dwell among the data. The warning of this *Black Mirror* episode is straightforward: we are not the sum of our data. But might the message actually be that we are not yet capturing enough information about ourselves?

The aspirations of the quantified self-movement are anti-curatorial, resisting calls to record only the significant and let the rest go. If these speculative futures are going to come about, we need to preserve everything about our selves. What role will archivists play in this future? If Booms is correct that appraisal stands at the center of archival theory and practice, then what work remains after donors explicitly reject its presuppositions? Will curatorial work turn into data curation, that is, not appraisal of the value of the data but the lending of technical assistance to making it available, sharable, and reusable by others? Realistically speaking, preserving quantitive data at scale would shift the locus of collecting away from libraries toward corporations, from the Library of Congress toward Amazon Web Services. What kinds of collecting institutions will emerge and thrive after any societal resolution of this disagreement? And what function would be left to librarians and archivists if we enter this post-curatorial age?

The contemporary dispute about the value of curation cuts deeper than the ancient disagreement over memory and memoranda. At stake is which reveals the essential truth about ourselves: (phenomenological) self-reflection or data science? But the truth we seek is shaped by the means we use to uncover it. How we resolve this dispute influences who we become. The warning Husserl presciently issued in the *Crisis of European Sciences* finds a renewed pertinency in the age of big data: "merely fact-minded sciences make merely fact-minded people."[44] That is, by externalizing ourselves as data, converting ourselves into streams of quantifiable information that we gather and analyze, we become the kind of narrow beings Husserl worried that modern science was inadvertently

---

43 I thank Hannah Reichel of Princeton Theological Seminary for calling my attention to the significance of this episode for this paper.

44 Husserl, *The Crisis of European Sciences*, 6.

creating by virtue of its very success. By returning to the venerable tradition of exercises in memory, the phenomenological guards against this existential constriction—but at a steep price, namely, by consigning most of what we experience to oblivion.

# 7: Collecting the Cultural Memory of Palmyra

*Erin L. Thompson*

O N THE FOURTH DAY of December 1893, Joseph Friedrich Nicolaus Bornmüller bent down and picked leaves from a low shrub with small white flowers. Bornmüller was on a botanical collecting trip through the Middle East, and he had just discovered a new species of pennycress. The dried specimen of *Thlaspi syriacum* he preserved on a sheet of paper is now housed in the herbarium of the Berlin-Dahlem Botanical Museum of the Freie Universität Berlin. These crumbling leaves are the holotype of the *Thlaspi syriacum* species. The word holotype is derived from the Greek ὅλος—"whole, entire." Bornmüller's sample was the basis for the description of the whole species. Every subsequent identification of an individual plant as *Thlaspi syriacum* or not *Thlaspi syriacum* is, in theory, based on whether or not that individual conforms to the appearance of the leaves Bornmüller plucked somewhere in what is now Syria. Holotypes are artificial. Bornmüller's hand was not guided to the most perfect specimen of *Thlaspi syriacum*. Rather, he anointed one individual plant to be the representation of a schema of botanical collecting and categorizing. This artificial creation and use of a holotype works for botanists, since they (usually) care more about the ways in which individual plants of the same species are similar rather than the ways in which they are different. They ignore the differences between individual embodiments (this patch of *Thlaspi syriacum* by the side of the road) and the abstract generalization (the Berlin holotype).

Cultural artifacts do not admit of so easy a negation of the value of the individual. We would rightly hesitate to discard even very similar cultural artifacts. Even reprintings of the same text can each have different value. The text of Alexander Pope's poem "The Rape of the Lock" is the same in the volume of John Bell's *Travelling Poetic Library*, bound in elaborately gilt calfskin and purchased in Paris in October 1785 by Thomas Jefferson for his twelve-year old daughter Martha, and in the battered paperback that I bought for a dollar from the bins of a used bookstore. But each of these volumes has a different history and a different set of relationships with the people who produced and used them. Some of these histories are more interesting than others. Rereading my pretentious annotations on the poem, written when I was not much older than Martha Jefferson, is worthwhile only to myself, while contemplating how Jefferson's recommendation of Pope as an educational text not only for his own daughter but, later, for female education in general, is to see a piece of the shaping of American educational policy. But whether more or less interesting, these different histories are revelatory of the lives of people connected to the artifact.

While cultural artifacts are not plants, sometimes we collect them as if they were. Besides its tragic human victims, the ongoing conflict in Syria has damaged or destroyed many aspects of cultural heritage, either as accidental, collateral damage or as part of deliberate destruction. Of the deliberate acts, the destruction of several well-preserved Roman-era temples and other structures in the archaeological area of Palmyra, Syria, particularly caught the attention of Western audiences. These losses have inspired a number of projects that use new technologies to recreate Palmyra's lost heritage—to collect, in a manner of speaking, what has been lost. It is important to examine these projects not just for the sake of Palmyrean or Syrian heritage, but because they are examples of a rapidly forming consensus on how we will use new technologies to collect cultural heritage. Or perhaps "consensus" is the wrong word. While the projects seem to agree on how to use technology, this agreement has been reached without much, if any, sustained debate about who should control, participate in, and share any profit from digital recreations of destroyed cultural heritage. And as the artist and activist Morehshin Allahyari has repeatedly insisted, we cannot ignore the power structures that come into play when we seek to use technology to collect culture produced by other communities, lest these projects reproduce the structures of colonialism in digital form.[1]

Digital technologies offer expanded capacities to collect, index, and access large and unwieldy volumes of varied information of all types, including images, texts, and audio recordings, in multiple languages from multitudes of sources. Digital technology can collect the various and the varying: the disagreements, personal perspectives, idiosyncratic and minority views on the past. And yet many of the Palmyra-inspired projects act as if they were forming a collection of holotypes. These projects permit only a single, cohesive view of each monument. They ignore the mess of all the personal meanings that flowed from and around these monuments. In so doing, they ignore the human and thus miss the very value of paying attention to Palmyra at all.

I will begin by summarizing the activities of various Palmyra-related digital projects. I will then discuss the stated goals of these projects and

---

1    Claire Voon, "What's the Value of Recreating the Palmyra Arch with Digital Technology?," *Hyperallergic* (April 19, 2016), https://hyperallergic.com/292006/whats-the-value-of-recreating-the-palmyra-arch-with-digital-technology/?wt=2.

point out both some of the problems standing in the way of achieving these goals and problems with the goals themselves. I will pay special attention to the issue of how the often-stated goals of open participation and access can be achieved in the face of the realities of the limitations of online access in the Global South, including Syria. I will conclude by discussing a few examples of digital projects that have aimed to collect cultural memory rather than supposedly objective holotypes of cultural monuments.

## Digital Monuments

In mid-2015 a radical group calling itself the Islamic State (IS) deliberately destroyed several pieces of monumental architecture in Palmyra, including a Roman-era arch built at the intersection of two of the city's columnated streets. In April 2016, a recreation of this arch was unveiled in a temporary installation in Trafalgar Square, London.[2] The replica was a creation of the Institute for Digital Archaeology.[3] The Institute had collected enough pre-destruction photographs of the arch to produce a digital model, which was then used as the template for machine cutting the scale replica from marble. Only a few of the projects responding to IS's destruction at Palmyra have had such tangible products. The few exceptions have generally used digital modeling to 3D print restorations for irreparably broken segments of restored monuments, such as the Lion of Al-lāt, a 15-ton sculpture from Palmyra that had been broken into pieces by IS.[4] More often, the final product remains digital. Indeed, the recreated arch itself was a type of advertisement for the Institute's main project, the *Million Image Database*. The Institute has distributed Wi-Fi-equipped cameras to volunteers to capture detailed photographs of at-risk cultural heritage in conflict zones. The cameras automatically upload the images to the Institute's servers, where they will eventually be turned into digital models.

Digital recreation projects can either use preexisting data or produce their own, if the target monument still exists. CyArk uses 3D scanners to measure monuments by bouncing laser light off their surfaces.[5] These

---

2    Jennifer Baird and Zena Kamash, "Remembering Roman Syria: Valuing Tadmor-Palmyra, from 'Discovery' to Destruction," *Bulletin of the Institute of Classical Studies* 62, no.1 (2019): 1–29.

3    Institute for Digital Archaeology, *Triumphal Arch*, http://digitalarchae ology.org.uk/.

4    See Sarah Cascone, "Nearly Destroyed by ISIS, the Ancient City of Palmyra Will Reopen in 2019," *Artnet* (August 27, 2018), https://news.artnet. com/art-world/syria-isis-palmyra-restoration-1338257.

5    CyArk, https://www.cyark.org/.

measurements are combined to produce a digital model, which is then colored based on photographs of the surfaces of the monument. CyArk has done a number of projects around the world, but only one so far in Syria, at the site of Ninevah. Iconem, http://iconem.com/en/, a French agency working in collaboration with the Syrian Directorate-General of Antiquities and Museums, is similarly capturing data to build digital models of threatened sites, including the eighth century CE Great Mosque of Damascus and the ancient sites of Ugarit and the Jabley amphitheater.[6]

Other projects have concentrated on compiling open access databases of images and bringing together volunteers to work collaboratively to turn these images into digital models. Rekrei, founded as Project Mosul, has for example collected geotagged images from sharing sites like Flickr.[7] The #NEWPALMYRA project aims at bringing together a community of developers and modelers to create a complete digital model of Palmyra as it might have looked originally.[8] This project aims to continue the wishes of Bassel Khartabil, a Syrian who began taking photographs of Palmyra in 2005 with the goal of creating digital models of its monuments, although his files were lost when he was arrested (and later executed) by the Syrian regime. Khartabil's wife, Noura Ghazi, visited him in prison and told him about the IS destruction in Palmyra. She reports that he told her that he wanted "to collect everything there is about Palmyra and try to keep it alive with images on the Internet . . . [to] protect Syrian memory and identity from the disfiguration underway."[9] The #NEWPALMYRA project continued even after Khartabil's death was confirmed when Barry Threw, a San Francisco-based technologist, took over its direction and attempted to continue with this goal.

The other current projects have similarly phrased intentions—to collect, protect, and keep alive or preserve. However, it is important to note the differences in the objects of these verbs. In Khartabil's phrasing, the goal is to collect "Syrian memory and identity." Most other projects focus on "shared" or "universal" cultural heritage. Thus, for example, Alexy Karenowska, Director of Technology for the Institute for Digital Archaeology, explained that the purpose of the display of the recreated arch in Trafalgar Square was "to contextualize issues of shared cultural heritage, of what cultural heritage means to people, and the significance of these objects to people's everyday life," https://hyperallergic.com/

---

6   Iconem, http://iconem.com/en/.
7   Rekrei, https://projectmosul.org/.
8   #NEWPALMYRA, https://www.newpalmyra.org/.
9   Dominique Soquel, "Tech World Takes on Icon-Smashing Islamic State with a Virtual Palmyra," *Christian Science Monitor* (November 24, 2015), https://www.csmonitor.com/World/Middle-East/2015/1124/Tech-world-takes-on-icon-smashing-Islamic-State-with-a-virtual-Palmyra.

292006/whats-the-value-of-recreating-the-palmyra-arch-with-digital-technology/?wt=2.

But what, exactly, is the stuff of heritage? I have written elsewhere about the objective slippages between destroyed heritage and digital models, when technology does not quite yet live up to what has been promised or claimed about it: project organizers often describe digital models as perfect representations of the modeled object or monument, but they simply are not.[10] Here, however, I am more interested in thinking not about the failures in what these projects set out to do representationally, but the gaps in what they consider worth representing. What almost all of the current projects have in common is that they create visual representations of unpeopled sites. The represented sites are almost always ahistorical; they exist not at some particular moment in time, but in a vague period (for example, Palmyra at its height or before the destruction). If there is text, it is presented as a depersonalized, authoritative, truth-dispensing vehicle. The images and text work together to present the facts of the represented monument, just as the dried leaves and written annotations on the *Thlaspi syriacum* holotype present it as the representative of its species. These models generally leave out disagreements, debates, first person accounts, or any of the accumulated impressions, emotions, and interpretations that constitute cultural memory.

This omission of cultural memory is all the more striking because many of the founders of these projects were moved to act out of sympathy with the Syrian civilian population, besieged by conflict or fleeing it as refugees. And yet only a vanishingly small number of Syrian voices are associated with these digital collections of Syrian cultural heritage. Instead, the sites are treated as if from an archaeological perspective—as if their populations were long dead.

The elision of the Syrian people in the current attention to Syrian historical monuments may well be unintentional, but it is not accidental. Heritage, as David Lowenthal wrote, "exaggerates and omits, candidly inverts and frankly forgets."[11] The frank forgetting of the contemporary population of Palmyra is hardly surprising, given the long history of leaving them out of representations of the site disseminated in the West. This is true even from the first European popularization of Palmyra in the modern age, which occurred thanks to Robert Wood's 1753 publication of *The Ruins of Palmyra, Otherwise Tedmor, in the Desart*, after his expedition to the site with another Englishman, James Dawkins, who measured the ruins, and an Italian draftsman, Giovanni Borra, who made

---

10   Erin Thompson, "Legal and Ethical Considerations for Digital Recreations of Cultural Heritage," *Chapman Law Review* 20, no. 1 (Spring 2017): 153–76.

11   David Lowenthal, *The Heritage Crusade and the Spoils of History* (Cambridge: Cambridge University Press, 1998), 121.

the drawings that became the basis for the book's lavish engravings. As Jennifer Baird and Zena Kamash have pointed out, Borra's drawings, and thus the subsequent engravings, omit any trace of any modern human occupation of Palmyra, although at that time (and indeed, until 1932), an entire modern village lived within the walls of the site's largest sacred complex, the Temple of Bel. Tellingly, the people who are depicted in these representations "are exoticized figures or decorative *staffage*, who belong in a tradition of paintings of picturesque ruined landscapes."[12] Wood claims that Dawkins, when measuring Palmyra, was "indefatigable in his attention to see everything done accurately."[13] This claim of exact accuracy is echoed again and again in the discussion of the current wave of digital Palmyra projects. Yet what type of accuracy is it that results from omitting the human?

Baird and Kamash also point out that Wood's text, written to accompany the engravings, also "silences many of the contemporary Syrian voices he encountered" by "conflating past and present inhabitants; by writing out the Arab historians from the historiography of Tadmor-Palmyra; by generally denigrating the people he meets and with whom he travels; and by taking a highly Eurocentric view of the ruins, with comparisons to Rome and, especially, Athens."[14] Instead of listening to what any residents of Palmyra might have to say about the site, Wood claims that Palmyra has "out-liv[ed] any account," and is "left to tell [its] own story."[15] Baird and Kamash point out that, of course, the silencing of contemporary voices other than his own means that Palmyra's story "was not told by those mute stones but by Wood himself," and that this hostility "set the stage for future disregard" of contemporary inhabitants of the area.[16]

This model of disregard was eagerly followed. While Wood seems not to have had any conscious agenda in bringing Palmyra to Western attention, another eighteenth-century traveler, Constantin François de Chasseboeuf, the Comte de Volney, had an explicitly political goal for writing about Palmyra. Volney had seen Palmyra during his travels in the 1780s, but rethought the importance of the site in the later context of the French Revolution. In 1791 he published *Les ruines, ou méditations sur les révolutions des empires*, which compares the crumbling French monarchy to the ruins of Palmyra.[17] To point this comparison, in which Palmyra

---

12  Baird and Kamash, , "Remembering Roman Syria," 8.

13  Robert Wood, *The Ruins of Palmyra, Otherwise Tedmor, in the Desart* (London, 1753), preface.

14  Baird and Kamash, "Remembering Roman Syria," 10.

15  Wood, *The Ruins of* Palmyra, 1.

16  Baird and Kamash, "Remembering Roman Syria," 20 and 16.

17  Blake Smith, "Ruins and Revolution: Volney, Palmyra, and ISIS," *Age of Revolutions* (March 7, 2016), https://ageofrevolutions.com/2016/03/07/

serves as a dead city, killed by aristocratic rule, Volney also had to ignore the contemporary life at the site. With the distance of time, the voices of Wood and Volney can be identified, speaking through the mask of Palmyra. It is not so easy to identify the messages of the current projects representing Palmyra, but we must accept that they, too, are not as neutral as they might claim or seek to be. As Gramsci theorized, hegemonic representations of the world are averse to counternarrative and thus legitimate the powerful and dominant groups who produce them.[18]

## Representation and Access

One way to see the significant gap between collecting heritage conceived of as shared, versus as exclusively or proprietarily Syrian, is to look at the different intended audiences for these projects. Who should see the results of the projects—primarily Syrians or the world as a whole? The latter would seem to encompass the former, but in reality, the projects that conceive of Palmyra as shared heritage generally focus on reaching audiences that already have access to the means used to disseminate the project. This is most clear in the case of physical objects, like the recreated arch, placed in Trafalgar Square—a location not likely to feature a high percentage of Syrians. The issue of who has access becomes fuzzier for those projects with digital outputs, like #NEWPALMYRA's virtual model. Threw has stated that he conceives of this project's goal as "freeing Palmyra digitally to turn agency over this cultural heritage to the Syrian and global communities, following Bassel Khartabil's visionary work of transparency, open Internet, and free culture for the advancement of the Syrian people."[19] This idea—that an open access project using networked communication (through online social networks such as Twitter, Facebook, Sketchfab, or platforms specially constructed for cultural heritage purposes) will result in agency for Syrians as well as everyone else in the global community—is a common assumption in current digital cultural heritage projects. This principle of open access can be used to counter the claim that it is problematic that the demographics of the prime movers of current Palmyra digital projects mirror the demographics of the prime movers of the digital world as a whole—that is, white and Western. Their bias could be erased by wider participation. But the mere availability of access to participate in a crowd-sourced or otherwise open

---

ruins-and-revolution-volney-palmyra-and-isis/.

18  Antonio Gramsci, *Prison Notebooks*, ed. and trans. Quintin Hoare and Geoffrey Nowell Smith (New York: International, 1971).

19  El Salem, "#NEWPALMYRA: Breathing Life Lost into Syria's Ancient City" (July 25, 2018), https://www.progrss.com/design/20180725/newpalmyra-syria/.

digital project does not by any means guarantee participation. The rise of online networked communication led to hopes that, as Harvard Law Professor Lawrence Lessig put it, technology would finally "equalize the opportunity that people have to access and participate in the construction of knowledge and culture, regardless of their geographic placing."[20] It was hoped that people in the Global South would be able both to access and contribute to networked and codified knowledge of all sorts. But this promise has not been realized.

The latest figures available, for 2017, indicate that only around 34 percent of Syrian citizens use the Internet regularly.[21] This is already a lower percentage than accords with the ideals of universal participation in heritage projects, but it is also important to think about differences in the way that people use the Internet when they do have access to it. The *Whose Knowledge?* project has investigated disparities in production of online networked knowledge, and has found that "most public knowledge online has so far been written by white men from Europe and North America."[22] Graham et al. analyzed geotagged Wikipedia articles to discover that most articles about the Global South are written in English, and mostly by editors living in the global North.[23] This matters because such articles "shape what is known and what can be known, which in turn influences the myriad ways in which knowledge is produced, reproduced, enacted, and re-enacted" and allows "dominant groups to fix distinct forms of representations onto otherwise contested places while maintaining an outward appearance of rationality and objectivity."[24] All this follows faithfully the patterns of the pre-digital age, when codified knowledge in the forms of, for example, books and newspapers, were far more often published in the global North.[25]

---

20   Lawrence Lessig, "An Information Society: Free or Feudal?" World Summit on the Information Society, Geneva (2003), http://www.itu.int/net/wsis/docs/pc2/visionaries/lessig.pdf Contra, see, e.g., Payal Arora, *The Next Billion Users: Digital Life beyond the West* (Cambridge, MA: Harvard University Press, 2019).

21   World Bank, "Individuals Using the Internet (% of Population)," https://data.worldbank.org/indicator/IT.NET.USER.ZS.

22   Whose   Knowledge?,   "About   Us,"   https://whoseknowledge.org/about-us/.

23   Mark Graham, Bernie Hogan, Ralph K. Straumann, and Ahmed Medhat, "Uneven Geographies of User-Generated Information: Patterns of Increasing Informational Poverty," *Annals of the Association of American Geographers* 104, no. 4 (2014): 746–64.

24   Graham et al., "Uneven Geographies," 748.

25   Mark Graham, Scott A. Hale, and Monica Stephens, *Geographies of the World's Knowledge* Convoco! Edition (2011), https://www.oii.ox.ac.uk/archive/downloads/publications/convoco_geographies_en.pdf.

And it is not just the makeup of the participants; the design of networked communication sites by members of dominant groups often structures supposedly open sites in ways hostile to non-dominant ways of knowing. For example, oral knowledge is not citable on Wikipedia, where all additions to articles must be supported by written citations. Graham et al. list other pitfalls that stand between the ideal of universal participation and the reality of knowledge concentration, including "language barriers, connection speeds, technical impediments, cultural differences in what constitutes authority and in attitudes towards knowledge sharing, diffusion of the *notion* of participation, and a host of other factors."[26]

Thus the problem with depending on open access platforms to provide a truly diverse view of heritage is not so much a problem of access but of *representation* and *participation*.[27] Graham et al. conclude that, despite the recent rapid increase of Internet access in the Middle East, its residents "remain largely absent from websites and services that represent the region to the rest of the world."[28] The *Whose Knowledge?* project insists that such absences mean "that we do not adequately know each other, our histories and knowledges well enough in a rich, diverse, multilingual, multicultural world," and calls this a "hidden crisis of 'unknowing.'"[29]

## Alternative Structures, Alternative Narratives

Thus far I have argued that, given the history of Western-produced representations of Palmyra, it is not surprising that the current crop of projects also leaves out Syrian cultural memory of the site, despite the promise new forms of technology offer to increase the ease of including Syrian voices. There are, fortunately, many projects that have succeeded in collecting cultural memory. These projects should be models for Palmyra-related digital reconstructions.

Some of these potential models use more traditional forms of communication, such as the labels in the permanent collection display of the National Museum of the American Indian (New York), which include commentary from members of descendant communities, even for quite ancient objects. Other models have made eloquent use of digital technologies to capture individual reactions to sites and monuments, over and above merely representing artifacts themselves. For example, "The

---

26  Graham et al., "Uneven Geographies," 750.

27  Eszter Hargittai and Gina Walejko, "The Participation Divide: Content Creation and Sharing in the Digital Age," *Information, Communication and Society* 11, no. 2 (2008): 239–56.

28  Graham et al., "Uneven Geographies," 750.

29  Whose Knowledge?, "Decolonizing the Internet," https://whoseknowl edge.org/initiatives/decolonizing-the-internet/.

Last Goodbye" traveling exhibit asks viewers to wear a headset to experience immersive virtual reality, following the Holocaust survivor Pinchas Gutter on his final trip to the concentration camp where his parents and twin sister were murdered.[30] Gutter explains the functions of the buildings viewers see as they proceed through the camp, and the experience ends with him reciting prayers in front of the site's mausoleum. Similarly, although less immersive, New York's National September 11th Museum not only includes audio and video recordings of survivors talking about their memories of the attacks but also features recording booths to allow visitors to tell their own stories. Video games also offer interesting models for presenting a cultural site along with its cultural memory. Sites as various as the controversial psychiatric hospital of Volterra, Italy, and a factory providing employment for disabled veterans of World War I have been memorialized using not only photographic records to recreate the space but also oral histories and archival materials to allow players to learn about the lives lived in these spaces.[31]

The *Diarna Project* is an even more directly applicable model.[32] It aims to document and preserve the history of Sephardi Jewish communities in the Middle East and North Africa, especially in Iraq, Syria, Yemen, and Libya, where the majority and sometimes the entirety of the Jewish community left decades ago.[33] Diarna ("Our Homes" in Judeo-Arabic) is an interactive online museum. The project collects oral histories to create digital maps to guide users on interpretive tours of monuments—whether still existing or vanished. For example, users might see a road running between a Christian and a Muslim cemetery in Sulaymaniyah, Iraq, but learn that the road was built over what had once been the Jewish section of a formerly undivided burial ground. The project's goal is for displaced community members and descendants to learn more about their family origins, and for everyone to learn about a part of the history of

---

30　Museum of Jewish Heritage. "The Last Goodbye," https://mjhnyc.org/exhibitions/the-last-goodbye/.

31　Florence Smith Nicholls, "Exploring the Afterlife of Historical Sites in Video Games," *Eurogamer* (July 7, 2019), https://www.eurogamer.net/amp/2019-07-07-exploring-the-afterlife-of-historical-sites-in-video-games; see also José Antonio González Zarandona, Adam Chapman, and Darshana Jayemanne, "Heritage Destruction and Videogames: Ethical Challenges of the Representation of Cultural Heritage," *Transactions of the Digital Games Research Association* 4, no. 2 (2018): 173–203.

32　Diarna Project, http://diarna.org/.

33　Ross Ufbergnov, "How One Organization Is Using Google Maps to Save History in the Middle East," *Pacific Standard Magazine* (November 18, 2016), https://psmag.com/news/how-one-organization-is-using-google-maps-to-save-history-in-the-middle-east#.hzyky9g5h.

pluralism in areas where the existence of religious minorities is currently often ignored or repressed.

There are currently a few attempts to collect Syrian voices speaking about the current conflict, such as the Syrian Archive and the Syrian Oral History Project.[34] Only a few current projects focus specifically on preserving the cultural memory of Palmyra. Yet these projects have already shown the richness of such material. One such project is a BBC podcast, the *Museum of Lost Objects*, which has interviewed, among others, a man seeking to find out the fate of his family's home in Aleppo's heavily damaged Old City, a Syrian art historian who lived inside the Temple of Bel, and Salam al-Kuntar, whose mother was born inside the temple, who explains that the meaning of heritage is "not only architecture or artifacts that are representing history, it's these memories and ancestral connection to the place."[35]

The podcast has also interviewed Zenobia al-Asaad, whose father, Khaled al-Asaad, directed the archaeological site of Palmyra for forty years before being imprisoned and then executed by IS, reportedly for not revealing the location of antiquities he had hidden to protect them from looting.[36] Zenobia, who was named for a third century CE queen of Palmyra, described walking the site with her father, "checking on things, laughing, talking, and the way he talked about Palmyra made me love the city even more, because I know he loved it."[37] She says she cannot bear to return to Palmyra, because the destruction of its monuments is linked with her father's death: "Palmyra the ancient city will always be a part of me, but I can't really imagine going back to Palmyra, walking along the paths, looking at the sites, without my father. . . ."[38] Another project, Zena Kamash's *Postcard to Palmyra*, invited viewers of the Institute for Digital Archaeology's recreated arch in Trafalgar Square to write their thoughts about the display on postcards.[39] Although most of those who identified themselves were English, a few were Syrian. One postcard,

---

34  Syrian Archive, https://syrianarchive.org/en. For the Syrian Oral History Project see Daniela Blei, "'We Can't Save Syrians Anymore, but We Can Save the Truth': An Ambitious Oral History Project Will Determine How the War in Syria is Remembered," *Foreign Policy* (December 27, 2018), https://foreignpolicy.com/2018/12/27/ugur-umit-ungor-syria-oral-history-project/.
35  Kanishk Tharoor and Maryam Maruf, "Museum of Lost Objects: The Temple of Bel," *BBC News Magazine* (March 1, 2016), https://www.bbc.com/news/magazine-35688943.
36  Tharoor and Maruf, "Museum of Lost Objects: The Temple of Bel."
37  Tharoor and Maruf, "Museum of Lost Objects: The Temple of Bel."
38  Tharoor and Maruf, "Museum of Lost Objects: The Temple of Bel."
39  Zena Kamash, "'Postcard to Palmyra': Bringing the Public into Debates over Post-Conflict Reconstruction in the Middle East," *World Archaeology* 49, no. 5 (2017): 608–22.

written in Arabic, read "Tadmor [Palmyra] the eternal . . . the green shoot of beauty, you will remain with us forever."[40]

Perhaps this paper will not persuade the technologists who, after all, frequently do recommend discarding books and other texts after digitization.[41] The cultural memory adhering to various copies of Pope's "The Rape of the Lock" might, to this audience, be as little interesting as the cultural memory of Palmyra seems to be to many people currently creating digital representations of the site. But we should think hard about what we are throwing away. Palmyra has different resonances in the memory of those who have lived nearby than to those who have visited as tourists or experienced it through photographs. Not all of these resonances are positive. Tadmor, the modern city linked to the archaeological site, is infamous for its prison, where many Syrians opposed to the regime government were tortured.[42] These differences in the memory and interpretation of the site are important to collect and preserve. In part this is true because Palmyra's fate is highly political; the ruins are, as Threw of #NEWPALMYRA has put it, a "symbolic battleground for control over the Syrian people."[43] The Syrian President Bashar al-Assad has claimed that his forces' "liberation" of Palmyra from IS occupation is "another indication of the success of the strategy pursued by the Syrian army and its allies in the war against terrorism."[44] Are those who oppose his regime expected to tolerate its human rights abuses in order to protect shared cultural heritage? We need to see many versions of Palmyra in order to prevent a single one from dominating.

---

40   Kamash, , "'Postcard to Palmyra,'" 619.

41   Nicholson Baker, *Double Fold: Libraries and the Assault on Paper* (New York: Random House, 2001); James A. Jacobs and James R. Jacobs, "Wait! Don't Digitize and Discard! A White Paper on ALA COL Discussion Issue #1a" (June 2013), https://www.freegovinfo.info/files/FGI-white-paper-response-to-COL-discussion.pdf.

42   Miriam Cooke, "Tadmor's Ghosts," *Review of Middle East Studies* 47, no. 1 (2013): 28–36.

43   Salem, "#NEWPALMYRA."

44   Adam Taylor, "The Problem with Rebuilding a Palmyra Ruin Destroyed by ISIS—Does it Simply Help Assad?," *Washington Post* (April 20, 2016), https://www.washingtonpost.com/news/worldviews/wp/2016/04/20/the-problem-with-rebuilding-a-roman-ruin-destroyed-by-isis-does-it-simply-help-assad/; see also Lynn Meskell, *A Future in Ruins: UNESCO, World Heritage, and the Dream of Peace* (Oxford: Oxford University Press, 2018), 176–81.

# 8: Conservation in the Digital Age

*Jessica Walthew*

## Introduction

CONSERVATION IS A COMPLEX FIELD that draws on many different disciplines. Broadly speaking, conservators are concerned with the future of the past. While we are primarily focused on preserving material aspects of objects (that is, artworks, artifacts, specimens, and other historic documents), we are also concerned with the meanings present in objects, and how those objects are used to tell histories. Conservators work in a wide variety of contexts, ranging from archaeological sites to libraries, national parks, museums, and private practice studios (these conservators in turn work for galleries, private collectors, artists, historic homes, auction houses and so on). Acting as translators between different fields, we must manage different professional languages and collaborate with a variety of partners. Despite our field's deep roots in archaeology and art history, conservators' vocabulary has been augmented with new approaches to contemporary and media art—and this new lexicon also helps to understand emerging approaches to the conservation of historic works better. In discussing the evolving language of conservation, this lexicon can be understood in both a narrow sense (that is, recent terms coined in the conservation of time-based media and contemporary art) and in a broader sense. In this more expansive definition, fluency in multiple languages functions as a metaphor for how conservators codeswitch between different skill sets and vernaculars to manage interactions with diverse professional collaborators.

While we are adept at mediating between different professional languages, this is not the only codeswitch that informs the practices of modern conservation. Foundational coursework in American conservation training programs includes learning the history of conservation practices across specialties. My own training was focused on archaeological and anthropological collections, a subfield of object conservation (sculpture, decorative arts, artifacts, and so on) with its own particular history, practices, and ethics. Now working at Cooper Hewitt, Smithsonian Design Museum, I work with an interdisciplinary team confronted with many challenging new digital acquisitions. While there have been perceptive articles on the links between the conservation of contemporary art and cultural materials collections,[1] contemporary design requires a new hybrid approach that draws on many other subcultures of conservation.

The field of conservation has been revolutionized once again by technological changes, but only recently have we started to register the changes in our practice and theory engendered by the inventions of the twentieth and twenty-first centuries. Despite a legacy of "traditional" restoration techniques that still forms the basis of our training and the public perception of our work, technological tools and our technical terminology in fact define the practices of modern conservation. This paper attempts to chart a path from the history of conservation to its future. It will explore how the challenges of collecting and conserving digital design interface with existing frameworks (histories, theories, and practices) of conservation intervention. Case studies from the Cooper Hewitt, Smithsonian Design Museum collection will demonstrate how our tactics and lexicon are evolving to suit twenty-first century needs.

## Conservation and Archaeology

The professions of archaeology and conservation have long been closely aligned, sharing similar theoretical foundations and developmental trajectories. As a starting point, the birth of scientific conservation—with the introduction of chemists to the museum setting when Friedrich Rathgen's laboratory in Berlin was founded in 1888—followed on the heels of the adoption of the scientific method for archaeological excavation.[2] In the past, vocational archaeological treasure hunting without regard for

---

The text of this chapter is a work of the US Government.

1    See Kelly McHugh and Anne Gunnison, "Finding Common Ground and Inherent Differences: Artist and Community Engagement in Cultural Material and Contemporary Art Conservation," *Studies in Conservation* 61, no. sup 2 (2016): 126–29. doi:10.1080/00393630.2016.1181349, and Renata F. Peters, "The Parallel Paths of Conservation of Contemporary Art and Indigenous Collections," *Studies in Conservation* 61, no. sup 2 (2016): 183–87. doi:10.1080/00 393630.2016.1200839.

2    Alexander Scott was appointed at the British museum in 1919—on the history of conservation at the British Museum see Harold J. Plenderleith, "A History of Conservation," *Studies in Conservation* 43, no. 3 (1998): 129–43—and William Young at the MFA Boston in 1929, see Susan E. Schur, "Laboratory Profile: The Boston Museum of Fine Arts' Research Laboratory," *Technology and Conservation* (1977): 1–5. For a discussion of Rathgen's influence, see Mark Gilberg, "Friedrich Rathgen: The Father of Modern Archaeological Conservation," *Journal of the American Institute for Conservation* 26, no. 2 (1987): 105–20, https://cool.conservation-us.org/jaic/articles/jaic26-02-004_1.html.

stratigraphy (today considered looting) was matched with vocational restoration that sometimes (inadvertently or not) falsified objects' histories, creating pastiches and resulting in many "over-cleaned" or "over-restored" artifacts, as judged by today's standards.

Throughout its history, the field of conservation has struggled to understand what constitutes proper conservation activity. Early conservation theorists, including John Ruskin, Eugene-Emmanuel Viollet-le-Duc, Alois Riegl, and Cesare Brandi, focused their attention on buildings, monuments, and wall paintings and were concerned with how restoration might interfere with interpretation. Brandi's work has had a long legacy, and the tension between wholeness (recuperated through restoration) and authenticity (held by the original itself, however fragmented) remains a central concern for conservators.[3] How visible should restorations be to allow viewers to best appreciate the works? Unethical or improper interventions compromise the original in favor of a current interpretation which could later prove incorrect. Thus, clear distinctions between original and in-fill or replacement materials, "reversibility," and "retreatability" became cornerstones of conservation ethics.[4]

Conservation as a distinct field is defined by the use of scientific methods with the aim of understanding the history and technology of artist's materials.[5] Conservation (vs. restoration) was born in the late nineteenth century and came to universities in the United States as a formal academic

---

3    Brandi's influence has been strong particularly in Italy but also in English-speaking countries since his work has been translated into English; see Frank Matero, "Loss, Compensation and Authenticity in Architectural Conservation," *Journal of Architectural Conservation* 12, no. 1 (2006): 71–90, and Sebastiano Barassi, "Dreaming of a Universal Approach: Brandi's Theory of Restoration and the Conservation of Contemporary Art," Paper Presented at the Seminar Conservation, Principles, Dilemmas and Uncomfortable Truths, Royal Academy of Arts, September 24, 2009, 1–5, http://www.icom-cc.org/54/document/dreaming-of-a-universal-approach-brandis-theory-of-restoration-and-the-conservation-of-contemporary-art/?id=777#.Xs_Ji9NKjMI.

4    See Barbara Appplebaum, "Criteria for Treatment: Reversibility," *Journal of the American Institute for Conservation* 26, no. 2 (1987): 65–73, cool.conservation-us.org/jaic/articles/jaic26-02-001.html 1987; and Frank Matero, *Heritage Conservation and Archaeology: An Introduction*, AIA site preservation programme, 2008, www.archaeological.org/news/hca/89Matero.

5    While technical examination and treatment of artworks are considered key competencies, "conservation terminology" (i.e., "The nomenclature or language of technical terms used in conservation") is actually the first essential competency as defined by the *American Institute for Conservation*, "Defining the Conservator: Essential Competencies" (2003), www.conservation-us.org/docs/default-source/governance/defining-the-conservator-essential-competencies.pdf.

field only in the post-World War II period.[6] In the early twentieth century, however, ultraviolet light, X-rays, and analytical chemistry were introduced into museums as harbingers of this new scientific conservation discipline.[7] Emphasis on technical investigation, empirical observation, and material testing also drove a divergence with traditions of restoration, as conservation labs began to replace restorer's studios.[8] Today, conservators inhabit a world of interdisciplinarity, balancing the historic, material, and conceptual values (among others) of works under our care.[9]

The methods and ethics of both professions evolved over the twentieth century and continue to change in the twenty-first: archaeologists

---

6     For a history of The Conservation Center at New York University's Institute of Fine Arts (founded 1960) see Craig Hugh Smyth, "The Conservation Center: Origins and Early Years," in *Training in Conservation: A Symposium on the Occasion of the Dedication of the Stephen Chan House. October 1, 1983*, ed. Norbert S. Baer (Institute of Fine Arts, New York University, 1989), 7–16.

7     Francesca G. Bewer, *A Laboratory for Art: Harvard's Fogg Museum and the Emergence of Conservation in America, 1900–1950* (Cambridge, MA: Harvard Art Museums, 2010), 11–13. Bewer gives a full account of the history of Harvard's *Fogg Museum*. Most articles from the late nineteenth and early twentieth century on scientific techniques were published in the Museum Journals (British or American) or science journals prior to the founding of conservation-specific literature. See also James Rorimer, *Ultra-Violet Rays and Their Use in the Examination of Works of Art* (New York: Metropolitan Museum of Art, 1931), and Julia Leonardos, "X-Ray Visionary," *Harvard Art Museums Index Magazine* (September 28, 2016), www.harvardartmuseums.org/article/x-ray-visionary.

8     I do not mean to imply that this transition from studio to lab was completed. There are still many conservation "studios" and several subfields of conservation in which "traditional" materials and techniques are still critical to conservation practice, for example furniture and Asian paintings.

9     "Values based conservation" was introduced in the 1990s concurrent with values-based and community-based archaeological practice; see Erica C. Avrami, Randall Mason, and Marta De la Torre, *Values and Heritage Conservation: Research Report* (Los Angeles, CA: Getty Conservation Institute, 2000), hdl.handle.net/10020/gci_pubs/values_heritage_research_report. "Values" and "significance" are also reflected in the Venice (1964) and Nara (1994) charters, https://www.icomos.org/charters/. The *AIC Essential Competencies for Conservators* (2003) included the following: "An understanding and appreciation of the aesthetic, cultural, economic, historical, political, religious, scientific, and social values of objects, buildings, and sites are critically important when devising preservation and conservation plans, strategies, and treatments. When caring for and treating cultural heritage, the conservator must be aware of and consider knowledge relating to these values, on the basis of which society establishes the significance of cultural heritage. Although conservation and preservation decisions may be viewed as technical in nature, the conservator must be aware that these decisions are themselves profoundly influenced by past, present, and future societal attitudes and values."

and conservators alike receive professional training at the post-graduate level, and have been quick to adopt new technologies and incorporate them into research.[10] The traditional tools of conservation practice (cotton swabs, solvents, tiny paint brushes) now include digital documentation tools (microscopes, cameras, dataloggers, 3D scanners). Over time, conservation and archaeological practices have advanced to emphasize context, documentation, and stakeholders' input.

# New Tools

Digital tools help conservators and archaeologists generate new readings of old evidence, and allow for non-destructive investigation. Computational photography techniques, along with GPS and laser scanning, have contributed to better documentation and interpretation of archaeological remains (both objects and sites). One prevalent example is photogrammetry, a tool that combines photographs from different angles to calculate the three-dimensional shape of the object or scene pictured. Aerial photogrammetry is a key technique for military surveillance, emergency first responders, the agricultural industry, and archaeological survey alike. In conservation, photogrammetry and other documentation technologies promise to track change over time more accurately; higher resolution 3D images promise to help us monitor smaller degrees of change. Another popular computational photography technique is Reflectance Transformation Imaging (RTI), which allows interactive close-range viewing of surface topology.[11] These technologies have uses that are descriptive, reflecting qualities of the works or sites we document, such as to look at toolmarks or generate scaled drawings, but are increasingly used in aiding and presenting interpretations.

Successful use of these tools requires employing best practices for capturing, processing, and archiving the data. These data do not stand on their own merits; rather, they are interconnected, dependent on hardware and software, and require a great degree of expertise to understand and interpret them.[12] In the archaeological field there has been much dis-

---

10 Several of the conservation training programs are also closely aligned with archaeology programs: University College London Institute of Archaeology (founded 1937), New York University's Institute of Fine Arts (founded 1960) and the UCLA-Getty Interdisciplinary Program (founded 2005).

11 The non-profit Cultural Heritage Imaging (CHI) provides training to conservators and archaeologists in both technologies (RTI and Photogrammetry) and has worked to develop and implement robust standards for capture and processing.

12 As many other authors have pointed out (see Erin L. Thompson in this volume), photogrammetry and 3D scanning are techniques of representation like any other, and need to be used with care.

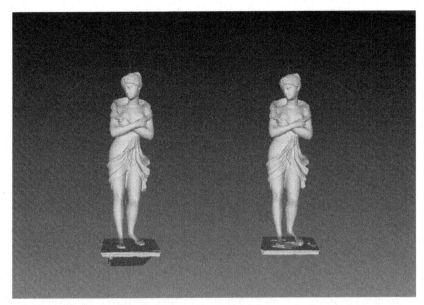

Figure 8.1. Caption: 3D scans were part of an extensive conservation treatment (i.e., cleaning and stabilization) of an *ormolu* table centerpiece, likely commissioned by Napoleon. Two figures were compared by blue-light laser scanning performed at NYU's Laguardia Lab. The three-dimensional scans were presented along with Reflectance Transformation images in a touchscreen interactive in the gallery. Image: Cooper Hewitt, Smithsonian Design Museum.

cussion of how digital tools fundamentally change how we relate to the objects and sites we uncover. Indeed, a vocal contingent has emerged in archaeology that is critical of the agendas hidden in the untempered adoption of digital technology, which comes with its own coded language and creates "digital divides."[13] While I am an enthusiastic adopter of digital

---

13  Huggett questions whether digital technologies make us better interpreters, or merely mask and reinforce existing hierarchies of power, which determine the interpretation and ownership of sites and museum objects alike. See Jeremy Huggett, "Archaeology and the New Technological Fetishism," *Archeologia e Calcolatori* 15 (2004): 81–92; and Hugget, "A Manifesto for an Introspective Digital Archaeology," *Open Archaeology* 1, no. 1 (2015): 86–95, doi:10.1515/opar-2015-0002, and more general commentary on digital archaeology on his blog, http://introspectivedigitalarchaeology.com/. On digital divides and digital technology in teaching, see Bill Caraher, "Digital Approaches to Teaching the Ancient Mediterranean: Dissecting Digital Divides," *Mediterranean World blog* (September 19, 2018), mediterraneanworld.wordpress.com/2018/09/19/digital-approaches-to-teaching-the-ancient-mediterranean-dissecting-digital-divides/.

technology tools in conservation, there remain many philosophical problems with 3D data (e.g., models as digital surrogates, intellectual property issues, and ownership of and access to data).[14] Some of these ontological concerns have their roots in twentieth-century questions about reproductions and their relationship to originals, often invoked in dialogues about contemporary art practices.[15] Since these technologies now serve multiple roles in conservation, from documentation to producing stand-ins for display, these are critical topics for cross-disciplinary discussion. In the introduction to James Rorimer's *Ultra-Violet Light in the Examination of Works of Art* (1931), Joseph Breck (Curator of the Decorative Arts department and Assistant Director of The Metropolitan Museum) hinted at the long-standing tension pitting traditional connoisseurship against modern tools of investigation:

> Science has placed at the disposal of the expert various aids for the examination of works of art, such as chemical analysis, micrography, photography, examination by x-rays, and the like. To these may now be added as of established value the ultraviolet rays. For the layman a word of warning is perhaps desirable. None of these aids, invaluable as they may be—when used by the trained observer—in helping to establish identity and in recognizing fraud and repairs, is of itself endowed with intelligence. These aids supplement the discerning eye; they do not replace it.[16]

Let us heed this warning to not lose sight of our goals by focusing too much on our tools. These new tools, while they are not a panacea, are useful for us to better comprehend the objects of our study, and better communicate our findings to wider audiences. New vocabularies also enable us to engage critically with our actions and interpretations in novel ways.

---

14  For a further discussion in the context of archaeological conservation, see Jessica Walthew, Alison Hight, David Scahill, Anna Serotta, and Evelyn Mayberger "Collaboratively Thinking Forward: 3D Data in Conservation and Archaeology," in *Engaging Conservation: Collaboration across Disciplines,* ed. Nina Owzcarek, Molly Gleeson, and Lynn Grant (London: Archetype, 2017), 266–78.

15  See Bruno Latour and Adam Lowe, "The Migration of the Aura or How to Explore the Original Through Its Facsimiles," in *Switching Codes,* ed. Thomas Bartscherer (Chicago: University of Chicago Press, 2010), 275–97, and the *Tate Papers,* which gather diverse perspectives on reproductions and replication in conservation, *Inherent Vice: The Replica and Its Implications in Modern Sculpture Workshop, 18–19 October 2007,* ed. Bryony Bery. *Tate Papers* 8 (Autumn 2007), www.tate.org.uk/research/publications/tate-papers/08.

16  Rorimer, vii.

# New Vocabularies

Approaches developed for the conservation of digital, time-based, and variable media[17] have contributed to the broader conservation discipline precisely because conservation is a small and close-knit field, and because workshops and online publications have disseminated the work widely. Pioneering initiatives in museums including Tate, the Museum of Modern Art (MoMA), San Francisco Museum of Modern Art (SF MoMA), and the Guggenheim in the late 1990s and early 2000s established the basis for the practices and theories of media conservation.[18] In 2003, the program in Moving Image Archiving and Preservation (MIAP) was founded at New York University's Tisch School of the Arts, drawing from the fields of media studies as well as film and sound archiving. These institutions helped to establish the primary strategies for conserving complex works, which have been ably summarized below by the Variable Media Initiative, and more thoroughly discussed in Pip Laurenson's seminal article "Authenticity, Change and Loss in the Conservation of Time-Based Media Installations":[19]

> The four associated preservation strategies as defined by the Variable Media methodology range from traditional to radical. Storage is the default strategy for most museums. In its most basic definition, it means to put the work in a climate-controlled environment. For time-based media like film and video, this means keeping original projectors and hardware running for as long as possible, and stockpiling old machines. For these types of works, migration is often seen as a more successful strategy. To emulate a work is to devise a way of imitating the original look of a piece by completely different means.

---

17 Variable media, which has been an area of great growth in the conservation world often alternately called time-based media or electronic media, includes performance, installation, kinetic, electronic, light-based, and other types of art. These "specialties" are represented by the Electronic Media Group and also by the new Contemporary Art Network of the American Institute for Conservation, the United States' professional body of conservators.

18 These initiatives are well-archived online. See Variable Media Initiative, www.variablemedia.net/e/index.html, and Matters in Media Art, https://www.moma.org/collection/about/conservation/matters-in-media-art.

19 Pip Laurenson, "Authenticity, Change and Loss in the Conservation of Time-Based Media Installations," *Tate Papers* 6 (Autumn 2006), www.tate.org.uk/research/publications/tate-papers/06/authenticity-change-and-loss-conservation-of-time-based-media-installations. Laurenson's most important assertion is that "Time-based media installations allow for greater parameters of change than many more traditional objects of fine art. The degree to which the artist 'thinly' or 'thickly' specifies the work is relative to the specific work and the practice of the artist."

The term can be applied generally to a refabrication of an artwork's components, but also has a specific meaning in the context of digital media, where emulation offers a powerful technique for running an out-of-date computer on a contemporary one. By far, the most radical strategy is to reinterpret the work each time it is recreated.[20]

Documentation, storage, migration, emulation, replication, and reinterpretation: these key terms have contributed immensely to our broader discussions of conservation ethics and practice, as we are often forced to renegotiate values of the "original" in our work, as well as determine who has the expertise and authority to make decisions. One of the major conceptual and practical shifts in conservation's development from the twentieth to the twenty-first century has been a refocusing of the conservator's primary responsibilities from intervention to documentation, monitoring, and prevention. As the field has matured and evolved, the balance between prevention and intervention has played a large part in defining ethical behavior (despite the pervasive and misleading use of "minimal intervention," even in current conservation writing).[21] A focus in the contemporary field on artist interviews has been influential in negotiating authority and decision-making involving artists and their agents or estates along with the museum's professional conservators and curators.[22] Understanding the work's conceptual and material aspects in great detail at the time of acquisition also enables conservators to understand which parts can or should be replaced in the future. "Iteration reports" are now standard museum practice for complex installation works, documenting how and why choices were made.[23] The long-term planning that museums undertake far outlasts any given technology and also outlasts artists, conservators, and curators—museum professionals must plan for a future without us, in which the documentation will need to stand in for both the creators' and institution's knowledge.

Migration or reformatting from one unstable medium to another medium with better longevity is a cornerstone of the conservation of film

20 Guggenheim Museum. *Variable Media Initiative*, www.variablemedia.net/.

21 See Caroline Villers, "Post-Minimal Intervention," *Conservator* 28, no. 1 (2004): 3–10, doi.org/10.1080/01410096.2004.9995197. Minimal intervention is one of conservation's most misused codewords. It can signify such a great range of actions that it is becoming a meaningless term.

22 *Voices of Contemporary Art* (VoCA) and other artist interview projects at the Menil Collection, Whitney, and SF MoMa have provided resources for artist interviews tailored for conservators. See also Fernando Domínguez Rubio, "Preserving the Inpreservable: Docile and Unruly Objects at MoMA," *Theor Soc* 43 (2014): 617–45, doi.org/10.1007/s11186-014-92334.

23 Joanna Phillips, "Iteration Report, 2012," *Time Based Media*. Guggenheim Museum, www.guggenheim.org/conservation/time-based-media.

and archival materials. Unstable early plastics like cellulose nitrate and cellulose acetate were used widely as film stocks in the early twentieth century. Today, accepted conservation practice is to digitize the content of these works to preserve them. In this circumstance, the content may be divorced from the material and transferred to another format, though there also exist many artworks that are conceptually incompatible with format changes. Digital files or programs may also be transferred from one format to another, but this can introduce a wealth of problems or artifacts that must be carefully considered and remediated if possible. For example, a software-based artwork may run at the wrong clock-speed when moved to a newer machine with increased graphics processing capabilities. As in many conservation interventions, only a perceptive audience will notice certain details, so some migration artifacts could go unnoticed by the larger public. Previous documentation to work from and clear disclosure to audiences is important in permitting migration to work successfully.

When artworks present complexities that make migration unsuitable, the strategies of emulation, replication, and reinterpretation become more appealing. Emulation imitates the original look of a piece but substitutes another way of functioning, presenting a work-around for obsolete (non-functional) or fragile components.[24] Programmable minicomputers like Mac minis or Raspberry Pis, and microcontrollers like Arduinos can run *sub rosa* hidden inside pedestals and platforms, imitating the original appearance of a work by running a virtual machine or program. The burgeoning field of software-based and Internet-based art preservation also relies heavily on being able to emulate characteristics of earlier software and web browsers.[25]

Replication and refabrication may be part of a work by definition, particularly for installation and performance works which are reassembled according to an accepted "score" for each exhibition, as Laurenson outlines. Sculptures might be refabricated as a conservation strategy when

---

24   As early as 2004, the Guggenheim displayed interactive works alongside emulations in the exhibition *Seeing Double, Emulation in Theory and Practice*, March-May 2004, https://www.guggenheim.org/exhibition/seeing-double-emulation-in-theory-and-practice; "emulation" may be just one small part of a more complex conservation treatment, as in the case of *Lovers* by Teiji Furuhashi, described in Ben Fino-Radin, "Art in the Age of Obsolescence: Rescuing an Artwork from Crumbling Technologies," *MoMA Stories* (December 21, 2016), https://stories.moma.org/art-in-the-age-of-obsolescence-1272f1b9b92e.

25   Rhizome (a digital preservation organization in residency at the New Museum) is the current leader in web-based artwork (net-art) preservation. They have introduced Webrecorder, an archiving tool for websites, as well as host http://oldweb.today/, a tool that allows exploration of web archives through emulated legacy browsers.

the original material manifestation no longer represents the artist's work. The Whitney Museum's interdisciplinary Replication Committee is charged with negotiating and managing such conservation challenges.[26] Refabricating a work in its entirety goes even a step further than refinishing or repatination—two drastic interventions which must be carefully considered and are undertaken only with great care.[27] Among professional conservators, refinishing is seen as an extreme intervention as opposed to consolidating and inpainting losses to the original surface. Refabrication is even rarer, and, depending on its extent, may legally require the artist's (or estate's) permission. While making exhibition copies to permit gallery interactivity also falls under the rubric of replication/refabrication, in contrast, this usually implies that the original is preserved.[28] When drastic interventions or substitutions are necessary to convey the original meaning or experience of a work, conservators are tasked with understanding and preserving more than merely the material aspects.

## From Archaeological Conservation to Conservation in a Design Museum

From the perspective of a conservator at a design museum, the strategies discussed above can apply to a wider range of objects and artworks than they were originally introduced to serve. As conservators, our professional responsibility is to define what constitutes acceptable change over time—this work depends on our understanding of how viewers perceive age and damage. These perceptions are conditioned as much by our professional and institutional cultures as by the art market and our culture at large. Within conservation practice, each object is conserved for a particular context and purpose. In the past, archaeological objects

---

26 See Margo Delidow, Clara Rojas Sebesta and Farris Wahbeh, "Whitney Replication Committee: Transparency in the Age of Reproduction," American Institute for the Conservation of Historic and Artistic Works Annual Meeting, Houston, TX, 2018 (Conference Presentation), and Ben Lerner, "The Custodians: How the Whitney is Transforming the Art of Museum Conservation," *New Yorker* (January 11, 2016).

27 For a discussion of refinishing, see Narayan Khandekar et al., "The Re-Restoration of Donald Judd's *Untitled* (1965)," in *Modern Paints Uncovered: Proceedings from the Modern Paints Uncovered Symposium*, ed. Thomas J. S. Learner et al. (London: Getty Conservation Institute, 2008), 157–64.

28 Exhibition copies were made of Lygia Clark's works for a 2014 *MoMA* retrospective (Cindy Albertson, Roger Griffith, Eric Meier, and Margo Delidow, "The Abandonment of Art: The Abandonment of Conservation, A Lygia Clark Retrospective at MoMA," presented at the American Institute for Conservation of Historic and Artistic Works, Miami, FL, 2015, and for Lygia Pape's works for the *Met Breuer*'s 2017 exhibition *A Multitude of Forms*.

were reconstructed to appear complete by replacing missing parts. By the early twentieth century, however, interest in archaeological context and the historic and material nature of artifacts (as reflected by Riegl's definitions of age and historic values in works of art) led to a new paradigm in archaeological conservation.[29] In the post-war period, a renewed interest in ruins and fragments reconceptualized damage as evidence of historic authenticity, leading to de-restoration of many artifacts. Prominent examples include the Aegina marbles at the Munich Glyptothek or the many noses removed from classical sculptures in the Ny Carlsberg Glyptotek in Copenhagen.

Conserving archaeological objects today usually gives more latitude for damage and incompleteness than decorative arts, for example, where we continue to privilege completeness and aesthetic integration. As noted above, another set of expectations and approaches is required for the conservation of contemporary art, which may involve less allegiance to original material in favor of preserving conceptual integrity. Likewise, for modern and contemporary "functional" design objects appropriate treatment may foreground use and function, potentially at the expense of original material, usually held sacrosanct. Competing paradigms of conservation are at play every day in museums, as each case plays out in its own history and trajectory along a wide spectrum of possibilities between these divergent limit cases. Conserving contemporary design (and especially works with digital components) requires a fluidity between the approaches of these different historical and institutional regimes of conservation.

The following case studies from the Cooper Hewitt, Smithsonian Design Museum highlight new concerns raised by digital media, and were carried out primarily by the time-based-media conservation consulting firm Small Data Industries during a survey of digital materials in the Cooper Hewitt collection and their special needs. Cooper Hewitt's collection focus makes it unique in many ways from our peer institutions in the larger museum field. Design objects can be mass produced, while art objects are rarely so. Industrial design objects may have distributed authorship, with many individuals and sometimes companies involved in their production. They may be factory-made rather than hand-made, though the collecting interests at Cooper Hewitt include prototypes and process materials which blur this boundary. Finally, and critically,

---

29  Alois Riegl, *Der moderne Denkmalkultus: Sein Wesen und seine Entstehung* (1903). Translation, "The Modern Cult of Monuments: Its Character and Its Origin, trans. Kurt W. Forster and Diane Ghirardo," *Oppositions* 25 (1982): 21–51. Riegl defined newness-value, age-value, historic value, and memory value. A slew of additional values are now understood in conservation's parsing of values and significance.

design objects are functional and offer the possibility of interactivity to a user—indeed, they are meant to be used, not just viewed in a vitrine. To conserve and display aspects of digital design opens up new twenty-first century problems. The role of the museum's conservators is to mediate between paradigms and practices derived from other contexts and make them applicable to Cooper Hewitt's collection and conservation ethos.

## Case Study: GRiD Compass Laptop

The following case study makes clear the difficulties of conserving personal computers, in which the function and interaction aspects are inherently fragile and difficult to access, yet critical to interpretation. The GRiD Compass was one of the first laptops, and was designed by Bill Moggridge, then the head of the international design firm IDEO. The design was quite unique in that it was the first "clamshell" case for laptops and had a bright orange display. It also used a form of non-volatile memory, now obsolete, called magnetic bubble memory (unlike solid-state or spinning hard drives we are most familiar with today). The interaction prototype GRiD Compass in our collection also comes with its own special aura, since the example came straight from Moggridge, the revered director of Cooper Hewitt for two short years before his death. While the computer's exterior case materials and its physical structure seem to be in good condition overall, the laptop is no longer functional. Several critical vulnerabilities exist for any consumer computer. There are physical vulnerabilities, such as plastic casings, batteries, and capacitors that degrade and can cause damage, and functional ones, i.e., software and operating systems becoming obsolete.

In order to safely examine the GRiD Compass to understand its condition, we needed to call in expertise outside the institution. Our digital media conservation consultants invited a collector specializing in historic computers to assist with condition assessment. They planned to (if possible) copy the bubble memory—revealing whether the computer in our collection had any original material directly from Moggridge remaining on it, then migrate the information to a more stable and more common digital format. For many historic consumer electronics, physical adapters between current and previous systems are not available, and preserving information can require performing a series of stepwise translations to get from one format to the currently accepted archival standard (i.e., digital files in specific file types, archived in remote, distributed storage and checked frequently for data integrity).

To understand whether the computer could be safely opened and examined, we also needed experience with other examples. Conservators often use replicas as tools for investigation and stand-ins to test treatments. We could not risk using the Cooper Hewitt GRiD's power supply,

Figure 8.2. GRiD Compass laptop computer disassembled for
condition check. Image: Small Data Industries.

particularly with its original capacitors (in poor condition, visibly bulg-
ing) and its battery in place. Even though these computers were commercially released, it is usually not within museum budgets or priorities
to purchase additional sacrificial consumer electronics to dismantle in the
name of practice and investigation. In another case study for the museum
concerning the Motorola Envoy, an early personal digital assistant, or
PDA, our consultant did just that (later donating the second Envoy with
its original packaging to the museum). Using a second GRiD computer
owned by the private collector enabled testing components one by one.
The screen is still functional, but the investigation found that the bubble
memory was not readable. While we understood that bubble memory was
a fringe technology and very little was known about its long-term durability, this demonstrates the danger with digital loss: it is often total. Now
that the migration strategy has failed, we are left wondering what more
there is to conserve than the physical material. The laptop looks exactly
the same, yet it has suffered an irreparable and arguably significant loss.

How the museum will eventually display the GRiD is still unclear.
Preserving the original material in long-term archival storage is different than conserving it for display. In most cases the museum displays
such objects under vitrines, and they are not touchable or interactive.
However, there is strong curatorial interest in displaying a duplicate
object for interaction, creating a physical stand-in, or using purely digital emulation. Duplicates or substitutes are becoming a more common

strategy at Cooper Hewitt where many of the contemporary objects we display are commercially available and can be acquired in duplicate without great expense. Of course, this is not a circumstance shared by many art museums. Does presenting a duplicate object that can be touched by visitors in lieu of the one behind glass constitute conserving the original? Operating system emulators are available for some historic software applications, but to create them from scratch is an enormous undertaking. Displaying an emulator on a separate digital screen alongside the object divorces the interface from its hardware, but arguably permits a clearer reading of what is original and what is emulated for didactic purposes. Where do these strategies of surrogates or duplicates fit into the taxonomies of conservation discussed above?

Consumer electronics in museums straddle a line by being both unique and relatively rare (each single example in the collection is a unique object) but also deriving their importance from their mass production and ubiquity at a certain point in the past. As Cooper Hewitt continues to collect contemporary consumer electronics, we are faced with new challenges with regard to the interactivity and increasingly digital-hybrid nature of these objects. Clearly, the museum's interpretive and preservation strategies are mutually dependent, each significantly impacting how the collection is understood.

## Case Study: Planetary iOS app

The first iOS application collected by the Smithsonian, Planetary by Bloom Studios, visualizes songs and artists in the user's iTunes library as stars and planets in space. The app was displayed on two first-generation iPads running iOS 5. In 2012, there were already known bugs and the creators ceased updating the app before it was acquired. Apps are particularly difficult to collect and preserve because they are highly dependent on hardware and software (i.e., each build is designed for certain platforms), which are each updated on short time scales.[30] As Sebastian Chan (then director of the Digital and Emerging Media at Cooper Hewitt) phrased it: "Like all software, Planetary has been skirting obsolescence almost from the moment it was released. Software and hardware are

---

30 App maintenance is a much more costly endeavor than was understood at the time of acquisition. For the perspective at the time of acquisition, see Sebastian Chan and Aaron Cope, "Planetary: Collecting and Preserving Code as a Living Object," Cooper Hewitt Labs (August 26, 2013), www.cooperhewitt.org/2013/08/26/planetary-collecting-and-preserving-code-as-a-living-object/. A more thorough analysis of the work and its current conservation status is related in a recent internal report by consultants Small Data Industries. *"Planetary" Digital Collections Materials Preservation Report,* Internal Report (September 8, 2018).

ſ

separate but inescapable companions that exact a sometimes profound and warping, and sometimes destructive, influence on one another."[31] In order to preserve an app, the internal workings (its architecture) must be clearly understood so that as changes to the software and hardware occur, the app can be modified to continue working. For this reason, the source code for the app was collected as part of the acquisition, and it was published online on Github, a platform that hosts repositories that track development changes and errors, and allows users to submit newer "branched" versions of software code. Some changes to the source code to retain functionality could be considered trivial and others more critical to the essence of the work, and this distinction needs to be carefully considered.

In order to upgrade the Planetary iOS app to a functional version for display on contemporary iPads we would require a specialized developer to investigate and make a new version of the original code. Appealingly, these changes are registered as "versions" or iterations, and the "original" is unaffected—it lives on as an archive in perpetuity (in this case, both online and printed out in OCR readable text in our storage). The biggest conceptual shift needed for collecting apps is that it is wiser (and much less costly) to make smaller stepwise transitions rather than try to migrate from iOS 5 to iOS 12 in one step. Unlike most conservation interventions, which happen intermittently, these apps might require instead a "gardening" approach of scheduled maintenance. One problem presented by the idea of treating a historical object like a living being is that a multitude of tiny changes, each acceptable on their own, could threaten the identity of the work over time.[32]

Perhaps anticipating these issues, Chan and Cope suggested that Planetary was not bound by its platform:

> Bloom's choice to develop Planetary for Apple's iOS operating system and the iPad (but not the iPhone) helps us to understand the technological landscape in which Planetary was conceived although it is important to realize that Planetary is not, first, an iPad application. Instead, we believe that Planetary is foremost an interaction design that found its "then-best manifestation" in the iPad. What might that choice look like today?[33]

While this is an attractive way of avoiding the conceptual problems app migration poses, we are now looking back with a few years' greater

---

31   Chan and Cope, "Planetary," 2013.

32   This example calls to mind the philosophical conundrum of The Ship of Theseus. It has inspired many conservators since conservation by its nature needs to find a compromise between old and new, original and restoration.

33   Chan and Cope, "Planetary."

distance. In a world of streaming music and therefore an entirely different sense of what a collection of music could be, it seems even more imperative to preserve the fully contained iTunes interaction as Planetary was originally designed, rather than to conceive of it as a platformless visualization. A particular challenge for collecting the contemporary is that given our native digital fluency today and the quick pace of technological change, it is hard to predict what the most significant or vulnerable features will be (i.e., those most deserving a conservator's attention), or how sensitive future viewers will be to changes we may make in the name of preservation.

## Conclusion: How Is Conservation Adapting to The Challenges of The Future?

As demonstrated above, the language of conservation is influenced by the many disciplines that feed into it. In the examples from the Cooper Hewitt collection, the particular challenges of a laptop and an app show that conservators today need to develop fluency in many different languages. In each case the investigation required combining historical evidence with curatorial input, as well as locating and working with outside experts. Electricians, software engineers, 3D printers, and master craftsmen are all part of our extended network. In this way, twenty-first century conservation is a natural outgrowth of the same work conservators have been engaging in for decades. Conservation remains about material stability and risk management, but it has become more collaborative. Our galleries are increasingly filled with touchable samples and as our collections and exhibitions become more process-oriented we will continue to face these challenges of balancing functional, material, and conceptual values in conserving collections objects.

The strategies for facing these new challenges are to work with outside experts as needed, as brokers or translators, and to increase our base of knowledge in these areas. Conservators are already talented at reverse-engineering and learning about new technologies. Our most common shared characteristic is a restless curiosity that is never satiated. However, conservation norms for modern and contemporary design are not yet fixed and must evolve with our cultural expectations as these objects become historic. Conservators need greater acknowledgment of the critical role preservation plays in interpretation and vice versa.

The complexity of contemporary art and design has affected our view of historic works in unexpected ways; we can now use a broader vocabulary to describe the intentions and the effects of conservation interventions. The introduction of terms to reconcile approaches to conserving non-material aspects of works with the traditions of conservation has allowed greater engagement on the part of conservators to understand how our work negotiates meanings between artists' and designers' intentions, material evidence, museum contexts, and public perceptions.

Postscript: As this article was being submitted for publication, the museum received an email out of the blue that a programmer had "remastered" the Planetary app and re-released it on the Apple app store. The degree to which this pro-bono intervention might constitute conservation via migration, emulation, or reinterpretation has yet to be assessed, but it attests to the possibilities of opening up museum collections to external users; they may eventually become our collaborators.

# Part III.

# Virtuality

# 9: Music and the Limits of Collectibility

*Rolf J. Goebel*

## 1

COLLECTING IS A CULTURAL PRACTICE characterized by an uncanny dialectic of violence and preservation. It willfully tears helpless objects out of their original and presumably "natural" context in order to integrate them into the new framework of the collection, whose selection criteria, values, and goals reflect the individual collector's subjectivity or the policies of cultural-political institutions like museums and archives. In many ways, collecting is the desperate attempt to reign in the dispersion, fragmentariness, and enigmatic aura of artifacts that seem to have an elusive life of their own. In his "Passagen-Werk" (Arcades Project, 1927–40), Walter Benjamin sketched a general theory of collecting that points to the illusory nature of this practice. In fragment H 4 a, 1, he juxtaposes the archetype of the modern collector with the Baroque allegorist. These supplementary types are defined by differences while also sharing some of each other's attributes. The "most deeply hidden motive" of the collector, Benjamin suggests, is his "struggle against dispersion." Collecting is motivated by the futile attempt to impose an order and a systematic meaning over the widely scattered objects of the collector's fascination; this order, however, is something the allegorist's passionate gaze of reflective contemplation, willfully dislodging things from their original contexts, has long abandoned. But, as Benjamin stresses, "in every collector hides an allegorist, and in every allegorist a collector." What the collector shares with the allegorist is the acknowledgment that a collection can never be complete. His discovery of "just a single piece missing" reveals that the collection "remains a patchwork," resembling the ruinous landscape of dispersed fragments pondered by the melancholic allegorist. Conversely, the allegorist, intent on deciphering objects as "keywords in a secret dictionary," shares with the collector the intimation that he "can never have enough of things": harboring, in other words, an unfulfillable desire for ideal completion, order, and shared significances.[1]

---

1 Walter Benjamin, *The Arcades Project*, trans. Howard Eiland and Kevin McLaughlin (Cambridge, MA: Belknap Press of Harvard University Press, 1999), 211.

This dialectic of assemblage and dispersal applies equally to the gathering of pictorial objects (pictures, sculptures, coins, stamps, etc.) and textual documents (books, autographs, newspaper articles, and so on). But does it also apply to sonic phenomena, especially to music? Can music be collected, and if so, in what form and in what ways? What are the implications with regard to aesthetic value, social function, and media-technological reproduction when music is considered in terms of collectibility? At a time when museum studies and theories of collecting tend to focus primarily on the tangibility and visible presence of spatial objects, the attempt to listen to music in this context may appear strange and wayward. But if we do listen in this way, we begin to understand why music has indeed been considered by musicologists, philosophers, and media theorists as a potential object of collecting, but only in order to raise more questions and doubts than to give definitive answers concerning the controversial and contradictory notion of musical collectibility itself.

Of course, since the Gutenberg galaxy of print media, the collecting of music as physical objects has been facilitated by written scores, which can be archived in libraries and museums and, in the area of classical music, exert considerable authority over performance practices, especially in the shape of critical *Urtext* editions that are crucial for historically informed interpretations. But if we define the musical work as a complex, historically unfolding, and often discontinuous process involving the original act of composing, various live or studio performances, and diverse listening experiences, then not only the written score but also music's reproducibility are important facets of collecting musical artifacts. In the age of digital reproducibility, whether in the area of classical music or popular genres, the instantaneous availability of music files on our laptops, smartphones, and iPods drastically redefines the human subject's capabilities of collecting music, in a way destabilizing the written score's representational authority. Nowadays, we can easily download a seemingly endless amount of sonic data, whose tracks we may delete or keep or shuffle according to our habitual tastes, impromptu listening desires, and market-directed consumer preferences. Our mobile computers serve as the virtual libraries and imaginary museums of the postmodern age.

Whereas architectural museums are public institutions supported by the professional expertise of curators responsible for preserving the canon of traditional art or for promoting the avant-garde, the digital music collection is highly personal, random, and destabilized, seeking to match the arbitrary repeatability of technologically reproduced sound data with the inherent temporality of music as a performative art.[2] As the virtual

---

2    See also Don Ihde, *Listening and Voice: Phenomenologies of Sound*, 2nd ed. (Albany: State University of New York Press, 2007), for an extensive

museums of infinite and unpredictable explorations, platforms like YouTube create the illusion of extending the private music file collection of the personal computer into the seemingly infinite universe of musical diversity, where users, guided by ingenious algorithms tracking previous listening choices to make ever-changing recommendations, can always discover new songs they did not even know existed. All this would be unthinkable without the invention of MP3 technology. Borrowing terminology from Martin Heidegger's philosophy of the "thing," Jonathan Sterne has analyzed this format, typical of today's mobile listening devices, as something ready-to-hand in matching innovative technologies of sound storage, portability, and wide circulation with new user practices affording greater possibilities of pleasure.[3] Sterne also stresses that despite the micro-materialization effected by MP3 technology, users still treat music recorded in this format as "things" that can be possessed as part of a collection.[4]

Before the invention of this kind of subject-centered electronic mobility, users had to purchase tangible objects of sound storage—the vinyl record, the magnetic tape cassette, the compact disc. Until listeners were able to order these online, they had to go to an actual music store where they were able to select what they wanted from well-appointed shelves and catalogs. Thus, despite the fact that it is ontologically a temporal art, the consumption and collectibility of music through media of technological reproduction was originally connected to the listening subject's prior conquest of urban space—the walk or car ride from one's home or office to the seller's premises. Moreover, the satisfaction of the traditional collector's musical desires was to some extent pre-programmed by the limited stock in the music shop or the current availability of specific items through specific mail-order sites. These restrictions corresponded roughly to the architectural limitations of the collector's home or office, whose shelves could never accommodate all the vinyl records, cassettes, and compact disks that the owner may have wished to display. Still, gramophones, record players, tape recorders, and CD players were able to facilitate the assembly of collectible music, whereas earlier, there were only live concert and opera performances, which had to be retained, more or less vividly and authentically, in the individual listening subject's memory. These events could thus be recollected but not collected, because, with the exception of player pianos, barrel organs, and other mechanical

---

phenomenological analysis of the temporality of sound and the auditory experience in relation to spatiality, visual perception, and verbal language.

3    Jonathan Sterne, *MP3: The Meaning of a* Format (Durham: Duke University Press, 2012), 221.

4    Sterne, *MP3*, 214.

devices, the temporality of live music could not yet be converted into the spatially defined objects of technological reproducibility.

Thus the possibility of collecting music unfolds through the tension between the temporality, even evanescence, of music as a performative art on the one hand, and, on the other, the fixation of its sonic data through devices of mechanical or electronic reproduction. As Sterne remarks, despite being in many ways an object that retains "many of the trappings of the commodity form," music "also exceeds any definition of a thing as it always has—it contains irreducible dimensions of social practice," not least because of its widespread accessibility: "If copyright law has served to create an economy of artificial scarcity for recorded music, file-sharing has announced an age of musical abundance."[5] But even the very difference between the collectible storage of acoustic data and the temporality of the listening experience is marked by instability and uncertainty, because listening is a historically fluctuating practice changing with the development of new technologies. Don Ihde has suggested that "just as the live performance of chamber or concert music is the medium, the historical and actual context in which the classical form of music developed, so the transistor and the amplifier are the context of the harder forms of youth culture's music" in the popular arena.[6] And as Sterne explains, citing Keir Keightley, with the popularization of the LP format after the Second World War, the audiophonic hi-fi boom came to be associated with a masculine, sophisticated, and elitist connoisseurship contrasted with the presumably feminine mass taste for television. Whereas hi-fi promised "opportunities for immersion and transcendence through contemplative listening," the digital age brought about the integration of audiovisual technology centered on the television set, leading to new consumer practices for whom "portability, modularity, malleability, access" replaced the (post-Romantic) ideal of solitary contemplation, even though the nostalgic resurgence of vinyl record collections and the LP record player seem to counteract this trend.[7]

Since listening habits, then, are intrinsically connected to changes in sonic technologies and cultural circumstances, I propose that the current possibilities of digital music collections can best be understood in the context of historical discourses on musical musealization and memory production as they emerged before the invention of electronic devices. I will therefore trace the tradition of collecting music back to what is perhaps the single most decisive turning point in the history of Western art music, the time around 1800, when the Romantic metaphysics of music promoted the ideal of the self-contained musical work to be collected

---

5    Sterne, *MP3*, 224.
6    Ihde, , *Listening and Voice: Phenomenologies of Sound*, 230.
7    Sterne, *MP3*, 238–39.

in imaginary museums. I will then connect this moment to Theodor W. Adorno's reflections on the phonographic record as a collectible item. Finally, I will relate these positions to Pierre Schaeffer's theory of the sonorous object as the imaginary storage of sound snippets detached from their visually ascertainable source, and to Michel Chion's analysis of the temporality of sonic events. I look back in time, because it seems to me that it is nearly impossible to grasp the implications of collecting music in the age of digital technologies and big data without at least a fragmentary understanding of its pre-electronic history.

# 2

As Lydia Goehr has argued in her controversial study *The Imaginary Museum of Musical Works*,[8] a new concept emerged around 1800 that spoke "of the arts as separated completely from the world of the ordinary, mundane, and everyday."[9] This "separability principle," as Goehr terms it, led to the development, especially promoted by German Romanticism, of the metaphysical ideal of musical autonomy, which raised serious questions concerning music's collectibility. As Goehr explains, around 1800, the separability principle was employed "to consider how and where works of fine art should be presented and exhibited" as aesthetically privileged objects in public museums, art galleries, and concert halls.[10] Stripping art objects of their local contexts and historical origins, museum collectors reframed art as purely aesthetic objects for public contemplation. Thus by "estranging the work of art from its original external function," curators projected the idealistic notion "that its artness would now be found within itself" only.[11] According to Goehr, the musealization of the plastic and pictorial arts as autonomous objects created a particular legitimacy problem for music. Seeing itself as equally autonomous in comparison to other art forms, "music came to replicate some of the characteristics of the plastic arts of painting and sculpture."[12] Music had to identify a way

---

8    Lydia Goehr, *The Imaginary Museum of Musical Works: An Essay in the Philosophy of Music*, rev. ed. (Oxford: Oxford University Press, 2007). Goehr's controversial study has provoked a long critical debate as to her central idea that the concept of the self-contained musical work emerged around 1800. In his nuanced survey of this debate, Gavin Staingo proposes that "the full development of the work–concept does not only allow for the *identification* of its origins in times prior to 1800; in a sense, the development of the work–concept actually *creates* its origins." See his "The Musical Work Reconsidered, In Hindsight," in *Current Musicology* 97 (Spring 2014): 81–112, here 104.

9    Goehr, *The Imaginary Museum*, 157.

10   Goehr, *The Imaginary Museum*, 173.

11   Goehr, *The Imaginary Museum*, 173.

12   Goehr, *The Imaginary Museum*,. 173.

of commodifying itself as a kind of object that could become part of a collection analogous to the art objects exhibited in the museum. "Neither transitory performances nor incomplete scores would serve this purpose," Goehr continues, and therefore, the notion of the musical work was invented as an autonomous creation, partitioned off from other works, each revealing the Infinite and the Beautiful in its self-contained form.[13]

But, as Goehr stresses, this legitimation of the music work as a collectible object proved to be challenging on practical (and ontological) grounds: "Since music was a temporal and performance art, its works could not be preserved in physical form or placed in a museum like other works of fine art."[14] Therefore, music, as a cultural institution, sought to reconcile its inherently temporal and intangible form with listeners' desire to replicate the conditions of public exhibition of plastic arts. Music "had to replicate the conditions of the plastic arts and, at the same time, render them appropriate to its temporal and ephemeral character."[15] Musical culture accomplished this task by creating its own form of display, a metaphorical or "imaginary museum of musical works" analogous to the architectural and experiential physicality of pictorial art museums.[16] The imaginary nature of this type of collectorship corresponded to the auratic vocabulary employed by musicians advocating the foundations of actual museums for the performance of musical works. As Goehr explains, in 1835 Franz Liszt proposed that every five years the best compositions "be ceremonially performed every day for a whole month in the Louvre"; as early as 1802, J. S. Bach's biographer Johann Nicolaus Forkel thought that the public performance of the Baroque master's compositions would "raise a worthy monument to German art," and in 1809, Carl Maria von Weber saw possibilities for a recently founded museum in Stuttgart to offer professional and amateur artists a forum for cultivating their "artistic taste."[17]

# 3

Eventually, however, this early nineteenth-century mode of preserving music in the collective imagination of composers, performative practices, concert halls, and educated audiences changed sharply with the invention of mechanical reproduction technologies. Looking back to the outdated gramophone record, Theodor W. Adorno reconsidered this medium in its cultural function as a collectible object. Terming it, in 1934, "an

---

13  Goehr, *The Imaginary Museum*, 174.
14  Goehr, *The Imaginary Museum*, 174.
15  Goehr, *The Imaginary Museum*, 174.
16  Goehr, *The Imaginary Museum*, 174.
17  Goehr, *The Imaginary Museum*, 205.

artistic product of decline," Adorno sees the record as the "first means of musical presentation that can be possessed as a thing," much like photographs. Indeed, the nineteenth century introduced collectible "phonograph record albums alongside photographic and postage-stamp albums," intended to preserve "in the smallest space" human recollections that would otherwise disappear.[18] Retrospectively, the invention of the gramophone record turns the "evanescence and recollection" associated with the nostalgically outdated barrel organ, which Adorno rediscovers as a precursor to modern sound reproduction, into a "tangible and manifest" object.[19]

For Adorno, then, the most incisive change effected by phonography is the removal of music from the realms of live production and artistic activity into the petrifying domain of technological collectibility. But despite this objectification, music, as Adorno speculates, also possesses a kind of redemptive temporality. For through its material traces in the grooves of the record needle, music approaches "its true character as writing," that is, as a language of authenticity and truth, because the record, by directly preserving the traces of specific sounds in the physicality of the grooves, relinquishes the arbitrary and hence presumably less truthful relation of verbal signifier and signified.[20] Thus, it seems to me, Adorno seeks to discover the positive side of the potentially alienated status of mechanically recorded music. While in the era of mechanical reproducibility live music becomes subject to objectification, because it can be gathered like photographs, postage stamps, and other things, it is the same media technology that also engages profoundly in the temporality of human history, linking the fateful dispersal of arbitrary tongues after the fall of the Tower of Babel with the utopian ideal of a universal language of truth. Thus Adorno invests the vinyl record with a metaphysical significance that goes beyond the storage medium's mere materiality as a collectible and commodified object.[21]

Goehr's reconstruction of the historical emergence of the musical work under the auspices of the idealist notion of musical autonomy shares, I think, some important and suggestive insights with Adorno's metaphysical implications of mechanical sound reproduction as a nonverbal medium of universal truth. Both writers identify a cultural desire to submit music to specific parameters—Goehr's public institution of the classical museum

---

18  Theodor W. Adorno, "The Form of the Phonograph Record," in *Essays on Music*, ed. with an introduction by Richard Leppert, trans. Susan H. Gillespie et al. (Berkeley: University of California Press, 2002), 277–82, here 278–79.

19  Adorno, "Phonograph Record," 279.

20  Adorno, "Phonograph Record, 280.

21  See also the wide-ranging discussion of Adorno's views on phonography by Thomas Y. Levin, "For the record: Adorno on Music in the Age of Its Technological Reproducibility," in *October* 55 (Winter, 1990): 23–47, esp. 31–42.

on the one hand, Adorno's private collections of phonographic records on the other—that promote the spatial objectification of musical temporality. But this desire, as Goehr's term of the imaginary museum suggests, is exactly this—it is imaginary in the sense that it cannot ever achieve a state of physical permanence, gathering together music as a collection of items that sooner or later must reveal itself as an elusive fantasy. In this sense, music is especially phantasmagoric, because its subjective experience always exceeds and escapes the materiality of its media-technological reproducibility. While phonographic records, magnetic tapes, or compact discs can be collected in our library and MP3 files can be stored on our computers or smartphones, music as a temporally unfolding performance and listening experience cannot; its intangible evanescence lends music a sensuous and spiritual excess, a hermeneutic surplus that can never be arrested by even the most advanced media technologies.[22]

# 4

The desire to capture this fleeting incommensurability of musical experience motivates the theory of Pierre Schaeffer, the pioneer of musique concrète, an avant-garde style assembling music from pre-recorded snippets of a wide variety of sounds. Starting from the premise that radio, recording devices, and electro-acoustic transformers are able to separate sound from its putative, visually ascertainable sources, Schaeffer defines these acousmatic sonorities as self-referential, autonomous objects that, especially when listened to repeatedly through media of phonographic reproduction, enhance the subject's perceptive sensibilities and insights. As Schaeffer explains, somewhat echoing the imaginary status of the musical work of Classicist and Romanticist aesthetics, this sonorous object is not identical with the magnetic tape (his reference technology at the time); the storage device only contains the magnetic traces of the sonorous object, not the object itself: "The object is not an object *except* to our listening, it is relative to it. We can act on the tape physically, cutting it, modifying its replay speed. Only the act of listening by

---

22 See also Ihde's analysis of the "auditory imagination" in relation to visual perception and inner speech (Ihde, *Listening and Voice: Phenomenologies of Sound*, 131–36 and 203–15). This excess is akin to the material traces of what Jacques Lacan has called the Real—the elusive subversion of the Symbolic and the Imaginary that, according to Friedrich A. Kittler, "has the status of phonography." See his *Gramophone Film Typewriter*, trans. Geoffrey Winthrop-Young and Michael Wutz (Stanford, CA: Stanford University Press, 1999), 15–16. See also Rolf J. Goebel, "The Musical Ineffable Revisited: Hermeneutics, Psychoanalysis, and Media-Technological Reproducibility," *Journal of Musicology* 38, no. 4 (2021): 419–435.

a listener . . . can provide us with an account of the perceptible result of these manipulations. Coming from a world in which we are able to intervene, the sonorous object is *nonetheless contained entirely in our perceptive consciousness.*"[23] Thus, despite its media-technological reproducibility, the sonorous object is essentially a matter of the listening subject's imagination, possessing an ontological status of irreducible fragility, fleetingness, and intangibility, which subverts any desire to fixate on it as a collectible object.

Seeking to differentiate sound from visual objects, Michel Chion's critique of Schaeffer argues that "sound objects remain . . . more difficult to observe than visible objects because they are incorporeal and inscribed within a given length of time."[24] Therefore, he believes that it is not "possible to describe sound in the form of a voluminous object captured in a system of three-dimensional coordinates."[25] As "a vital process, an active energy," sound "makes its initial appearance in our culture as an object of language, as a shattered object, indeed as an impossible object, hard to reify."[26] For sound, there is no equivalent of the cinematic shot in the sense of a "cohesive unit" that would allow the listener to "zoom in" on a specific sound while "others resonate simultaneously with a similar force."[27] Moreover, Chion continues, it seems difficult even for the most attentive listener "*to take up a disinterested attitude when faced with sounds*" because the "purest of sonic delights," for instance for the opera enthusiast, can at any moment surprisingly "tip over to torture" when the bel canto singer makes a mistake or when the recording technologies falter: "jammed cassette decks, damaged portable devices, worn-out speakers, excessive loudness, the startling squeal of audio feedback."[28] Consequently, Chion distinguishes the irreducibly temporal but often overwhelming intrusiveness of sonic events from the spatiality of visual objects and their contemplation from a distance. Especially in the age of electronic technologies and virtual reality scenarios that explore new territories of the interface between the human subject and media technologies, as Frances Dyson argues, "digital audio implicitly defines sound in terms of a 'thing,'" but "that 'thing' is no longer an object (of the concrete kind) but a stream of information constituted by zeros and ones that are

---

23 Pierre Schaeffer, "Acousmatics," in *Audio Culture: Readings in Modern Music*, rev. ed., ed. Christoph Cox and Daniel Warner (New York: Bloomsbury, 2017), 95–101, here 99 (emphasis in the original).

24 Michel Chion, *Sound: An Acoulogical Treatise*, trans. and ed. James A. Steintrager (Durham: Duke University Press, 2016), 173.

25 Chion, *Sound*, 184.

26 Chion, *Sound*, 187 and 194.

27 Chion, *Sound*, 200.

28 Chion, *Sound*, 201 (emphasis in the original).

approximations of discrete samples of audio waves."[29] Moreover, whether in traditional situations of live performances or in digitally mediated formats, it seems to me that sound exerts its most powerful effects not on the listening subject's consciousness but on its unconscious desires, fantasies, dreams, and repressions. Elusive, confusing, and enigmatic, these psychological experiences may never reach the level of reflective awareness—the only level of the self where sound may be controlled, analyzed, and collected.

## Conclusion

To offer a tentative conclusion: Being a cultural institution of the public sphere defined by the tensions between its aesthetic properties, performance practices, and technological mediation, music is deeply divided and contradictory to itself. As suggested by Goehr's historical survey of the ideal of an imaginary museum of musical works, by Adorno's metaphysical speculations on the vinyl record and its redemptive promises of being a universal language, and by Schaeffer's relocation of the sonic object from its material facticity to the interiority of human imagination, the discourse about music is haunted by the desire to turn it into a thing to be collected and preserved while at the same time having to admit that this longing must necessarily remain unsatisfied. Certainly, music (and other sounds) can be collected in the material forms of musical scores, analytical commentaries, and poetic representations. In the age of technological reproducibility, the acoustic data of music themselves can be collectibles, as they can be stored in the visual grooves of vinyl records, as magnetic traces on tapes, or, in the digital files of CDs and MP3 files on computers. In this way, technological media turn the aesthetic value of music into a material commodity for the modern culture industry's mass consumer market where easy accessibility is essential.

But it is exactly this objectifying tendency of the collection that inevitably points to what it can never assemble or master: the immediacy and spontaneity of the musical experience, which, through the sheer power of the subjective imagination, transforms the raw data of the fixating collection into the composition's elusive meanings, collective values, and cultural contexts. The musical experience defies collectibility because in its totality of compositional intentions, performance practices, and audience responses, it is ontologically different from physical objects.[30] Unfolding

---

29  Frances Dyson, *Sounding New Media: Immersion and Embodiment in the Arts and Culture* (Berkeley: University of California Press, 2009), 137–38.

30  See also Sterne, who distinguishes between those who argue that music can produce artifacts in the shape of recordings but cannot "be objectified as a thing, except as a kind of reduction," and those who "refer to music as a thing"

unpredictably in time rather than being located as a visible object in space, the musical experience possesses an elusiveness that subverts the objectifying hegemony governing any museum exhibition or private collection. These institutions must privilege the spatiality and tangibility of sculptures, pictures, or books to legitimate themselves in the eyes of the public seeking the immediate satisfaction of its desires of visual consumption, but they can never manage to store, display, and arrest the evanescence of music as a performative art.[31]

This elusiveness of the musical experience, then, points to the ontological groundlessness of collecting—not just of music but of any art form or medium. In his essay "Ich packe meine Bibliothek aus" (Unpacking My Library), Walter Benjamin characterized the book collector's passion as one that "borders on the chaos of memories." For Benjamin, a collection of books is little more than an illusory order of collectibles whose "accustomed confusion"—the ultimately arbitrary assemblage of disparate volumes—reflects "the chance, the fate" of the collector's own historical past.[32] Benjamin alludes to "people whom the loss of their books has turned into invalids" and to "those who in order to acquire books become criminals"; the obsessive passions of such collectors reveal that

---

by virtue of its technological form, its commodity status, or essence independent of its performance. Sterne himself defines music "as a bundle of affordances, thus borrowing some of the process language and some of the thing language" (Sterne, *MP3*, 189).

31 Arguing in the context of the posthuman redefinition of the interface of the human subject and media technologies, Kramer notes five "casualties" that the posthuman paradigm has affected in the area of traditional listening: music as a "quasi-thing"; the notion of the musical work as an "integrated totality"; music as an address to the embodied listener from a contemplative distance; the ideal notion of the musical work as an enigma requiring performative and explanatory interpretation; and music "as something to be listened to in an activity of nothing but listening"; Lawrence Kramer, "Classical Music for the Posthuman Condition," in *The Oxford Handbook of New Audiovisual Aesthetics*, ed. John Richardson, Claudia Gorbman, and Carol Vernallis (Oxford: Oxford University Press, 2013), 39–52, here 45. In this context, the live performance of classical music, he continues, "might . . . be restored as the medium of the exceptional event, a museum of vanishing acts." Listened to anew outside of the repeatability of recording technologies, music attains a fresh sense of "singularity" because "the live concert may restore this music to perceptual integrity and sensory vividness" even while being inevitably affected by the ubiquity of digital media culture (Kramer, "Classical Music for the Posthuman Condition," 50).

32 Walter Benjamin, "Unpacking My Library: A Talk about Collecting," in *Selected Writings*, vol. 2, ed. Michael W. Jennings, Howard Eiland, and Gary Smith, trans. Rodney Livingstone et al. (Cambridge, MA: Belknap Press of Harvard University Press, 1999), 486–93, here 486.

any order, no matter how consistent or durable it seems to be, is really "nothing more than a hovering above the abyss."[33]

The sometimes self-destructive irrationality of Benjamin's book collectors, then, lends their practice a value that is illusory and abysmally uncertain, but for these very reasons all the more imaginative, existentially enriching, and aesthetically meaningful. The groundlessness of Benjamin's passion of collecting old books—whether canonical masterpieces or the writer's beloved, half-forgotten children's books—is analogous to the paradox facing Goehr's late eighteenth-century musicologist trying to forge the elusive temporality of the musical work into quasi-museal canonicity. In either case, the order imposed upon the collected items—the individual physicality of the rare book editions favored by Benjamin or the autonomy of the musical work idealized by the Romantic metaphysics of art—is as imaginative as it is imaginary, since neither the dispersal of visual or tangible objects in cultural space nor the evanescence of musical works and their aesthetic experience in history can ever be completely stabilized by any conceptual order, hermeneutic discourse, or media of technological reproduction. Benjamin talks of the "most profound enchantment" that the collector senses when locking the prized objects "within a magic circle in which they are frozen" when the "final thrill" of acquisition passes over them under the gaze of the collector pondering the "magic encyclopedia" of the collectible's history.[34] Similarly, the musical experience, thoroughly embedded in social situations and yet irreducibly personal and subjective, discovers in the very midst of sonic evanescence an auratic realm of aesthetic beauty, moral values, and spiritual redemption that the Romantic Idealists—unjustly assigned to the dustbins of metaphysical speculation by the materialist ideology of media analysis—discovered to be the hidden essence of music. Thus the imaginary museums of musical productivity always tend to deconstruct their own modes of preservation, thereby liberating the musical experience from the acoustic material and technological mediation that it nonetheless relies on for its ever-imperfect self-preservation.

---

33 Benjamin, "Unpacking My Library," 487. As Muensterberger proposes from a psychoanalytic perspective, collecting can amount to an obsessive longing that uses a fetishistic object to compensate for a deeply felt loss, anxiety, uncertainty, or trauma, expressing a fantastical mix of desire and recurrence that can never be satisfied; Werner Muensterberger, *Collecting: An Unruly Passion. Psychological Perspectives* (San Diego: Harcourt, Brace, 1994), 3–13.

34 Benjamin, "Unpacking My Library," 487.

# 10: Cat Art and Climate Change: Collecting in the Data Anthropocene

*Edward Dawson*

WHAT DOES IT MEAN to collect in the digital age? Abundance inheres in digital objects through the possibility of their limitless duplication, a fact which should represent a challenge for collection. In this essay I will consider an attempt to make digital objects collectible by artificially imbuing them with scarcity, and thus making them discrete. Manufacturing that "digital scarcity" will in turn depend on an enormous energy investment, on the mobilization of collections of natural resources for the production of data. This process serves as an example of what I term the Data Anthropocene, the condition in which humans have taken on geological agency, and in which our data appear as a primary locus of that agency. In this time, a different sort of collection, the gathering together of water and mineral deposits, powers both digital abundance and digital scarcity, and the question of the collection of digital objects recedes behind the question of the collection of natural resources. My essay thus moves from the question of collecting in the digital age to the question of digital collecting in the Anthropocene.

## Collecting Digital Cats

If our current moment is remembered at all, will it be remembered as the golden age of cat imagery? So great is the present glut of digital cats that "cat video" has become a byword for gratuitous digital imagery in general, and the mammal threatens to become little more than a corporeal extension of the meme. "The contemporary Internet was designed, in no small part, for the dissemination of cute pictures of cats," writes Ethan Zuckerman, without a hint of hyperbole.[1] The shift to "Web 2.0," in

---

1    Zuckerman's point is that websites like Facebook.com, geared towards what he calls "expressive" discourse (e.g., the dissemination of cat pictures) ultimately serve the ends of "influential" discourse (e.g., political protest) better than sites specifically intended for the latter purpose, as these latter sites can more easily be censored, and as political discourse on the "cute cat" pages is more quickly

which platforms like Facebook, YouTube, and Twitter depend on users' uploaded content in remaking the landscape of the Internet, relies on the proliferation of digital objects—whether cat video, 3D tour, album track, or discursive essay—that are understood as having little inherent value. These websites, as we are by now all too aware, sell not their content to users but their users to advertisers. The value resides not in the cat video, but in the cat video watcher. Cat pictures, like all digital objects, thrive under the sign of abundance, appearing as weightless and free.

It should come as a surprise, then, that on September 4, 2018, a user paid some $170,000 for a digital cat. How can this be? Under the conditions of digital feline abundance, why would anyone pay money for an image of a cat? Irrational as art markets may be; irrational as the ubiquity of digital cat imagery may be; irrational as the intersection of these two vectors of contemporary capitalist irrationality surely is, the sale of digital cat pictures for large sums of money—indeed, for any sum of money—appears so irrational as to make us aware of the limits of our thinking, rattling the bars of our epistemic prison. The sale of cat pictures raises questions about the conditions of possibility for knowledge construction today.[2]

To be sure, there are aspects of this specific transaction that help account for its staggering price, including the supposition that the purchase may have been a cover for some sort of illicit activity.[3] But this

---

picked up by the general public (Ethan Zuckerman, "Cute Cats to the Rescue? Participatory Media and Political Expression," in *From Voice to Influence: Understanding Citizenship in a Digital Age*, ed. Danielle S. Allen and Jennifer S. Light (Chicago: The University of Chicago Press, 2015), 131–54, here 135–36. Writing in 2013, Zuckerman is primarily interested in the potential of cute cats to promote democratic involvement, though his occasional skepticism at least begins to anticipate the kinds of anti-democratic and propagandistic ends towards which his "Cute Cat Theory" has been put, as became especially apparent in online political discourse in 2015 and 2016.

2    In his famous preface to *The Order of Things*, Foucault reacts to the bizarre classification system of Borges's fictional Chinese encyclopedia: "In the wonderment of this taxonomy, the thing we apprehend in one great leap, the thing that, by means of the fable, is demonstrated as the exotic charm of another system of thought, is the limitation of our own, the stark impossibility of thinking *that*," Michel Foucault, *The Order of Things: An Archaeology of the Human Sciences* (London: Routledge, 2006), xvi. The idea of paying money, a lot of money, for a digital cat picture is similar, as we recognize that this transaction has occurred within a system as exotic to us as Borges's encyclopedia.

3    For an account of the $170,000 sale, see Mark Serrels, "Someone Just Bought a Cryptocurrency Cat for $172,000," *CNET* (September 4, 2018), www.cnet.com/news/cryptokitties-bought-a-digital-cat-for-172000/. For speculation about the potentially criminal motivation, see Neer Varschney, "Someone Paid $170,000 for the Most Expensive CryptoKitty Ever," *Hard Fork | The Next*

purchase was just one of some half-million digital cat transactions that have taken place since November 2017 on the digital cat marketplace known as "CryptoKitties," and while the sale of this particular cat may have involved untoward motivations, the median price of CryptoKitties is about $12.[4] The CryptoKitties market represents an especially odd corner of the cute-cat-picture digital world in which those cute cat pictures are exchanged for money. Even paying $12 for a digital cat seems unthinkably strange, because paying any money whatsoever for digital objects has proved a hard sell, even when those digital objects might appear to have intrinsic value.[5]

Such an exchange becomes thinkable because of blockchain technology. Best known for powering cryptocurrencies like Bitcoin, blockchains make it possible to precisely and uniquely link a digital object to an individual owner without reliance on traditional arbiters of property ownership like banks or governments. They do this through distributed ledgers of transactions, lists held in common by countless computers, which jointly account for the ownership of every single object and bit of currency in the network of that blockchain. When a new transaction is made, all the computers which hold the ledger recognize the transaction by adding a new block of code to the chain. Hence the name blockchain. The $170,000 cat, whose name is "Dragon," was actually bought for 600 Ether, the currency of a blockchain called "Ethereum," and the Ethereum ledger identifies the original owner. Everything about Dragon can be copied and reproduced, but the ledger cannot. What Dragon's owner purchased, then, is not so much an original digital object as the idea of that object's originality.

The makers of CryptoKitties refer to their creation as a game, though they are also quick to point out that the Zentrum für Kunst und Medien (ZKM) in Karlsruhe, Germany, put on a CryptoKitties exhibition, and that a CryptoKitty was displayed at the Schinkel Pavillon in Berlin. CryptoKitties, they insist, are "literal works of art." Above all, however, they seem to focus on the possibility of investment, pointing to the volume of transactions and total worth of CryptoKitties, and to the fact that, in addition to the half-billion sales over Ethereum, a CryptoKitty was sold

---

*Web* (September 5, 2018), https://thenextweb.com/hardfork/2018/09/05/most-expensive-cryptokitty/.

4    See Kitty Sales, https://kittysales.herokuapp.com/.

5    The rise of CryptoKitties coincides with the collapse of iTunes, the great exemplar of an attempt to carry on older forms of media collection in the digital age through the sale of discrete digital objects to be individually possessed, a model which ultimately could not survive in the age of shared digital collections (e.g., Spotify). The vinyl LPs stored in the attic morphed first into cassettes, then CDs, then files on hard drives, before vanishing altogether, the individual collection becoming subsumed into the collective collection.

for $140,000 at a public auction connected to Christie's.[6] Writing in *The New Yorker* in October 2018, Nick Paumgarten described CryptoKitties as "a virtual-pet-collection racket."[7] While it is certainly possible, perhaps likely, that some CryptoKitties exchanges involve people transferring money in the form of CryptoKitties sales to cover the actual sale of something else, Paumgarten's description misses the revolutionary fact that, as original digital objects that appeal to both an artistic sense and an investment potential, CryptoKitties have become digital collectibles.[8]

The idea of a digital collectible overturns a basic assumption of the Internet age: that digital objects can be infinitely and perfectly reproduced. In his classic study of digital materiality, Matthew Kirschenbaum draws on a model of the digital object put forth by the now retired director of the Electronic Records Program at the National Archives, Kenneth Thibodeau. This tripartite model understands a digital object on three levels, a physical, a logical, and a conceptual level, with only this last corresponding to what we typically perceive as "the object," that is, the image we see on screen of a digital photograph.[9] The other two levels refer to the object as addressed by software (logical) and as inscribed into a physical medium, which Kirschenbaum will later refer to as a digital object's "inscribed remainder."[10] Those digital objects for which the conceptual level, what we normally think of simply as *the object*, and the physical level, the "inscribed remainder," remain in 1:1 relation we might call "traditional" digital objects.

By virtue of their assumed perfect reproducibility, traditional digital objects can be amassed, but not collected. In the most obvious reading, digital technology brought the ideas of technical reproducibility outlined in Walter Benjamin's famous artwork essay to perfection. Any lingering objections to Benjamin's claim that "the technique of reproduction detaches the reproduced object from the domain of tradition" wither in the face of digital objects that can be copied without change a theoretically infinite number of times.[11] Digital technology obliterates

---

6    CryptoKitties, "Herding One Million Cats," *Medium* (September 19, 2018), https://medium.com/cryptokitties/herding-one-million-cats-7dbec6c77476/.

7    Nick Paumgarten, "The Stuff Dreams Are Made Of," *New Yorker* (October 2018): 62–75, here 74.

8    CryptoKitties, it should be noted, are more than just images of cats. The pictures are accompanied by short "biographies," and two CryptoKitties have the potential to "breed" additional CryptoKitties. This entails the obvious possibility of investment potential.

9    Matthew Kirschenbaum, *Mechanisms: New Media and the Forensic Imagination* (Cambridge, MA: MIT Press, 2008), 3.

10    Kirschenbaum, *Mechanisms*, 234.

11    Walter Benjamin, "The Work of Art in the Age of Mechanical Reproduction," in *Illuminations*, ed. Hannah Arendt (New York: Schocken Books, 1986), 217–52, here 221.

any remaining ideas of authenticity or originality, and whatever last ves-
tige of aura may have still hung about photographic negatives or film reels
has been lost forever.

Or so, prior to the blockchain, one might have thought. Now, the
domain of tradition returns as the ledger of transactions. A rather good
definition of this ledger might be a document that "determine[s] the
history to which it [the work of art] was subject throughout the time
of its existence."[12] This is of course Benjamin's formulation of what the
unique existence of the work of art was, its presence in time and space
which mechanical reproduction could not replicate but which technical
reproduction rendered meaningless. The blockchain appears to inject this
unique existence, this attachment to history, back into digital objects, and
thus to make them collectible.[13]

## From Cloud to Chain: Digital Abundance and Digital Scarcity

Making digital collectibles is not easy and depends on what blockchain
enthusiasts call "digital scarcity." Because of the nature of digital objects,
anyone should be able to make additional copycat CryptoKitties indistinguishable from the originals, and these CopyKitties would nullify the
value of CryptoKitties as collectibles. The concept of scarcity so fundamental to market capitalism should not exist for digital objects, which
are always characterized by abundance, or at least *potential* abundance.
Indeed, a central mechanism of profit-making with digital objects is
through realizing this potential abundance, by selling backup storage
media, either directly to consumers in the form of external hard drives,
or indirectly as so-called "cloud storage." Your precious digital objects
could be more abundant, more redundant, and therefore more secure, so

---

12   Benjamin, "Work of Art," 220.

13   Blockchain technology could in this sense be seen to invest digital objects
with a revenant form of aura, and it is not a coincidence that the language of
religion is deployed in explaining the blockchain. Paumgarten quotes the creator
of Ethereum, Vitalik Buterin, explaining how even in the institutionless world
of blockchains, authority returns in a different form: "There's definitely, in all
blockchains and cryptocurrencies, some notion of what I call the high priest"
(Paumgarten, "Stuff Dreams Are Made Of," 72). Paumgarten also quotes an
engineer at a blockchain startup describing the workings of the blockchain in dis-
tinctly mystical terms: "At a certain point, you break through it, you come to
understand it all, and then the door closes behind you, and then you just get it
but can't explain it" (Paumgarten, "Stuff Dreams Are Made Of," 73). Intriguing
as this connection may be, my argument does not rely on recourse to an idea of
auratic art, although revenant capitalistic forms will later appear in the guise of
resource extraction and the collection of natural resources.

goes this reasoning, apparently nullifying the possibility of uniqueness in the process.

Making digital objects collectible requires recasting as a bug what has generally been seen as a feature of digital objects: their abundance. Before considering how digital scarcity attempts to overcome digital abundance, that is, to "fix" the bug, I want to pause and consider how the digital abundance it seeks to undo is itself connected to scarce resources. Shane Brennan has described the way our "backup culture" imagines data as at risk while obscuring that data's material dimension and thus the environmental risks that it poses. When we follow the call to realize the potential abundance, and hence security, of our data, the resultant "digital 'sustainability' is achieved by multiplying the amount of data stored in energy-consuming server farms, leading to more carbon emissions and making the overall system less environmentally sustainable," the final irony being that environmental fears then raise demands for ever-greater protection of data.[14]

Brennan's is one of a number of recent studies that have uncovered a very different bug in digital abundance: its operation as a baffle to recognizing the materiality of digital objects.[15] The "light and airy image of the digital cloud," belies a substantial material weight.[16] In one of the most comprehensive considerations of this weight, Tung-Hui Hu's *A Prehistory of the Cloud* explores the materiality of the modern Internet from the cables and telecommunications infrastructure connecting computers to the storage bunkers in which the massive material substrate of our digital objects reside, finding that "the cloud is a resource-intensive,

---

14 Shane Brennan, "Making Data Sustainable: Backup Culture and Risk Perception," in *Sustainable Media: Critical Approaches to Media and Environment*, ed. Nicole Starosielski and Janet Walker (London, New: Routledge, 2016), 56–76, here 57.

15 These recent studies draw on a long history of considerations of digital materiality. As early as 2002, Matthew Kirschenbaum had coined the term "tactile fallacy" (elsewhere "haptic fallacy") for the widespread belief that "electronic objects are immaterial simply because we cannot touch them," going on to call for scholars to "begin cultivating a critical sensibility in which knowledge of material matters matters," Matthew Kirschenbaum, "Editing the Interface: Textual Studies and First Generation Electronic Objects," *Text* 14 (2002): 15–51, here 43. While a focus on "material matters" in media studies dates back at least to the seminal work of Friedrich Kittler, Kirschenbaum's call came at the beginning of what Nicole Starosielski and Janet Walker refer to when they write in 2015 that "environmental media studies has taken its own materialist turn," Nicole Starosielski and Janet Walker, "Introduction: Sustainable Media," in *Sustainable Media*, 1–19, here 12.

16 Allison Carruth, "The Digital Cloud and the Micropolitics of Energy," *Public Culture* 26, no. 2 (2014): 339–64, here 339, doi: 10.1215/08992363-2392093.

extractive technology that converts water and electricity into computational power, leaving a sizable amount of environmental damage that it then displaces from sight."[17]

Resource extraction has long been central to the production of value in capitalist economies, and it has always been the case that the resources extracted are measured not only in ounces or barrels, but also sweat, blood, and bodies. Digital objects depend on resource extraction most obviously in the form of metals and other materials that make up the physical storage systems and the electricity that powers them, although this is only the tip of the material and bodily iceberg.[18] The idea of digital abundance vastly increases the material accretions of our digital objects, turning the relationship of digital object to physical basis—that is, in Thibodeau's tripartite model, the relationship of conceptual to physical object—from 1:1 (your file to your hard drive) to 1:x, where x is always increasing, and in the case of the cloud, unknowable in size.[19]

---

17  Tung-Hui Hu, *A Prehistory of the Cloud* (Cambridge, MA: MIT Press, 2015), 146. A common denominator among many of these studies is the recognition that our understanding of digital objects as ethereal and ephemeral, as cloud-like, has obscured more than just physical infrastructure. Starosielski's *The Undersea Network*, a cultural and environmental history of the ocean-crossing cables that carry nearly all international Internet traffic, thus finds that not only the cables themselves are hidden, but also "labor, economics, culture, and politics," Nicole Starosielski, *The Undersea Network* (Durham, NC: Duke University Press, 2015), 2. Hu similarly finds that the Cloud "covers up the Third World workers who invisibly moderate . . . websites and forums" (Hu, *Prehistory*, xii).

18  For a fuller account of the various rare and toxic minerals involved, the hazards of mining them, and the impossibility of recycling them, as well as powering IT infrastructure, see Richard Maxwell and Toby Miller, *Greening the Media* (Oxford: Oxford University Press, 2012). In their rich "Anatomy of an AI system" Kate Crawford and Vladan Joler look specifically at the Amazon Echo device, mapping its manifold extraction of minerals, energy, and human labor: "As we see repeated throughout the system, contemporary forms of artificial intelligence are not so artificial after all. We can speak of the hard physical labor of mine workers, and the repetitive factory labor on the assembly line, of the cybernetic labor in distribution centers and the cognitive sweatshops full of outsourced programmers around the world, of the low paid crowdsourced labor of Mechanical Turk workers, or the unpaid immaterial work of users. At every level contemporary technology is deeply rooted in and running on the exploitation of human bodies," Kate Crawford and Vladan Joler, "Anatomy of an AI System: The Amazon Echo as an Anatomical Map of Human Labor, Data and Planetary Resources," *AI Now Institute and Share Lab* (September 7, 2018), https://anatomyof.ai.

19  Crawford and Joler note that Amazon AWS does not even disclose information about its environmental footprint, let alone the number of backup copies of a file. Brennan similarly finds the cloud storage platform Dropbox avoiding any specificity about the quantity of copies (Brennan, "Making Data Sustainable,"

However, despite the continuity in its dependence on paleotechnical resource extraction, the cloud has also challenged a number of older capitalist constructions of value—as the entrepreneurs like to say, it allows new business models to disrupt older ones, a process that largely consists of replacing products and services once sold for money with "free" digital versions. This, of course, is part of the Internet's outsize footprint, for it holds the resource extraction constant on the side of production of goods, while eliminating payment for those goods, making the environmental destruction once claimed necessary for some general prosperity the basis of prosperity for an increasingly small group. In this context, the rise of the blockchain, with its artificially constructed authenticity and its digital scarcity, could appear as a palliative, poised to return to an older, less unequal form of capitalism.

Such a view misses the fact that so-called digital scarcity does not overturn digital abundance, but rather depends upon it. In order to make digital objects unique and therefore collectible, blockchains ensure the historical memory of an object's originality through the ledger, and to guarantee the inviolability of that ledger without recourse to a traditional institution (such as a bank), the ledger is distributed to innumerable nodes on a large network, and can only be modified through shared action on the basis of rather complicated cryptographic analysis. In other words, to have only one possible owner of a digital object, the blockchain creates limitless copies of another digital object in the form of the ledger, which depends on the worldwide network of computers, that is, on cloud computing. Digital scarcity is unthinkable without digital abundance. The chain is unthinkable without the cloud.

## The Data Anthropocene

The collection of digital objects is tied to the same vast resource extraction on which the cloud depends. Collecting digital cats has an enormous carbon footprint, depends on unprecedented levels of resource extraction, and requires vast amounts of underpaid labor by some of the most marginalized people on the planet for all the same reasons that any of our interactions with digital cats do. These are base conditions of the contemporary Internet that apply to all of our engagements with digital objects. In addition to the ways in which our idle hours spent watching cat videos depend ultimately on the vast and hidden infrastructure of the cloud, however, collecting digital cats on the blockchain goes further, tying value *directly* to resource extraction.

---

68). We do not know, indeed, *cannot* know, the material shape of our digital objects.

In the process that Bitcoin calls *mining*, computing systems compete to complete the cryptographic analysis necessary to add blocks to the ledger, and the first system to do it is rewarded with a fraction of the value created. While this system has led some to suggest that Bitcoin (and blockchain technology more generally) has "created billions of dollars of value out of thin air," this value is in fact created by enormous amounts of digital work.[20] The competition for high end computational power necessary to do this work is so great that some estimates suggest Bitcoin demands approximately the same amount of annual electricity as the country of Ireland.[21] Cryptocurrency miners must build power-hungry, heat producing "rigs," and the rig that consumes the most electricity will mine the most digital currency. Miners build these rigs where either electricity is cheap to obtain (often because of hydropower) or where cooling is inexpensive. Paumgarten thus writes of "open-air warehouses in remote corners of sub-Arctic Canada, Russia, and China, with machines whirring away on the tundra, creating magic money, while the permafrost melts."[22] The addition of Bitcoin mining rigs, with their incredible energy demands for the manufacture of digital scarcity, to the already vast energy demands (and concomitant carbon footprints) of the data bunkers, server farms, and networks of cables that encircle the globe to connect all these components, raises the carbon footprint of our apparently ethereal data to the absurd. In what appears as a revenant form of the gold standard, the manufacture of digital scarcity ties value directly to resource depletion.

Riffing on Nadia Bozak's use of "resource image" to highlight the environmental entanglements of a single filmic image, Brennan uses the term "resource data file" to describe how our digital objects are accompanied by a range of environmental dependencies of which we are rarely aware.[23] While the resource data file addresses the material weight of individual digital objects, I am most interested in understanding the larger situation of which these objects are only instantiations. That the digital objects and data we think of as lightweight, ethereal records of our activity may leave more substantial material traces than our paper archives reminds us that the digital not only takes part in, but takes a leading role in, the inscription of the human into the geology of the planet.

This inscription of human into planet has been termed the "Anthropocene." Initially suggested as a new geological epoch by the

---

20  Brian Patrick Eha, *How Money Got Free: Bitcoin and the Fight for the Future of Finance* (London: Oneworld, 2017), 9.

21  Alex de Vries, "Bitcoin's Growing Energy Problem," *Joule* 2, no. 5 (May 2018): 801–05, doi: 10.1016/j.joule.2018.04.016.

22  Paumgarten, "Stuff Dreams Are Made Of," 66–67.

23  Brennan, "Making Data Sustainable," 58.

Nobel Prize–winning chemist Paul J. Crutzen, the Anthropocene describes a condition of human geological agency beginning in the eighteenth century, at the dawn of the industrial age.[24] Geological agency names a condition far grander than the biological agency humans have always had—the power to shape the living and non-living things around ourselves, to destroy forests, plant trees, eradicate species, bring new ones into existence, and so forth. The impact of our species on our world has now become so vast that we modify not only regional environments but the entire planet. The temperatures rise, and indeed, the very globe spins more slowly, as a result of human activity. The days grow hotter and longer, and the face of the earth has changed.

There is a certain self-aggrandizing gesture in calling this condition the Anthropocene. Naming a geological epoch after ourselves seems to manifest exactly the kind of hubris which, per the argument of the Anthropocene, got us into this mess in the first place. Moreover, talking about an "Anthropocene" appears to elide social disparities, making all of us *anthropoi* commonly culpable, and equally capable, when in fact climate change, as Rob Nixon has been especially forceful in pointing out, exacerbates the inequalities between human beings. In one of the most important articulations of the Anthropocene from a humanities perspective, Dipesh Chakrabarty recognizes this point as he argues that combating climate change will require not only critiques of capital but also an address of species history, because we have begun to

> destabilize conditions (such as the temperature zone in which the planet exists) that work like boundary parameters of human existence. These parameters are independent of capitalism or socialism. They have been stable for much longer than the histories of these institutions and have allowed human beings to become the

---

24 The idea that humanity has taken on such significance as a geological force as to end the epoch of the Holocene and launch an Anthropocene has not been universally accepted, and even where it has been accepted, the dating varies widely. I follow Chakrabarty (and also Crutzen's original suggestion) in placing the beginning of this epoch in the eighteenth century, at the dawn of the industrial revolution and the time when ice core samples first index human-caused increases in atmospheric carbon dioxide, Dipesh Chakrabarty, "The Climate of History: Four Theses," *Critical Inquiry* 35, no. 2 (January 2009): 197–222, doi: 10.1086/596640. While Paul Crutzen's article "Geology of Mankind," *Nature* 415, no. 23 (2002), is credited with having launched the concept, Eugene Stoermer had already informally talked about the Anthropocene in the 1980s. The concept of global human agency has a longer history still, with the nineteenth century articulations of George P. Marsh and Antonio Stoppani appearing as particularly strong anticipations of current discussions; see Jussi Parikka, *A Geology of Media* (Minneapolis: University of Minnesota Press, 2015), x and 115–19.

dominant species on earth. Unfortunately, we have now ourselves become a geological agent disturbing these parametric conditions needed for our own existence.[25]

In seeking to understand geological agency, one of the most important suggestions made in Chakrabarty's essay is that any once-tenable distinctions between subject and object no longer cleanly obtain. While this central aesthetic distinction has long been unstable in the case of collecting, as the objects of collection present themselves as expressions of human subjectivity, the idea of geological agency expands this, taking the condition of the collector vis-à-vis their collection and recasting it as the condition of the human vis-à-vis the world. As Stacy Alaimo puts it: "What can it mean to be human at this time when the human has become sedimented in the geology of the planet?"[26] And we might add, what can it mean to collect at this time when we are already sedimented into any possible object of collection?

The conditions under which our apparently ethereal data play a leading role in sedimenting the human into the geology of the planet might be termed the Data Anthropocene. Collecting digital objects, objects apparently made only of "data," in fact entails remaking the planet. And this remaking has to do in a crucial way with resource extraction generally, and the use of fossil fuels in particular. As Chakrabarty writes: "The mansion of modern freedoms stands on an ever-expanding base of fossil fuel use."[27] Will Steffen, Paul Crutzen, and John McNeill make a similar point: "Hitherto humankind had relied on energy captured from ongoing flows in the form of wind, water, plants, and animals, and from the 100- or 200-year stock held in trees. Fossil fuel use offered access to carbon stored from millions of years of photosynthesis: a massive energy subsidy from the deep past to modern society, upon which a great deal of our modern wealth depends."[28] They focus especially on the shift in time scales involved, but also note a change from flow to storage or, we might say, a change from temporary use to collection.

25 Chakrabarty, "The Climate of History," 218.

26 Stacy Alaimo, *Exposed: Environmental Politics and Pleasures in Posthuman Times* (Minneapolis, MN: University of Minnesota Press, 2016), 1.

27 Chakrabarty, "The Climate of History," 208.

28 Will Steffen, Paul Crutzen, and John McNeill, "The Anthropocene: Are Humans Now Overwhelming the Great Forces of Nature," *AMBIO: A Journal of the Human Environment* 36, no. 8 (December 2007): 614–21, here 616, doi:10.1579/0044-7447(2007)36[614:TAAHNO]2.0.CO;2.

# Mines and Reservoirs:
# Collecting in the Data Anthropocene

Focusing on the environmental entanglements of collecting digital objects draws our attention to a number of continuities of the digital age. Where purveyors of digital technologies may focus on rupture, this focus looks past the deep material entanglements of these technologies, entanglements so well obscured that we often fail to notice them, even when they are explicitly named.

Mining, for example, has always been a dirty business in which human hands reshape the face of the earth, marring both the geological and biological in the process, and scarring the object as well as the subject of extraction. The "mining" that powers manufactured digital scarcity is every bit as dirty, and depends on actual mining, even if at often considerable remove.[29] The attempt to make the abundant digital into singular and collectible draws on the continuity of the relationship between human and Earth represented in resource extraction. In the Data Anthropocene, mineral seams and oil deposits rearranged by human hands into planet-encircling cables and vast data bunkers transform prehistoric geological patterns into aspects of human culture. Fiber-optic cables, as Nicole Starosielski has noted, reveal a "renewal of a spatial organization and set of ecological practices" that are decades old, following as they do older rail lines, telephone systems, and even networks of milk distribution.[30] And in their renewal of these practices, they are continuing the centuries-old habits of remaking past geological patterns and biological systems characteristic of the Anthropocene.

But resource extraction and fossil fuel burning alone are not sufficient to name the changes in human/planetary relations we call the Anthropocene. There is also a continuity in the practice of making the abundant collectible, in manufacturing scarcity which was central to the rise of capitalism. One example is of course the complex and ambivalent role of enclosure in creating new relationships between humans and the land.[31] More clearly related both to collecting and to human geological agency, however, is the process of river water collection undertaken on a massive scale beginning in the eighteenth century, and the building of

---

29  Parikka, *Geology of Mediai*, 24, makes nearly the same point I am making about Cryptocurrency mining with reference to text mining.

30  Nicole Starosielski, "Pipeline Ecologies: Rural Entanglements of Fiber-Optic Cables," in *Sustainable Media*, 38–55, here 42.

31  For an account of the role that enclosure played in the development of landscapes which would later be praised for their naturalness by the Romantics, see Catherine E. Rigby, *Topographies of the Sacred: The Poetics of Place in European Romanticism* (Charlottesville: University of Virginia Press, 2004), especially 60–66.

dams and reservoirs, at first for river regulation, and later for the production of electricity.[32] This process reveals a continuity in human power from flow to storage, for it depends neither purely on the flow of the river nor on the storage of photosynthesis-derived energy in trees or fossil fuels, but rather appears as a hybrid form. It is also responsible for one of the more dramatic examples of human geological agency: the slowing of the earth's rotation. By collecting large quantities of water in locations distant from (and generally north of) the equator, humans have caused our planet to turn more slowly in the same way a figure skater extends their arms to slow their spin. While this slowing is measurable only in fractions of seconds, it represents a human interference in geologic time at least as significant as the use of fossil fuels as discussed by Steffen et al. And while hydroelectricity is less and less frequently enumerated in lists of renewable energy resources due to the recognition of the scale of its impact, it is still an important source of cheap electricity for, among other things, Bitcoin mining.[33]

The Data Anthropocene is driven by collection. The collection of data undertaken by giants like Google and Apple is powered by the collection of natural resources. Perhaps the overt digital cat collection of CryptoKitties is little more than an obscene gimmick, a caricature of an outmoded form of collection. Even so, every engagement with digital cat imagery—one of the primary loci of contemporary aesthetic experience—remains an example of collection in the digital age, because it is connected to our species's act of collection in the form of resource control and depletion. The bunker, an erstwhile technology of human paranoia, has in the Data Anthropocene become a technology of human dominion. The algorithmic curation of our collective collection gradually reshapes the world, powered by the hydroelectrical dams that slow the planet's rotation and producing the heat that thaws the permafrost. As we fill our high-tech vaults with our apparent collections—endless copies of cat pictures, virtual reams of consumer metadata, logs of conversations between Twitter

---

32 David Blackbourn offers a thorough consideration of the human reworking of natural water flows in Germany beginning in the eighteenth century in his book *The Conquest of Nature: Water, Landscape, and the Making of Modern Germany* (New York: Norton, 2006), especially 228–49, on the consequences of hydropower and dam building in Germany and beyond.

33 In an article for *Motherboard*, Daniel Oberhaus tells the story of the city of Plattsburgh, NY, which placed a moratorium on Bitcoin mining after residents' energy costs began spiking because the new industry was using such a large percentage of the city's allotment of cheap electricity from a nearby 1950s hydroelectric dam. One mine alone was using roughly ten percent of the allotment for the city of 20,000. Daniel Oberhaus, "The City That Banned Bitcoin Mining," *Vice* (March 16, 2018), www.vice.com/en_us/article/8xk4e4/bitcoin-ban-plattsburgh-coinmint-mining).

bots—our actual collection appears elsewhere in the altered geography of our planet, remade through a process that breaks down the relationship between subject and object, so that the entire globe, like a collector's collection, becomes a manifestation of our subjectivity. If, indeed, our age is to be remembered at all—if our species is to be remembered at all—perhaps it will not be the cat pictures for which the Internet was designed, but rather the geological changes which it leaves behind that will be our enduring mark.

# Part IV.

# Economics

# 11: Doomed to Collect: Dataveillance as Inner Logic of the Internet

*Roberto Simanowski*

THE LEAD STORY in *Vanity Fair* on July 1, 2018, reads like the script of a Hollywood thriller, "Nearly three decades earlier, Berners-Lee invented the World Wide Web. On this morning, he had come to Washington as part of his mission to save it."[1] It was a day in summer 2018, just weeks after the Facebook-Cambridge Analytica scandal, which had made it decidedly clear to the public that their data was not in safe hands on the Web. Instead, each individual's personal thoughts and political preferences were analyzed by unknowns in the service of exploitative and manipulative third-party interests. A few months later, on the thirtieth anniversary of the WWW, Berners-Lee explains in an open letter: "While the web has created opportunity, given marginalized groups a voice, and made our daily lives easier, it has also created opportunity for scammers, given a voice to those who spread hatred, and made all kinds of crime easier to commit."[2] Berners-Lee's "pain in watching his creation so distorted," in the words of *Vanity Fair*, culminated in an appeal to take a stand for the Web—for the *Web We Want*—as his campaign came to be known. This campaign, started by Berners-Lee and the World Wide Web Consortium, which he founded on the twenty-fifth anniversary of the Web, begins:

> Against the backdrop of news stories about how the web is misused, it's understandable that many people feel afraid and unsure if the web is really a force for good. But given how much the web has changed in the past 30 years, it would be defeatist and unimaginative to assume that the web as we know it can't be changed for the better

---

1    Katrina Brooker, "'I Was Devastated': Tim Berners-Lee, the Man Who Created the World Wide Web, Has Some Regrets," *Vanity Fair*, www.vanityfair.com/news/2018/07/the-man-who-created-the-world-wide-web-has-some-regrets.

2    Tim Berners-Lee, "30 Years On, What's next #ForTheWeb?," *World Wide Web Foundation* (blog), March 12, 2019, https://webfoundation.org/2019/03/web-birthday-30/.

in the next 30. If we give up on building a better web now, then the web will not have failed us. We will have failed the web.[3]

The main problem for Berners-Lee is the centralization of the Web that has transformed it from a safe place for the exchange of knowledge and the interaction of its users into a constantly surveilling, data-consuming monstrosity. His response to this unwelcome change is a platform called *Solid*, which will, "reclaim the Web from corporations and return it to its democratic roots."[4] This reclamation occurs in terms of where the data is stored. Normally, when someone uploads a photo, comment, or other object to an application, that data resides within and is subject to use by that application. With *Solid*, this user-generated data is "decoupled" from the application and is instead stored on a server, or "Pod," of the user's own choosing and shared only with those individuals, websites, or applications that the user has selected.[5] No longer must the user surrender their data to platforms like Facebook as the cost of admission but can now block the sharing of their information at will, which fundamentally alters the balance of power on the Internet. At the end of 2018, Berners-Lee introduced the beta version of *Solid* and invited developers to create a social networking experience that supported the informational autonomy of its users. *Solid* is the decentralized alternative to Facebook, as Mastodon is to Twitter, a return to the future in which our data does not languish in the cloud but remains in the daily plebiscite of our own computers. It is as *Solid*'s allusive and hopeful proclamation goes: "One small step for the Web . . ."[6]

The most well-known opponent to the 63-year-old Berners-Lee is the 34-year-old Mark Zuckerberg, founder and CEO of Facebook, a social media platform that has to date brought together over 2.5 billion users. In his New Year's address on January 4, 2018—as rulers of such great empires sometimes feel entitled to address their public—Zuckerberg attempted to shift the focus from centralization to privatization and called encryption the work of the future.[7] On March 6, 2018, Zuckerberg published a privacy manifesto, a merger between Facebook, Instagram, and WhatsApp, that makes centralization—a red flag for privacy groups—a condition for the protection of data:

---

3    Berners-Lee, "30 Years On."
4    Brooker, "'I Was Devastated.'"
5    The Solid Project, "Solid," *Solid*, 2020, https://solid.mit.edu/.
6    Tim Berners-Lee, "One Small Step for the Web . . .," *Medium*, January 2, 2019, https://medium.com/@timberners_lee/one-small-step-for-the-web-87f92217d085.
7    Mark Zuckerberg, "Untitled," *Facebook*, January 4, 2018, www.facebook.com/zuck/posts/10104380170714571?pnref=story.

For example, lots of people selling items on Marketplace list their phone number so people can message them about buying it. That's not ideal, because you're giving strangers your phone number. With interoperability, you'd be able to use WhatsApp to receive messages sent to your Facebook account without sharing your phone number—and the buyer wouldn't have to worry about whether you prefer to be messaged on one network or the other.[8]

It is quite bold to try and sell the collection of even more data (because only when the call takes place in the network does one have metadata), as data protection. This kind of rhetoric is recognizable enough in the meantime and not only from Facebook. A response was inevitable. Just two days later on March 8, US Senator Elizabeth Warren explains that it would be time to break up Amazon, Google, and Facebook. Warren speaks of unfair competition and makes clear that their monopoly position leads these corporations to pressure states for tax breaks (like Amazon in New York) and to neglect the interests of their customers (as Facebook does with data privacy). Warren demands, like Berners-Lee, that control be restored to individuals as to where their data is collected, how it is shared, and to whom it is sold. Unlike Berners-Lee, Warren sees the problem not in defective programming that can be corrected through better coding,[9] but rather as a driving economic force that must be stopped with appropriately updated antitrust legislation.[10]

Even if this long overdue shift from the technical to the political were to occur, it would not go far enough, because the problem, according to Shoshana Zuboff, lies with capitalism itself: "Technologies are always economic means, not ends in themselves: in modern times, technology's DNA comes already patterned by what the sociologist Max Weber called the 'economic orientation.'"[11] This economic orientation directs these new technological possibilities into a paradigm of surveillance that calls

---

8   Mark Zuckerberg, "A Privacy-Focused Vision for Social Networking," www.facebook.com/notes/mark-zuckerberg/a-privacy-focused-vision-for-social-networking/10156700570096634/.

9   "While the problems facing the web are complex and large, I think we should see them as bugs: problems with existing code and software systems that have been created by people—and can be fixed by people." Tim Berners-Lee, "The Web Is under Threat: Join Us and Fight for It," *World Wide Web Foundation* (blog), March 12, 2018, https://webfoundation.org/2018/03/web-birthday-29/.

10   For more on this topic compare: Tim Wu, *The Curse of Bigness: Antitrust in the New Guilded Age* (New York: Columbia Global Reports, 2018).

11   Shoshana Zuboff, *The Age of Surveillance Capitalism: The Fight for a Human Future at the New Frontier of Power*, Paperback Reprint (New York: PublicAffairs, 2019), 15–16.

for the collection and analysis of data in the interest of monetization: "Surveillance capitalism is not an accident of overzealous technologists, but rather a rogue capitalism that learned to cunningly exploit its historical conditions to ensure and defend its success."[12] Surveillance capitalism is the primary concept that Zuboff uses to describe the current situation in her book of the same name, published in 2019. Surveillance capitalism wants to know everything about us—where and when we do something and with whom and why, because it seeks to monetize all our personal experiences. For this reason, the dismantling of Facebook alone is not a solution for Zuboff. Decentralization of data would result in the metastasis of surveillance corporations: "Calls to break up Google or Facebook on monopoly grounds could easily result in establishing multiple surveillance capitalist firms, though at a diminished scale, and thus clear the way for more surveillance capitalist competitors."[13]

The composite constructed by Zuboff out of surveillance and capitalism indicates a causal relationship. Surveillance is the consequence of capitalism that best serves capitalism's most basic law of profit generation. According to Zuboff, the logic of this neoliberal commodification of everything and everyone should be offset by adequate consumer protection of the private sector and the legal ban on the collection of private data. But principally it comes down to the resistance of citizens against the rule of wealth. The last subchapter of the book, entitled "Be the Friction," is just as vague as it is melodramatic as it ends by hinting at the fall of the Berlin Wall: "Above all it was because the people of East Berlin said, 'No more!' We too can be the authors of many 'great and beautiful' new facts that reclaim the digital future as humanity's home. No more! Let this be *our* declaration."[14]

With her critique of the political economy of the Internet, Zuboff goes much further than Warren or Berners-Lee in her error analysis. The technical is political; its usage, as Theodor Adorno emphasizes in his 1953 lecture "On Technology and Humanism," depends on the "objective structure of the society as a whole." For Adorno, technology can only realize itself in a humane setting.[15] The consequence of this logic leads us further than Zuboff is ready to go.[16] As a result, one must ask if the avoidance of the problematic tendencies of the Internet necessitate

---

12  Zuboff, *Age of Surveillance Capitalism*, 17.

13  Zuboff, *Age of Surveillance Capitalism*, 23.

14  Zuboff, *Age of Surveillance Capitalism*, 520 and 525.

15  Theodor Adorno, "Über Technik und Humanismus," in *Gesammelte Schriften*, vol. 20 (Frankfurt am Main: Suhrkamp, 2003), 310–17, 316.

16  Others would even consider the current use of digital technology a solution to most of the problems of contemporary capitalism, as Victor Mayer-Schönberger and Thomas Ramge claim in their *Reinventing Capitalism in the Age of Big Data* (New York: Basic Books, 2018).

a "change in the social balance of power between capital and labor," as left-leaning political observers say.[17] Next to the centralization of data, these problematic tendencies include the atomization of the subject, who is forced away from unionized relationships into precarious forms of self-employment through "click-work" and a platform economy. These new technological opportunities of a decentralized work force meet the neoliberal individualization of responsibility, as well as the gamification of competition through so-called "democratically" crowd-sourced ranking procedures. A look at these social consequences of new technologies raises the question as to whether the technical revolution requires in its completion—or its correction—a political dimension that converts digital capitalism into digital socialism.[18] Confronting the post-political illusion of consensus of interest by the social players would unmask the tech giants and the start-ups' rhetoric of bettering the world through technical advancement. The return to agonal and antagonistic politics is imperative also in the consideration and assessment of digitization.

At the same time, it must be asked whether another form of society really would be the solution to the present problem. Is the compulsion to networking not already embedded in Berners-Lee's invention of the hypertext that binds everything to everything else? Does such compulsion not demand from the central entities that oversee everything—including available hotels, taxis, and singles in a city, region, or country—in order to offer a service that would not be otherwise possible? Would another form of society in fact solve this problem, or would it only shift its cause from a consumption to a control doctrine, from an interest in profit to an ideological use? Is the measurement of everything and everyone and the centralization of data not already inscribed on the Web as its genuine message (to allude to Marshall McLuhan's famous statement "The medium is

---

17 Bernd Riexinger, "Wege zum Infrastruktursozialismus: Für eine neues Normalarbeitsverhältnis," *Luxemburg: Gesellschaftsanalyse und linke Praxis* 3 (2015): 82–87, here 82.

18 Robert W. McChesney, *Digital Disconnect: How Capitalism Is Turning the Internet against Democracy* (New York: New Press, 2013); John Bellamy and Robert W. McChesney, "Surveillance Capitalism: Monopoly-Finance Capital, the Military-Industrial Complex, and the Digital Age," *Monthly Review: An Independent Socialist Magazine* 66, no. 3 (July 1, 2014). See also the discussion on the prospect to use the feedback infrastructure of digital technology as non-market forms of social coordination in Daniel Saros, *Information Technology and Socialist Construction: The End of Capital and the Transition to Socialism* (Abingdon: Routledge, 2014); Erick Limas, "Cybersocialism: A Reassessment of the Socialist Calculation Debate," SSRN Scholarly Paper (Rochester, NY: Social Science Research Network, February 4, 2018), doi.org/10.2139/ssrn.3117890; and Evgeny Morozov, "Digital Socialism?," *New Left Review* 116/117 (June 2019), https://newleftreview.org/issues/II116/articles/evgeny-morozov-digital-socialism.

the message")? Is such measuring and centralization not the result of the "internal drive" of the Internet to take Georg Simmel seriously who, in his 1911 essay *The Concept and Tragedy of Culture*, speaks of an intrinsic logic in all products of the human imagination from which future generations will find escape very difficult. Both McLuhan and Simmel suggest that technology is always simultaneously a means of human self-control and self-disempowerment; using technology, human beings create a home for themselves in the world but are rarely lords of their own manor.

Is the relationship between technology and society to be determined with Simmel and McLuhan beyond Zuboff and Adorno? Do we face principles that are not anchored in politics but rather in technology? In the end, is it perhaps that technology is just an expression of an anthropological phenomenon? These questions are examined in the following sections in which centralization and acquisitiveness are described as the primary message of digital technologies, acquisitiveness being identified as the legacy of the Enlightenment, and finally, the New Deal for Big Data Society will be discussed as a response to change acquisitiveness productively.

## Birth Defects of the Web and Acquisitiveness as the Logic of Technology

The misery in which the World Wide Web now finds itself results from a birth defect that for the longest time was understood as a virtue. "Information wants to be free," is the fundamental conviction of web-activists like Berners-Lee, who, among others, holds that information is not a commodity out of which to shake profits. In the context of an information society, this sentiment takes on almost communist overtones: everyone gives according to their ability and takes according to their need. The unavoidable flipside of these allegedly free services is advertising that drives the process of surveillance and centralization, because the personalization of advertisements online is best optimized by knowing as much as possible about as many people as possible.

However, it is certainly not only the logic of advertising but also the logic of technology that pushes towards the centralization of data. Who actually wants to consult more than one app for finding books or flights? Is it not cumbersome enough as a scholar to have to maintain separate accounts on LinkedIn, ResearchGate, and Academia.edu? Does one really want more than one Twitter or WhatsApp? The demand for centralization also applies to those cases when local service operators provide better alternatives to monopolies like Uber, Airbnb, or booking.com. Even locally, a customer may only wish to consult a single ridesharing or apartment-finding app. And if one wants to maintain contact with new and old friends from afar, will not one regionally, nationally, or globally operating social network suffice? The more cosmopolitan we become, the more urgent it is to have a centrally operated social network like Facebook. Centralization introduces economies of scale that have an optimizing effect on services and process flows. This is the same for health apps, like WebMD, as much as for Google or Facebook.[19]

Many hopes bound to the Internet and Big Data—from perfecting translation programs and the optimizing of search engine results to the investigation of disease and behavioral patterns—entail a centralization of data. What use would *IBM Watson Health* be if it only used a fraction of the available medical data? What use is information on current road conditions if smart cars only use information from their own manufacturer and not from every other car underway in their respective location?

The counterpart to centralization is totalization: one wants to collect as much data as possible from as many sources as possible. Modeling and deductions from correlations occur only *en masse*. The information gain that will ultimately be monetized lies within the "virtual data," data that does not exist in a given database but is rather generated from a combination of data sources. This process of exploring data—In IT-jargon called "data finds data"[20]—results in the problem of nondescript data that we freely disclose to our social networks, facts that betray us, indiscretions that we would prefer not to make public. The most famous example is of the pregnant teenager in Minneapolis in early 2012, whose own father was unaware of her condition until the retailer Target sent directed advertisements to her home based on her buying behavior. Also, it is known that the ten likes I have given away on social media reveal more about me than my coworkers know, 150 likes reveal more than my parents know,

---

19  Even the most vehement critics of technology, like Evgeny Morozov, do not see it otherwise: "The fact that Google monitors my Web searches, my email, my location, makes its predictions in each of these categories much more accurate than if it were to monitor only one of them. If you take this logic to its ultimate conclusion, it becomes clear you don't want two hundred different providers of information services—you want just one, because the scale-effects make things much easier for users." Evgeny Morozov, "Socialize the Data Centres!," *New Left Review* 91 (February 2015): 45–66, here 63, https://newleftreview.org/issues/II91/articles/evgeny-morozov-socialize-the-data-centres. Important is Morozov's follow-up question, which we will come back to in the third section: "The big question, of course, is whether that player has to be a private capitalist corporation, or some federated, publicly-run set of services that could reach a data-sharing agreement free of monitoring by intelligence agencies."

20  Jeff Jonas and Lisa Sokol, "Data Finds Data," in *Beautiful Data: The Stories behind Elegant Data Solutions*, ed. Toby Segaran and Jeff Hammerbacher (Sebastopol, CA: O'Reilly Media, 2009), 105–18.

and 300 likes reveal more than my partner knows.[21] It is highly probable that over 1,000 likes reveal more about me than even I know about myself. The algorithm knows me better than I know myself, because it can compare my data with millions of other records. It is the psychoanalyst of the twenty-first century, who makes use of its own insights without ever informing its patients or asking them for consent.

"Liking" is, however, only one example of unconscious self-betrayal in digital media, which can be avoided if we do not use this form of feedback information. But can we really renounce our "Googling" which just as "liking" captures as much data, insofar as every query makes a statement about ourselves? Can we prevent Google's use of cookies to track us on more than half of the ten million most important websites on the Internet? The analysis of my Internet search behavior makes me a transparent, predictable person and establishes why Amazon had already in 2013 applied for a patent on "Anticipatory Package Shipping," which would send you a product that you had not yet ordered, but would probably purchase.

## The Measuring Society as the Legacy of the Enlightenment

The concept of a "transparent society" is an alternative term for Zuboff's idea of surveillance capitalism that at the same time denotes a conceptional difference. The primary category of description for this transparent society is that of the famous panopticon, which British philosopher and social reformer Jeremy Bentham described at the beginning of the nineteenth century and that Michel Foucault later used as a metaphor for his theory of governmentality. The digital panopticon, however, differentiates itself from the classical model insofar as it does not recognize a separation of the center from the periphery and does not consist of the isolated inmates of an institution but is rather based on similarly exhibitionistic and voyeuristic "hyper-communication" of everyone with everyone else: "The society of control achieves perfection when subjects bare themselves not through outer constraint but through self-generated need, that is, when the fear of having to abandon one's private and intimate sphere yields to the need to put oneself on display without shame."[22]

---

21 Wu Youyou, Michal Kosinski, and David Stillwell, "Computer-Based Personality Judgments Are More Accurate than Those Made by Humans," *Proceedings of the National Academy of Sciences* 112, no. 4 (January 27, 2015): 1036–40, doi.org/10.1073/pnas.1418680112.

22 Byun-Chul Han, *The Transparency Society*, trans. Erik Butler (Stanford, CA: Stanford University Press, 2015), 46.

The "transparency society," or "metric society" as Steffen Mau calls it,[23] is the result of one's own desire to be seen. This aspect complements Zuboff's critique of surveillance capitalism's desire to measure. At the same time, it must be asked if this desire to measure is part of the DNA of capitalism or that of modern humankind. Did not modern humans endeavor to know and measure the world that led to the development of the natural sciences that explore every aspect of the physical world, and then to the development of psychoanalysis, which seeks to lay bare the inner workings of humankind? That this drive to know has grasped society is facilitated by the new possibilities for accumulating and analyzing data, but cannot be explained alone this way. "Network Science," which has emerged from data science and "tries to understand people in the context of their social networks rather than viewing them as isolated individuals,"[24] is only the logical continuation of statistical pattern recognition processes using digital technology, as Armin Nassehi in his study *Muster: Theorie der digitalen Gesellschaft* (*Patterns: A Theory of the Digital Society*) makes clear. The desire to measure human behavior in order to control and regulate it is not the outcome of digitization but rather represents the drive to know and shape that characterizes the Enlightenment and the modern humans who emerged from it. Digitization, according to Nassehi, is also to be understood as a "sociological project" in the sense that the "calculating, therefore, digitally self-observing society" and the resulting self-control reacts to the "unpredictability of its free citizens," which begins with the modernization of society.[25]

A well-known representative of Network Science is the director of the MIT Media Lab, Alex Pentland, who explains the new field of Social Physics research: "Social physics functions by analyzing patterns of human experience and idea exchange within the digital bread crumbs we all leave behind us as we move through the world."[26] As Pentland emphasizes, these bread crumbs that we leave behind are, "very different from what is put on Facebook"; they are not, as in the case of postings on social networks what "people choose to tell each other, edited according to the standards of the day," but are rather *honest signals* that are hardly edited and of which users are largely unaware. Such honest signals have been the subject of Pentland's earlier research when, in his

---

23 Steffen Mau, *The Metric Society: On the Quantification of the Social*, trans. Sharon Howe (Medford, MA: Polity, 2019).

24 Alex (Sandy) Pentland, *Honest Signals: How They Shape Our World* (Cambridge, MA: MIT Press, 2008), ix–x.

25 Armin Nassehi, *Muster: Theorie der digitalen Gesellschaft* (Munich: C. H. Beck, 2019).

26 Alex (Sandy) Pentland, *Social Physics: How Social Networks Can Make Us Smarter* (New York: Penguin Books, 2014), 8.

book of the same title, he theorized that "people have a second channel of communication that revolves not around words but around *social relations*," and proposed to reveal and to understand this second channel that "profoundly influences major decisions in our lives *even though we are largely unaware of it*."[27] Honest signals are "so expensive or so directly connected to the underlying biology that they become reliable indicators that others use to guide their own behavior."[28] These signals allow insights about the individual over which they have limited control and as such are the caviar of sociological analysis. Social media is a tantalizing data source for those kinds of signals. And the Internet of things is another even more promising source of data. At the same time these signals can be targeted by the appropriate types of sensors or "socioscopes," the new tools of social science that consist of

> "smart" phones programmed to keep track of their owners' location and their proximity to other people . . . electronic badges that record the wearers' location (with 2 m typical accuracy), ambient audio, and upper body movement . . . microphone and software that is used to extract audio 'signals' from individuals, specifically, the exact timing of their vocalizations and the amount of modulation (in both pitch and amplitude) of those vocalizations.[29]

According to Pentland, these new tools "will revolutionize the study of human behavior," just "as the microscope and telescope revolutionized the study of biology and astronomy."[30]

Honest signals are *the* topic of sociological analysis in the age of digitization. The interest in these nonverbal, network-specific signs as the unmediated gateway to the inner life of individuals has established its own field of inquiry. Alongside the honest signals are biometric data like vocal register, facial features, gestures, and postures for which the MIT Media Lab has designated its own research group on *affective computing*.[31]

---

27  Pentland, *Honest Signals*, ix.

28  Pentland, *Honest Signals*, xii.

29  Alex (Sandy) Pentland, "Automatic Mapping and Modeling of Human Networks," *Physica A: Statisical Mechanics and Its Applications* 378, no. 1 (n.d.): 60–61.

30  Pentland, *Social Physics*, 10.

31  "MIT Media Lab: Affective Computing Group," Massachusetts Institute of Technology + Media Lab, https://affect.media.mit.edu/.

## The New Deal for a Big Data Society

In the atmosphere following the NSA scandal of 2013 there was an outcry demanding action to prevent a "data catastrophe" comparable to those envisaged by environmental protection movements.[32] The metaphor of environmental pollution by data builds rhetorically on its comparison to oil and points out that individual generosity—or perhaps promiscuity—with data has its social consequences because it contributes to the determination of statistical criteria and norms against which everyone, regardless of their willingness to disclose private data, will be measured.[33] The possibilities and dangers of data pollution are growing immensely with the production and popularity of "wearables," the minicomputers and electronic badges that we carry around with us in the form of devices like FitBits and smart watches, which constantly record all of our actions. With these devices, the individual resorts to a virtual labor and literally with each step enriches the data pool. On one hand, this labor often occurs voluntarily, as the market success of devices like Amazon's Alexa, or "little big brother," that we willingly have in our homes, demonstrates. On the other hand, it may happen involuntarily as exemplified by the West Virginia teachers' strike in spring of 2018. The strike, among other reasons, was a reaction to the undue pressure to use the *Go365* app, a "workplace wellness program" that tracked the physical movement of employees and penalized them with increased insurance costs if they failed to earn enough points.[34] The success of Amazon's Alexa and numerous other self-tracking devices, as well as the confirmed exhibitionist tendencies in social networks and a willingness to concede personal data in exchange for free or discounted services, prove that these apparent victims are frequently willing participants, even trendsetters, and shows that a transparent society in relationship to surveillance capitalism cannot simply be reduced to an us vs. them opposition.

32 Evgeny Morozov, "The Real Privacy Problem," *MIT Technology Review* (October 22, 2013), www.technologyreview.com/2013/10/22/112778/the-real-privacy-problem/. The former German interior secretary from the Free Democratic Party, Gerhart Baum, wrote in an op-ed: "We lack a citizen's movement for the protection of privacy as it existed and exists for the protection of natural resources." Gerhart Baum, "Ich will, dass wir beißen können," *FAZ.NET* September 24, 2013, www.faz.net/1.2589869.

33 See the discussion in Roberto Simanowski, *Data Love: The Seduction and Betrayal of Digital Technologies* (New York: Columbia University Press, 2016), ch. 4: Ecological Disaster, 17–23.

34 Adam Gaffney, "The West Virginia Teachers' Strike Is over. But the Fight for Healthcare Isn't," *Guardian* (March 7, 2018), www.theguardian.com/commentisfree/2018/mar/07/west-virginia-teachers-strike-healthcare.

However, rising expectations and impositions by employers and service providers regarding ready access to the private data of their employees and customers, as well as the increase in demand for specialized companies to collect and evaluate the enormous amounts of data, like Palantir, make it possible to speak of a "*coup from above*," as Zuboff describes surveillance capitalism: as an "overthrow of the people's sovereignty and a prominent force in the perilous drift toward democratic deconsolidation that now threatens Western liberal democracies."[35]

At the same time, this coup is to be understood as the continuation of the sociological project of self-knowledge through digital media. At least as expressed by the "digital bread crumb" collector Pentland, who Zuboff identifies as "high priest among an exclusive group of priests" that "helps to legitimate instrumentarian practices,"[36] who is rather keen on the opportunity to be able to better understand and organize social interaction using data analysis, as already shown by the title of his 2013 essay "How Big Data Can Transform Society for the Better."[37] Pentland in no way overlooks the risk of abuse—"A successful data-driven society must be able to guarantee that our data will not be abused"[38]—and proposed a "New Deal on Data" to the World Economic Forum as early as 2007.[39] This data deal contends that the framework for institutional controls, "must support and reflect greater user control over personal data, as well as large-scale interoperability for data sharing between and among institutions."[40] It finally demands that:

> Private organizations collect the vast majority of personal data in the form of mobility patterns, financial transactions, and phone and Internet communications. These data must not remain the exclusive domain of private companies, because they are then less likely to contribute to the common good; private organizations must be key

35    Zuboff, *Age of Surveillance Capitalism*, 21.

36    Zuboff, *Age of Surveillance Capitalism*, 417.

37    Alex (Sandy) Pentland, "How Big Data Can Transform Society for the Better," *Scientific American* (October 2013), www.scientificamerican.com/article/how-big-data-can-transform-society-for-the-better/.

38    Pentland, *Social Physics*, 177.

39    Alex (Sandy) Pentland, "Reality Mining of Mobile Communications: Toward A New Deal On Data," in *Social Computing and Behavioral Modeling* (Boston: Springer, 2009), 75–80.

40    Daniel Greenwood, Arkadiusz Stopczynski, Brian Sweatt, Thomas Hardjono, and Alex Pentland, "The New Deal on Data: A Framework for Institutional Controls," in *Privacy, Big Data, and the Public Good: Frameworks for Engagement*, ed. Julia Lane, Victoria Stodden, Stefan Bender, and Helen Nissenbaum (Cambridge: Cambridge University Press, 2014), 192–210, here 192, doi.org/10.1017/CBO9781107590205.012.

players in the New Deal on Data. Likewise, these data should not become the exclusive domain of the government. The entities who should be empowered to share and make decisions about their data are the people themselves: users, participants, citizens.[41]

The basic tenet of the New Deal on Data is private ownership, "balanced with the need of corporations and governments to use certain data:" "We need to recognize personal data as a valuable asset of the individual, which can be given to companies and government in return for services."[42]

The premise of the requested data security is not data scarcity, the expected outcome of a warning against environmental data pollution. With ownership comes responsibility, as a chapter title and its abbreviation in Pentland's *Social Physics* indicates, "Data for Development: D4D." Pentland explains: "A key insight that motivates the creation of a New Deal on Data is that our data are worth more when shared, because they can inform improvements in systems such as public health, transportation and government."[43] The dream of reality mining targeted by Pentland lies in the measurement of individual behavior in the interest of social optimization, "as we all know, what isn't measured can't be managed."[44] He explains using the prime example of the prevention of epidemics:

> For example, an app on a phone could quietly look for uncharacteristic variations in behavior, and then figure out if an illness is developing . . . By crowdsourcing this behavior information across a population, and then combining that information with data about where and when people went during the previous days, the infection risk of an entire area can be figured out.[45]

The corresponding data visualization "shows where people are most likely to become infected with the flu at a particular day and hour."[46] The generation of such an easily understandable visualization, such as a map, is in this case developed through the connection of behavioral and locational data and is the central aim from which an individual may not escape, insofar as assisting in the reduction of a pandemic risk is seen as the duty of every citizen. Pentland's rhetorical weapon, "some experts on infectious disease believe that this is one of the only hopes we have for avoiding hundreds of millions of deaths from the pandemics that are certain to

---

41 Greenwood et al., "The New Deal on Data."
42 Greenwood et al., "The New Deal on Data."
43 Pentland, *Social Physics*, 178.
44 Pentland, *Social Physics*, 106.
45 Pentland, *Social Physics*, 147.
46 Pentland, *Social Physics*, 147.

come,"[47] leaves no doubt of the obligation of individuals "to contribute to the common good"[48] with their own data. This responsibility to share data, and to install the corresponding apps in order to do so, is the logical consequence of the cooperative mandate.[49]

The New Deal on Data that Pentland suggests and which is supported by the European Commission and the United Nations has met sharp criticism as a "market-friendly 'new deal'" that "could help to forestall alternative attempts at imagining users as anything other than passive consumers of digital technology; they could enjoy their new status as hustling data entrepreneurs, but should aspire to little else."[50] This critique at the same time focuses on the smart city concept in which Pentland sees a promising future. He promotes smart cities as having the ability "to transform our cities into data-rich, dynamic, responsive organisms,"[51] while critics assert, "the current wave of 'smart' euphoria has resulted in many products traditionally classified as tools of surveillance and predictive policing being rebranded as essential components of the 'smart city' package."[52] Critics situate "smartness" in the context of the neoliberal evaluation and optimization models and demystify the technological retrofitting and upgrades of the city "as a continuation of the very same neoliberal agendas of privatization and outsourcing bulked up and extended by technological means."[53] In view of the economic necessities of impoverished local communities it is held that

> the appeal of quick technological fixes to city bureaucrats cannot be explained by their ideological confusion or technocratic faith alone, for there are actual structural factors which make the enlistment of technology firms in the business of running the city as well

---

47 Pentland, *Social Physics*, 149.

48 Pentland, *Social Physics*, 179.

49 In the meantime, the Corona-Pandemic has demonstrated how differently different countries see and enforce this duty. While in China and South Korea the installation of a Corona-Tracking-App is mandatory, in Germany privacy advocates achieved their goal of making the Corona-Tracing-App voluntary and only collects data anonymously and decentralized. This different approach demonstrates both notions made above with respect to Simmel and Adorno. On the one hand, society cannot escape the intrinsic logic of its technological inventions; on the other hand, the way this technology is used depends on the society's ideological model.

50 Morozov, "Digital Socialism?," 33–34.

51 Pentland, *Social Physics*, 153.

52 Evgeny Morozov and Francesca Bria, *Rethinking the Smart City: Democratizing Urban Technology* (New York: Rosa Luxemburg Stiftung, 2018), 8.

53 Morozov and Bria, *Rethinking the Smart City* (chapter 2, "Smartness and Neoliberalism").

as generating income for some of its inhabitants such an attractive choice.[54]

Tech companies not only will dominate the infrastructure but also, especially if they work with proprietary applications, are in possession of data (such as traffic data from Uber) that are important for future planning, which the city procures through financial contributions, concessions, or compromises.

Alternatives to the neoliberal smart city can be seen in the rejection of the data extraction model that is offered by service providers and that is at least initially lucrative for the city (either low- or no-cost services in exchange for data), in the insistence on free access to the accumulated data, or in the creation of communal alternatives to globally operated services. The primary requirement must be to reclaim technological sovereignty and ownership of data: "Cities must appropriate and run collective data on people, the environment, connected objects, public transport, and energy systems as commons."[55] If cities and citizens, not corporations, owned the data produced in the city, "it would make the rampant real estate speculation facilitated by the likes of Airbnb much more difficult," for it would allow "identifying the professional real estate developers who operate multiple properties but pass for ordinary users on Airbnb."[56] In addition to this demand to use the findings of data analysis in the interests of society, or of the municipality, there is a call for the abstention from collection and a recognition that individual behavioral patterns, which are exploited for the purposes of surveillance and commercial gain, should not be scrutinized: "There is no need for technocratic city managers to know everything . . . There is no danger in neglecting to learn certain elements or dimensions of a problem . . . There are many things our smart devices should not know, which in turn must be reflected in their design rather than relying on the goodwill of their operators."[57]

The suggestion of an abstention from measuring leads to the anthropological and evolutionary-theoretical aspect of the problem and to the question of who makes the decisions regarding the measure-worthiness of any given data. Another question is to what extent the measuring paradigm is only an expression of neoliberalism (or an authoritarian regime) or is it also the "message" or "intrinsic logic" of the new technology? Since criticism is focused not on the avoidance of data collection but rather on the ownership and usage rights of the data collected, the measuring paradigm appears likely to be a built-in feature of digital technology. The

---

54  Morozov and Bria, *Rethinking the Smart City*, 15.
55  Morozov and Bria, *Rethinking the Smart City*, 26.
56  Morozov and Bria, *Rethinking the Smart City*, 26 and 18.
57  Morozov and Bria, *Rethinking the Smart City*, 24.

solution is not primarily seen in the avoidance of data but instead on its socialization to ensure local control and to guarantee the ability of decentralized, local companies to compete.[58] This idea was already brought forward by political advisors and taken up by politicians in 2018 as an idea of a "progressive data-sharing mandate,"[59] and undermines the fundamental capitalist premise of the protection of property by declaring data that was obtained by tech monopolies the property of those entities from which it originated. The "citizens' rights to data as commons"[60] requires a new social contract regarding the ownership of data. The prospective alternative to socialization of data extracted through the large tech corporations like Uber or Airbnb is the local production of data through start-ups, small to medium-sized corporations, NGOs, cooperatives, and local communities carrying a "commons-based sharing economy which is data-centric, but where data is generated and gathered by citizens and public sensor networks available for broader communal use."[61]

The concept of *Platform Cooperativism* as the alternative to *Platform Capitalism*[62] raises questions that freely touch on the anthropological aspect beyond economic and political perspectives. The question is to what extent municipal start-ups and cooperatives are demonstrating morally superior behavior in comparison to tech giants, and are they as a result more advantageous for their respective communities or societies? This presumption is not anthropologically assured and can only be guaranteed politically by stricter regulations that could, for example, hinder a company (or cooperative) from using the data generated by its service beyond the community interest or that start-ups subsidized by public funds are not bought up by large tech corporations. The question is to what extent such control measures that obstruct private benefits of data ownership in the interest of the common good also weaken the profit-based economy

58   Morozov and Bria, *Rethinking the Smart City*, 26: "Cities and citizens, not companies, ought to own the data produced in cities and should be able to use said data to improve public services and put their policies into action."

59   Meyer-Schönberger and Ramge. In this spirit, the SPD-chairwoman, Andrea Nahles, called for "Daten für Alle" (Data for All) in the summer of 2018: Andrea Nahles, "Digitalisierung: Google und Apple gefährden den fairen Wettbewerb," *Handelsblatt* (August 13, 2018), www.handelsblatt.com/ meinung/gastbeitraege/gastkommentar-die-tech-riesen-des-silicon-valleys-gefaehrden-den-fairen-wettbewerb/22900656.html?ticket=ST-1080533-0V207YgUGROFd5HuhmAM-ap2.

60   Morozov and Bria, *Rethinking the Smart City*, 31.

61   Morozov and Bria, *Rethinking the Smart City*, 32.

62   *Ours to Hack and to Own: The Rise of Platform Cooperativism; A New Vision for the Future of Work and a Fairer Internet*, ed. Trebor Scholz and Nathan Schneider (New York: OR Books, 2016).

and thus question the foundations of the capitalist economic model.[63] It must, thus, be clarified as to what extent this economic model utilizes socialist methods of production and whether it can be more successful in the context of data production than the production of consumer goods under the conditions of actual socialism in the last half of the twentieth century.

There is no doubt regarding Morozov's conclusion that "future political battles" will not be reducible to data alone:

> The ownership and operation of the means of producing "feedback data" are at least as important as the question of who owns the data itself. The crucial battles ahead will involve the role of this "feedback infrastructure" in the reinvention of the political projects of both left and right.[64]

Morozov refers to the most well-known fundamental conflict between possession and usage of the means of production on which the Marxist social analysis rests its prediction of the future when he speaks of the "contradiction between collaborative forms of knowledge discovery and the private ownership of the means of digital production."[65] How this problem is to be resolved, remains to be seen, as well as to what extent the socialization of the "feedback infrastructure" requires the dispossession of its owners and how that is possible within a capitalist system.

## Conclusion: The Inescapability of the Archive

The principal locations from which the past ensures its power over the future are, on the one hand, the archive, and on the other, cultural memory as a whole. With respect to the ontology of media, we can draw a parallel that relates the archive to cultural memory in the same way that photography relates to painting. While a photo takes in everything at which the photographer may point the camera lens, the painter is selective in his labor, recording only those elements that are important to his perception. Thus for Siegfried Kracauer photography's inventory-like quality is a "barren self-presentation of spatial and temporal elements," which corresponds to historicism and which Friedrich Nietzsche associated to a

---

63 An indication of this consequence lies in the proposal to support, "projects which actually deliver value to residents, while discarding those which do not," with which business models are assessed not according to their marketability but rather their moral compatibility: Morozov and Bria, *Rethinking the Smart City*, 54.

64 Morozov, "Digital Socialism?," 52.

65 Morozov, "Digital Socialism?," 67.

third, "antiquarian" type of relationship with the past as a "blind mania for collecting," pedantic and passionless, that salvages the past for its own sake, while "monumental" and "critical" relationships to the past both treat the latter as being, respectively, emphatically either positive or negative.[66] The ideal archivist, typically, is not interested in a meaning-creating history in which diverse data assume the role of evidence. Archivists are not storytellers—out of respect for the material. However, even if archivists are more like "photographers" than "storytellers," the archive is not a photograph of the world. It cannot store everything that happens in the world, and it is no less determined by its choice of specific perspectives toward the world than photography. Unless, that is, the world itself is taking place in an archive.

This is increasingly the case as everything that exists in the Internet exists in digital form and is easily archived and accessible. The Internet radicalizes a process that Pierre Nora already noted in the late 1980s: "Memory has been wholly absorbed by its meticulous reconstitution. Its new responsibility is to record; delegating to the archive the duty of remembering."[67] There is still life outside the Internet, but on the Internet there is (almost) no life left outside of the archive. If photography was "the general inventory of a nature that cannot be further reduced,"[68] then the Internet is the general inventory of a digitally represented society. The Internet of things, which lets our cars, items of clothing, refrigerator, coffee machine, radio, heating system, lights, and so on, communicate with one another, substantially expands the terrain claimed by inventory by transforming even the smallest objects of daily life into powerfully effective archives that all lead towards the creation of one gigantic central archive. The Internet, less in its usage than its content, restores to the archive the innocence it had lost, at least since Michel Foucault's critical works on the archaeology of knowledge and the genealogy of power. The foreseeable future lies in the archiving of the entirety of existence, complete with all its everyday and less history-worthy details as a kind of 1:1 map that, unlike the 1:1 map in Jorge Luis Borges's story

---

66  Sigfried Kracauer, "Photography," trans. Thomas Y. Levin, *Critical Inquiry* 19, no. 3 (Spring 1994): 421–36, here 435; Friedrich Nietzsche, "On the Use and Abuse of History for Life," in *Untimely Meditations*, ed. Daniel Breazeale, trans. R. J. Hollingdale (Cambridge: Cambridge University Press, 1997), 77–79. This and the following paragraph take over thoughts and formulations from the chapter "Media Memory" in Roberto Simanowski, *Facebook Society: Losing Ourselves in Sharing Ourselves* (New York: Coulmbia University Press, 2018): 108–18.

67  Pierre Nora, "Between Memory and History: Les lieux de mémoire," *Representations* 26 (Spring 1989): 7–24. On the "obsession with the archive" in the late twentieth century, see also the issue "The Storage Mania" of the journal *Mediamatic* 8, no. 1 (Summer 1994).

68  Kracauer, "Photography," 61.

"On Exactitude in Science" or, before that, in Lewis Carroll's novel *Sylvie and Bruno*, is actually quite useful thanks to search engines and algorithms. The Internet brings with it a shift from the narrative paradigm to the database paradigm as the "new way to structure our experience of ourselves and of the world."[69]

The increasing accumulation of data and social analysis processes lies within the DNA of the modern human, in the possibilities of new technologies and, last but not least, in the resulting imperatives to a new business model of a sharing economy that is based on the protection of customer identity and reputation. The totality of the archive is inescapable. Whatever political framework a given society possesses, it will not find it disadvantageous to optimize its self-knowledge. Points of contention will not include the collection and analysis of data, but rather the use of the resulting findings.[70] Accordingly, the neoliberal model of data-hungry surveillance capitalism is not juxtaposed to lack of measurement, but rather with a radically democratic model of cybernetic governance that sees in data analytics a political potential for alternative social coordination.[71] The fact that in this context a social-credit model, like the one in China, is seen as having political potential for the future is as remarkable as it is disconcerting. It will lift the discussions on datafication, data mining, and dataveillance onto an entirely new level in a not so distant future.

*—Translated by Aurora B. Romero*

---

69  Lev Manovich, *The Language of New Media* (Cambridge, MA: MIT Press, 2002), 225. As I argue at length in *Facebook Society*: "The internet is the end of forgetting, to the extent that it potentially archives everything, but at the same time it is also the end of memory, to the extent that the unlost past is no longer a formed past at all. The stored information lacks the structure of narration and the perspective of the storyteller" (Simanowski, *Facebook Society*, 114).

70  In this sense, Morozov also notes: "Yet I believe there is a huge positive potential in the accumulation of more data, in a good institutional—and by that I mean political—setup . . . Public transportation would probably work much better if we could coordinate it based on everybody's location . . . I wouldn't want to oblige everyone to wear an electronic bracelet. But I am not against monitoring devices as such." Morozov, "Socialize the Data Centres!," 63.

71  Morozov, "Digital Socialism?," 61–63.

# 12: Data Collection in the Age of Surveillance Capitalism

*Douglas C. Schmidt*

## Surveillance Capitalism and Google Data Collection

THE PROLIFERATION OF personal computing devices—coupled with advances in network bandwidth, geolocation, "big data" analytics, and targeted advertising—has led to the rise of "surveillance capitalism," where large high-tech companies monetize personal data they collect by monitoring the online behavior and physical movement of their users around the world. The term "surveillance capitalism" was popularized by Shoshana Zuboff in the mid-2010s.[1] Surveillance capitalism constitutes practices conducted by large high-tech companies to monitor, predict, and control the behavior of consumers who use their products and platforms, either directly or indirectly.

Awareness of how personal data is collected by large high-tech companies is intensifying, with many people beginning to realize who is invested in knowing their online behaviors. For example, Facebook's enabling of data collection by Cambridge Analytica and the effect on the 2016 elections changed the conversation in the United States of America. Many people were rightly surprised by that vast collection and non-transparent use of their personal data, as well as the ways this information can be used to monitor, predict, and control many aspects of their lives.

Earlier means of monitoring, predicting, and controlling people relied on fear and shame to maintain order in society and ensure conformity with the interests of those in power. A classic example is the totalitarian

---

This paper is an extension of my earlier Vanderbilt Technical Report entitled "Google Data Collection": Douglas C. Schmidt, "Google Data Collection," in *Vanderbilt University Technical Report #ISIS-20-201* (August 15, 2018), www.dre.vanderbilt.edu/~schmidt/PDF/google-data-collection.pdf.

1 Shoshana Zuboff, "Big Other: Surveillance Capitalism and the Prospects of an Information Civilization," *Journal of Information Technology* 30 (2015): 75–89.

regime represented by "Big Brother" in Orwell's dystopian novel *1984*. In contrast, surveillance capitalism is based on a more subtle—and ultimately more pernicious—form of monitoring, predicting, and controlling what Zuboff calls "Big Other," which are digital networks trained to monitor and shape users' actions remotely based on machine learning technologies that are regulated by neither national nor international laws.[2]

At the forefront of today's surveillance capitalism practices is the world's largest digital advertising company, Google.[3] Included among its products and platforms are the most popular web browser,[4] mobile platform,[5] and search engine[6]—Chrome, Android, and Google Search, respectively—in the world. Google's video platform (YouTube), email service (Gmail), and map application (Google Maps) each have over 1 billion monthly active users.[7] The tremendous popularity and reach of Google's products enable it to collect detailed information about user online behaviors and physical movements that it then applies to target users with paid advertising. Google's revenues increase significantly as it refines its targeting technology and data collection methods.

Google collects data on its users by various means. The most obvious are "active" means, where the user directly and consciously conveys information to Google by logging in to any of Google's popular applications, such as YouTube, Gmail, Search, etc. Less obvious ways that Google collects data are its "passive" means, whereby its products are instrumented to gather information while they are running, possibly without user knowledge. For example, Google's passive data gathering methods arise from platforms (e.g., Android and Chrome), applications (e.g., Search, YouTube, and Maps), publisher tools (e.g., Google Analytics, and

2    Shoshana Zuboff, "The Surveillance Threat Is Not What Orwell Imagined," *Time* (June 6, 2019), https://time.com/5602363/george-orwell-1984-anniversary-surveillance-capitalism/.

3    "Google and Facebook Tighten Grip on US Digital Ad Market," *eMarketer* (September 21, 2017), www.emarketer.com/Article/Google-Facebook-Tighten-Grip-on-US-Digital-Ad-Market/1016494.

4    Statista, "Market Share or Leading Internet Browsers in the United States and Worldwide as of February 2018" (February 2018), www.statista.com/statistics/276738/worldwide-and-us-market-share-of-leading-internet-browsers.

5    Statista, "Global OS Market Share in Sales to End Users from 1st Quarter 2009 to 2nd Quarter 2017" (August 2017), www.statista.com/statistics/266136/global-market-share-held-by-smartphone-operating-systems/.

6    Statista, "Worldwide Desktop Market Share of Leading Search Engines from January 2010 to October 2017" (February 2018), www.statista.com/statistics/216573/worldwide-market-share-of-search-engines/.

7    Google 10K filings with the SEC, 2017, https://abc.xyz/investor/pdf/20171231_alphabet_10K.pdf.

AdSense), and advertiser tools (e.g., AdMob, and AdWords), all of which are discussed later in this article.

Although prior studies listed in Appendix A have explored the ways Google tracks users via active means, the extent and magnitude of Google's passive data collection has largely been overlooked. To help fill this gap, this study provides a detailed view of Google's data collection methods by drawing on (1) data intercepted as it is sent to Google servers while Google or third-party products are used and (2) Google's My Activity[8] and Takeout[9] tools, which describe information collected during the use of Google's user-facing products.

The remainder of this paper is organized as follows: Section 2 presents an example "day in the life" scenario, where a real user with a new Google account and Android phone goes through their daily routine to determine how much Google learns about their personal interests during a single day of typical Internet usage; Section 3 shows how Google's Android and Chrome products frequently send user location and device-related information to Google without direct user knowledge; Section 4 shows how purportedly anonymous advertising identifiers can get connected with a user's Google identity; Section 5 analyzes the results of an experiment that show how Google collects considerable information through its advertiser and publisher products, even if a user does not interact with any key Google applications; and Section 6 presents concluding remarks and summarizes lessons learned from research conducted for this paper.

## Evaluating Google Data Collection in Practice

To demonstrate the multitude of touchpoints between Google's data collection methods and an individual, as well as to showcase the extent of information collected during these interactions, an experiment was conducted where a user carried an Android phone, the LG X Power Android mobile device, during a day's activities. The device used for this experiment was (1) wiped clean to the default factory settings and given a new SIM card to ensure that no data was stored on the phone and that phone numbers could not be linked with any past usage, and (2) wiped by conducting a factory data reset, which deleted all log-in data for Google services and other accounts, system and app data and settings, all downloaded apps, digital rights management licenses, music, images, documents and backups, and other usage data from the internal storage of the device. A new Google account was created (username

---

8    Google, "My Activity," https://myactivity.google.com/myactivity.

9    Google, "Download Your Data," https://takeout.google.com/settings/takeout?pli=1.

"Jane"), so that Google had no prior knowledge of the user and had no advertising interests associated with the account. This user then went about a normal day using the mobile phone associated with this new Google account.

The data collected by Google was checked using two tools: My Activity and Takeout. The My Activity tool shows data collected by Google from any Search-related activities, use of Google applications (e.g., YouTube video plays, Maps search, Google Assistant), visits to third-party web pages (while logged in to Chrome), and clicks on advertisements. The Google Takeout tool provides more comprehensive information about all historical user data collected via Google's applications (e.g., it contains all past email messages on Gmail, search queries, location collection, and YouTube videos watched). The data was collected and used to depict key information collection events that were synthesized in the form of a "day in the life" of the user "Jane," as shown in figure 12.1.

In the activity shown in figure 12.1, as well as throughout the rest of this paper, the collected data is categorized in the following two broad subgroups:

1.  *Active data collection,* where information is directly exchanged between the user and a Google product. An example of active data collection occurred when Jane submitted a keyword in the Search tool bar and that search query was collected by Google.

2.  *Passive data collection,* where information is exchanged in the background without any obvious notification to the user. An example of passive data collection occurred when Jane's location was sent to Google after she entered a search query.

Analysis of key touchpoints during a normal day in Jane's life indicated that the "passive" data collection events outnumbered the "active" events by approximately two-to-one.[10]

Google analyzes the collected data to assess user interests and then applies it to target users with appropriate ads. For example, Google provides a list of interests it inferred from a user's activities, available via the "topics you like" section in the Google's Ad Personalization webpage.[11] Figure 12.2 shows the list that Google associated with Jane's account after a day's worth of activity. In total, Google attributed eighteen interests

---

10    Schmidt, "Google Data Collection."

11    Google, "Ads Personalization," https://adssettings.google.com/authenti cated.

## A DAY IN THE LIFE OF A TYPICAL GOOGLE USER

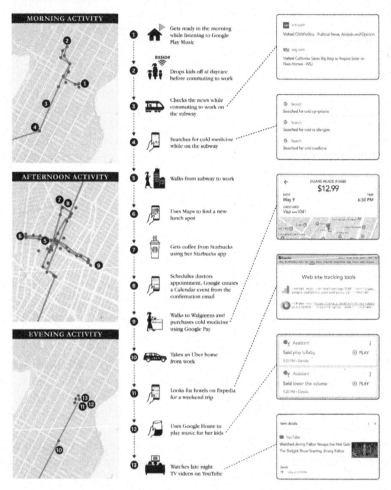

Figure 12.1. A Day in the Life of Jane, Highlighting Touchpoints Where Google Collects Data.

to Jane, eight of which (shown by highlighted borders) closely matched Jane's usage activities.[12]

---

12   It is unclear as to why other interests that have no connection with Jane's activities during the day show up in this list, though perhaps Google uses historical analysis of similar interests from other users to create associated recommendations.

**Interests Inferred by Google**

| | | |
|---|---|---|
| Action & Platform Games ⊗ | Books & Literature ⊗ | Business & Industrial ⊗ |
| Computer & Video Games ⊗ | Computers & Electronics ⊗ | Education ⊗ |
| Games ⊗ | Home & Garden ⊗ | Mobile & Wireless ⊗ |
| Movies ⊗ | Music & Audio ⊗ | News ⊗ |
| Online Communities ⊗ | Parenting ⊗ | Science ⊗ |
| Sports Games ⊗ | TV & Video ⊗ | TV Comedies ⊗ |

Figure 12.2. Google's Assessment of Jane's Interests at the End of One Day.

## Google Data Collection via the Android and Chrome Platforms

Android and Chrome are Google's primary platforms that collect significant user data due to their extensive reach and frequency of usage. By January 2018, Android captured 53% of the total US mobile OS market, whereas Apple iOS held 45%.[13] As of May 2017, there were more than 2 billion monthly active Android devices worldwide.[14] Google's Chrome browser held more than 60% share of all Internet browser usage in the world with over 1 billion monthly active users as reported in the 2017 Q4 10K filing. Both platforms facilitate the use of Google and third-party content (e.g., third-party websites and third-party apps) and hence provide Google access to a wide range of personal, web activity, and location information.

### Personal Information and Activity Data Collection

To download and use apps from Google Play Store on an Android device, a user must have (or create) a Google account, which becomes a key gateway through which Google collects personal information, including username, email, and phone number. If a user registers for services such as Google Pay,[15] Android also collects the user's credit card information, zip

---

13   Statista, "Subscriber Share Held by Smartphone Operating Systems in the United States from 2012 to 2018" (May 2018), www.statista.com/statistics/266572/market-share-held-by-smartphone-platforms-in-the-united-states/.

14   David Burke, "Android: Celebrating a Big Milestone Together with You," Google (May 17, 2017), www.blog.google/products/android/2bn-milestone/.

15   Google, "Google Chrome Privacy Whitepaper," www.google.com/chrome/privacy/whitepaper.html#payments.

code, and birth date. All this information becomes part of a user's personal information associated with their Google Account.

While Chrome does not mandate sharing additional personal information gathered from users, it does have the capability to capture such information. Chrome, for instance, collects a range of personal information via its form "autofill" feature, and such form fields typically include username, address, phone number, log-in name, and passwords.[16] Chrome stores form fill information on a user's local drive; however, if the user logs in to Chrome using Google Account and enables its "Sync" feature, this information gets sent to and stored on Google servers. Chrome could also learn about the language(s) a person speaks during their interactions with its translate feature, which is enabled by default.[17]

In addition to personal data, Chrome and Android send Google information about a user's web browsing and mobile app activities, respectively. Any webpage visit is automatically tracked and collected under user credentials by Google if the user is logged in to Chrome. Chrome also collects information about a user's browsing history, passwords, website-specific permissions, cookies, download history, and add-on data.[18] Android sends periodic updates to Google servers, including device type, cell service carrier name, crash reports, and information about apps installed on the phone.[19] It also notifies Google whenever any app is accessed on the phone (for example, Google knows when Android users access their Uber apps).

## User Location Data Collection

Android and Chrome platforms meticulously collect user location and movement information using a variety of sources. A "coarse location" assessment, for example, can be done by using GPS coordinates on an Android phone or through a network's IP address on a desktop/laptop device. The user location accuracy can be improved further ("fine location") through the use of nearby cell tower IDs or via scanning the device-specific base-station identifiers or basic service set identifiers, assigned to the radio chipset used in nearby Wi-Fi access points.[20]

---

16  Google, "Google Chrome Privacy Whitepaper" (March 6, 2018), www.google.com/chrome/privacy/whitepaper.html#autofill.

17  Google, "Google Chrome Privacy Whitepaper" (March 6, 2018), www.google.com/chrome/privacy/whitepaper.html#translate.

18  Google, "Google Chrome Privacy Notice" (March 6, 2018), www.google.com/intl/en/chrome/browser/privacy.

19  Google, "Privacy Policy," https://policies.google.com/privacy?hl=en&gl=us#infocollect.

20  To understand how location data is sent to Google servers in more depth, we analyzed the data traffic from a mobile phone from a user in motion.

Android phones can also use information from the Bluetooth beacons registered with Google's Proximity Beacon API.[21] These beacons indicate a user's geolocation coordinates and can also pinpoint exact floor levels in buildings.[22]

It is hard for an Android mobile user to "opt out" of location tracking, because even if a user turns off an Android device's Wi-Fi, the device's location is still tracked via its Wi-Fi signal. To prevent such tracking, Wi-Fi scanning must be explicitly disabled in a separate user action. The ubiquity of Wi-Fi hubs has made location tracking quite frequent. Even during a short 15-minute walk around a residential neighborhood, an Android device sent nine location requests to Google. The request collectively contained ~100 unique identifiers for public and private Wi-Fi access points. Google also ascertains with a high degree of confidence whether a user is standing still, walking, running, bicycling, or riding on a train or a car by tracking an Android mobile user's location coordinates at frequent time intervals in combination with the data from onboard sensors (such as an accelerometer) on mobile phones.

### Assessing Passive Data Collection by Google via the Android and Chrome Platforms

Active data that Android or Chrome platforms collect and send to Google as a result of users' activities on these platforms can be assessed through Google's MyActivity and Takeout tools. Of potentially greater interest, however, is the passive data that these platforms collect, which goes beyond location data and remains largely unrecognized by the users. To assess the type and frequency of occurrence of such collection in greater detail, an experiment was conducted that monitored traffic data sent to Google from mobile phones (both Android and iPhone). For comparison's sake, this experiment also included the analysis of data sent to Apple via an iPhone device.

For simplicity, the phones were kept stationary with no user interaction. On the Android phone a single Chrome browser session remained active in the background, whereas on the iPhone the Safari browser was used. This configuration provided an opportunity for systematic analysis of the background collection that Google performs purely through Android and Chrome, as well as collection that occurs in the absence of those (i.e., from iPhone device), without any additional collection requests generated by other products and applications (such as YouTube,

---

21 Google "Google Beacon Platform, Proximity Beacon API," https://developers.google.com/beacons/proximity/guides.

22 Ibid.

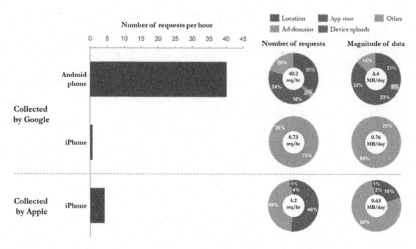

Figure 12.3. Traffic Data Sent from Idle Android
and iPhone Mobile Devices.

Gmail, and app usage). Figure 12.3 shows a summary of the results obtained from this experiment. The x-axis indicates the number of times the phones communicated with Google (or Apple) servers, whereas the y-axis indicates the phone type (Android or iPhone) and server domain type (Google or Apple) with which data packets were exchanged by the phones. The colored legend describes the broad categorization of the type of data requests identified by the domain address of the server.

During a 24-hour time period the Android device communicated ~900 data samples to a variety of Google server endpoints. Of these, ~35% (or approximately 14/hour) were location related. Google ad domains received only ~3% of the traffic since the mobile browser was not actively used during the collection period. The remaining ~62% of communications with the Google server domains were roughly divided between requests to Google's Play App store, Android's uploads of device-related data (such as crash reports and device authorization), and other data predominantly in the category of Google services background calls and refreshes.

Figure 12.3 shows that the iPhone device communicated with Google domains at more than an order of magnitude (~50x) lower frequency than the Android device, and that Google did not collect any user location during the 24-hour experiment timeframe via iPhone. This result highlights the fact that the Android and Chrome platforms play an important role in Google's data collection. Moreover, the iPhone device's communication with Apple's servers were 10x less frequent than the Android device's communications with Google. Location data made up a very small fraction (~1%) of the net data sent to Apple servers from the iPhone, with Apple receiving location-related communications once every day on an average.

Android phones communicated 4.4 MB of data per day (~130MB per month) with Google servers, about 6x more than what Google servers communicated through the iPhone device. This experiment was conducted using a stationary phone with no user interaction. As a user becomes mobile and starts interacting with their phone, the frequency of communications with Google's servers increases considerably. Section 5 of this paper analyzes results from such an experiment.

## Google Data Collection via Publisher and Advertiser Technologies

A major source for Google's user activity data collection stems from its publisher- and advertiser-focused tools, such as Google Analytics, DoubleClick, AdSense, AdWords, and AdMob. These tools have tremendous reach, e.g., over 1 million mobile apps use AdMob,[23] over 1 million advertisers use AdWords,[24] over 15 million websites use AdSense,[25] and over 30 million websites use Google Analytics.[26]

There are two main user groups of Google's publisher- and advertiser-focused tools:

1. *Website and app publishers.* Organizations that own websites and create mobile apps. These entities use Google's tools to (1) make money by allowing the display of ads to visitors on their websites or apps, and (2) better track and understand who is visiting their websites and using their apps. Google's tools place cookies and run scripts in the browsers of website visitors that help determine a user's identity, track their interest in content, and follow their online behavior. Google's mobile app libraries track use of apps on mobile phones.

---

23  Google, "AdMob by Google," www.google.com/admob/.

24  Google, "Hear from Our Happy Customers," https://adwords.google.com/home/resources/success-stories/.

25  BuiltWith, "Websites using Google Adsense," https://trends.builtwith.com/websitelist/Google-Adsense.

26  BuiltWith, "Google Analytics Usage Statistics," April 2018, https://trends.builtwith.com/analytics/Google-Analytics. Google has rebranded AdWords as "Google Ads" and DoubleClick as "Google Ad Manager," though there were no changes instituted in the core product functionalities including information collection by these products. Therefore, for the purpose of this paper the names are kept unchanged to avoid confusion that may occur with related domain names (such as doubleclick.net).

2. *Advertisers.* Organizations that pay to have banner, video, or other ads delivered to users as they browse the Internet or use apps. These entities apply Google's tools to target specific profiles of people for advertisements to increase the return on their marketing investments (better targeted ads generally yield higher click-through rates and conversions). Such tools also enable advertisers to analyze their audiences and measure the efficacy of their digital advertising by tracking which ads were clicked with what frequency and by providing insight into the profiles of people who clicked on ads.

Together, these tools collect information about user activities on websites and in apps, such as content visited, and ads clicked. They work in the background—largely unnoticeable by users. Figure 12.4 shows some of these key tools, with arrows indicating data collected from users and ads served to users.

The information collected by such tools includes a non-personal identifier that Google can use to send targeted advertisements without identifying the unique individual's personal information. These identifiers can be device- or session-specific, as well as permanent or semi-permanent. To provide users greater anonymity during information collection for ad targeting, Google has recently shifted towards using semi-permanent device unique identifiers, such as GAIDs, alphanumeric strings for Android and iOS devices that enable accurate targeted mobile ads.[27]

### Google Analytics and DoubleClick

Google Analytics and DoubleClick are Google's leading products in user behavior tracking and webpage traffic analyses on desktop and mobile devices. Google Analytics is used by ~75% of the top 100,000 most visited websites.[28] DoubleClick cookies are associated with more than 1.6 million websites.[29] Google Analytics uses short pieces of tracking code (called "page tags") embedded in a website's HTML code.[30] After a webpage loads per a user's request, the Google Analytics code calls an "analytics.js" program residing on Google's servers to transfer a "default" snapshot of user data at that moment, which includes visited webpage

---

27 Google "Best Practices for Unique Identifiers," https://developer. android.com/training/articles/user-data-ids.

28 BuiltWith, "Google Analytics Usage Statistics," April 2018, https:// trends.builtwith.com/analytics/Google-Analytics.

29 Datanyze, "DoubleClick Market Share," www.datanyze.com/market-share/ ad-exchanges/doubleclick-market-share.

30 GA or other tags can also be implemented through Google Tag Manage (GTM) without changing the functionality of the page tag.

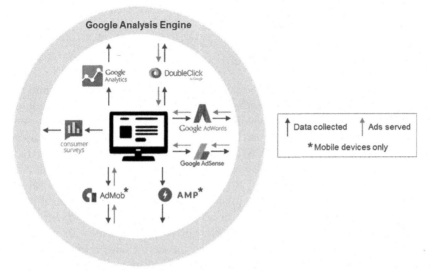

Figure 12.4. Google Products Aimed at Publishers and Advertisers.

address, page title, browser information, current location (derived from IP address), and user language settings. Google Analytics scripts use cookies to track user behavior.

The first time a Google Analytics script is run it generates and stores a browser-specific cookie on the user's computer. This cookie has a unique client identifier or Client ID.[31] Google uses the unique identifier to link to previously stored cookies that capture a user's activity on a particular domain as long as the cookie does not expire, or the user does not clear the cookies cached on their browser.[32]

While a Google Analytics cookie is specific to the domain of the website that a user visits (called a "first-party cookie"), a DoubleClick cookie is typically associated with a common third-party domain (such as doubleclick.net). Google uses such cookies to track user interaction across multiple third-party websites.[33] When a user interacts with an advertisement on a website, DoubleClick's conversion tracking tools (e.g., Floodlight) places cookies on a user's computer and generates a unique client ID.[34] Henceforth, the stored cookie information gets accessed by

---

31  Google "Cookies and User Identification," https://developers.google.com/analytics/devguides/collection/analyticsjs/cookies-user-id.

32  Ibid.

33  Google, "DoubleClick Search Help," https://support.google.com/ds/answer/7298761?hl=en.

34  Google "DoubleClick Search Help," https://support.google.com/ds/answer/2903014?hl=en&ref_topic=6054260.

the DoubleClick server if the user visits the advertised website, thereby recording the visit as a valid conversion.

## AdSense, AdWords, and AdMob

AdSense and AdWords are Google tools that serve ads on websites and in Google Search results, respectively. AdSense collects information about whether an ad was displayed on the publisher's webpage and how the user interacted with the ad, such as clicking an ad or tracking the curser movement over an ad.[35] AdWords enables advertisers to serve search ads on Google Search, display ads on publisher pages, and overlay ads on YouTube videos. To track user click-through and conversion rates, AdWords ads place a cookie on users' browsers to identify the user if they later visit the advertiser's website or complete a purchase.[36] AdSense and AdWords also collect data on mobile devices. Their ability to get user information on mobile devices is limited, however, since mobile apps do not share cookie data between them, an isolation technique known as "sandboxing."[37] It is therefore hard for advertisers to track user behavior across mobile apps.

To address this issue, Google and other companies use mobile "ad libraries" (such as AdMob) that are integrated into the apps by their developers for serving ads in mobile apps. These libraries compile and run with the apps and send data to Google that are specific to the app to which they belong, including GPS locations, device make, and device model when apps have the appropriate permissions. As observed through the data traffic analyses and confirmed through Google's own developer webpages,[38] such libraries can also send Google-users' personal data (such as age and gender) whenever app developers explicitly pass these values to the library. More than 15 million websites have AdSense installed to display sponsored ads.[39] Likewise, more than 2 million websites and apps

---

35  Google, "AdSense Help, Privacy and Security," https://support.google.com/adsense/answer/9897?hl=en.

36  Google, "Evaluating Ad Performance on the Search Network," https://support.google.com/adwords/answer/2404037?hl=en; and Google, "About Conversion Tracking," https://support.google.com/adwords/answer/1722022?hl=en.

37  This approach is similar to desktops, where cookies are not shared between browsers.

38  Google "Google APIs for Android," https://developers.google.com/android/reference/com/google/android/gms/ads/doubleclick/Publisher-AdRequest.Builder.

39  BuiltWith, "Websites using Google Adsense," https://trends.builtwith.com/websitelist/Google-Adsense.

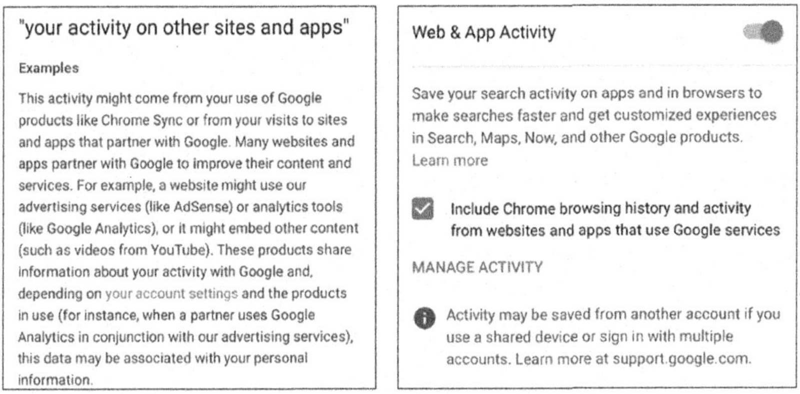

| "your activity on other sites and apps" | Web & App Activity |
|---|---|
| **Examples**<br><br>This activity might come from your use of Google products like Chrome Sync or from your visits to sites and apps that partner with Google. Many websites and apps partner with Google to improve their content and services. For example, a website might use our advertising services (like AdSense) or analytics tools (like Google Analytics), or it might embed other content (such as videos from YouTube). These products share information about your activity with Google and, depending on your account settings and the products in use (for instance, when a partner uses Google Analytics in conjunction with our advertising services), this data may be associated with your personal information. | Save your search activity on apps and in browsers to make searches faster and get customized experiences in Search, Maps, Now, and other Google products. Learn more<br><br>☑ Include Chrome browsing history and activity from websites and apps that use Google services<br><br>MANAGE ACTIVITY<br><br>ⓘ Activity may be saved from another account if you use a shared device or sign in with multiple accounts. Learn more at support.google.com. |

Figure 12.5. Google's Privacy Page for Third-Party Website
Collection and Association with Personal Info.

that make up the Google Display Network (GDN) and reach over 90% of Internet users[40] display AdWords ads.[41]

## Association of Passively Collected Data with Personal Information

As discussed above, Google collects data through publisher and advertiser products and associates such data with a variety of semi-permanent, anonymous identifiers. Statements made in Google's privacy policy, however, insinuate that Google can associate these IDs with a user's personal information. Excerpts of this policy are shown in figure 12.5.

The left text box in figure 12.5 clearly states that Google may associate data from advertising services and analytics tools with a user's personal information, depending upon the user's account settings. This arrangement is enabled by default, as shown in the right text box. Moreover, an analysis of data traffic exchanged with Google servers (summarized below) identified two key examples (one on Android and the other in Chrome) that indicate how Google can correlate anonymously collected data with users' personal information.

---

40 Google, "Google Ads Help," https://support.google.com/google-ads/answer/2404191?hl=en.

41 Google, "Google Privacy and Terms," https://policies.google.com/privacy/example/your-activity-on-other-sites-and-apps; and Google, "Activity Controls," https://myaccount.google.com/activitycontrols.

## Mobile Advertising Identifier May Get De-anonymized via Data Sent to Google by Android

Analyses of data traffic communicated between an Android phone and Google server domains suggest how anonymous identifiers (a "GAID" in this case) can get associated with a user's Google account. Data exchanges with Google servers from an Android phone show how Google can connect anonymized information collected on an Android mobile device via DoubleClick, Analytics or AdMob tools with the user's personal identity. During a 24-hour experiment, data collected from a stationary and dormant Android show phone two instances of check-in communications with Google servers were observed.

### DoubleClick Cookie ID Gets Connected with User's Personal Info on Google Account

Section 4.3.1 explained how Google can de-anonymize user identity via the passive, anonymized data it collects from an Android mobile device. De-anonymization can also occur on a desktop/laptop device, where anonymized data is collected via cookie-based identifiers (e.g., Cookie ID), which are typically generated by Google's ad and publisher products (e.g., DoubleClick) and stored on a user's local mass storage. The experiment presented below assessed whether Google can connect such identifiers (and hence information associated with them) with a user's personal information. This experiment involved the following ordered steps:

1. Opened a new (no saved cookies, e.g., Private or Incognito) browser session (Chrome or other);

2. Visited a third-party website that used Google's DoubleClick ad network;

3. Visited the website of a widely used Google service (Gmail in this case);

4. Signed into Gmail.

After completing steps 1 and 2, as part of the page load process, the DoubleClick server received a request when the user first visited the third-party website. This request was part of a series of requests comprising the DoubleClick initialization process started by the publisher website, which resulted in the Chrome browser setting a cookie for the DoubleClick domain. This cookie stayed on the user's computer until it expired or until the user manually cleared cookies via the browser settings.

Thereafter, in step 3 when the user visits Gmail, they are prompted to log in with their Google credentials. Google manages identity using a "single sign on (SSO)" architecture, whereby credentials are supplied to an account service (signified by accounts.google.com) in exchange for an "authentication token." This token can then be presented to other Google services to identify the users. In step 4 when a user accesses their Gmail account, they are effectively signing into their Google Account that then provides Gmail with an authorization token to verify the user's identity. The advantage of the extra authentication step is that the user's browser can later use the same authentication token to confirm user identity on other Google services (due to this process a sign-on in any particular Google application enables an automatic sign-on in all others in the same browser session).

In step 3 of this sign-on process, a request is sent to the DoubleClick domain containing the authentication token provided by Google and the tracking cookie set when the user visited the third-party website in step 2. Google uses these data to connect the user's Google credentials with a DoubleClick cookie ID. If users do not clear browser cookies regularly, therefore, their browsing information on third-party webpages that use DoubleClick services can be associated with their Google Account personal information.

## Amount of Data Collected during a Minimal Use of Google Products

This section examines the details surrounding Google's data collection through its publisher and advertiser services. To understand such data collection, an experiment was designed that entailed a user going through her daily life using a mobile phone (akin to "day in the life" described in section 2), while deliberately *avoiding* the use of any direct Google products (i.e., avoiding Search, Gmail, YouTube, Maps, etc.), except for the Chrome browser.

To make the experiments realistic, various consumer usage studies were used to form a daily usage profile of a typical mobile user.[42] Thereafter, any direct interactions with Google's products were omitted from the profile. The experiment was replicated on both Android and iOS devices and the HTTPS data sent to Google and Apple servers were monitored and analyzed using a similar method explained in previous sections. The results are summarized in figure 12.6. During the 24-hour

---

42 "Google, https://myaccount.google.com/activitycontrols"; and Nielsen, "Nielsen Provides Topline U.S. Web Data for March 2010" (April 2010), www.nielsen.com/us/en/insights/news/2010/nielsen-provides-topline-u-s-web-data-for-march-2010.html.

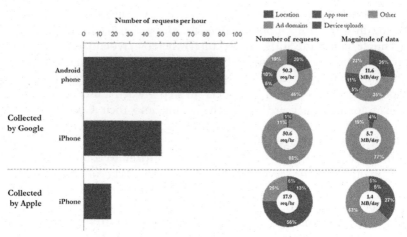

Figure 12.6. Information Requests from Mobile
Devices During a Day of Typical Use.

time period (including the nighttime stationary/dormant timeframe), most calls from the Android phone were made to Google's location and publisher/advertisement service domains (e.g., DoubleClick, Analytics). Google collected user location in ~450 instances, more than ~1.4x times the amount shown by the experiment presented in section 3 involving a stationary phone.

Google servers communicated a significantly lower number of times with an iPhone device compared to Android (45% less). The number of calls to Google's advertising domains, however, were similar from both devices, as was expected, since the usage of third-party webpages and apps was similar on both devices. One notable difference was that the location data sent to Google from an iOS device is practically non-existent. In the absence of Android and Chrome platforms—or the use of any other Google product—Google becomes significantly limited in its ability to track the user location.

The total number of calls to Apple servers from an iOS device was much lower, just 19% the number of calls to Google servers from an Android device. Moreover, there are no ad-related calls to Apple servers, perhaps stemming from the fact that Apple's business model is not as dependent on advertising as Google's. Although Apple does obtain some user location data from iOS devices, the volume of data collected is much (16x) lower than what Google collects from Android. Android phones communicated 11.6 MB of data per day (~350 MB per month) with Google servers. On the other hand, the iPhone device communicated just half that amount. The amount of data particularly associated with Google's ad domains remained quite similar across both devices. The iPhone device communicated an order of magnitude less data to Apple servers than what the Android device exchanged with Google servers.

Even in the absence of user interaction with Google's most popular applications, a user of an Android phone and Chrome browser still sends substantial amounts of data to Google. Much of this data is associated with location and calls to ad server domains. Although an iPhone user is insulated from Google's location collection in this narrow experiment, Google still captures a similar amount of ad-related data.

## Concluding Remarks

A large percentage of the world's population directly consume Google products that lead their markets globally and surpass 1 billion monthly active users. These products collect user data via various means that many typical users may not understand. Much of Google's data collection occurs "passively," i.e., while a user is not directly engaged with any of its products. While such information is typically collected without identifying a unique user, Google distinctively possesses the ability to utilize data collected from other sources to de-anonymize such collection.

The following summarizes the lessons learned from the research reported in this paper:

1. Google learns a great deal about a user's personal interests during even a single day of typical Internet usage. As shown by the "day in the life" scenario in section 2, Google collected data about Jane at numerous activity touchpoints, such as user location, routes taken, items purchased, and music listened to. Surprisingly, Google collected or inferred over two-thirds of the information through passive means. At the end of the day, Google identified user interests with remarkable accuracy.

2. Android is an essential enabler of data collection for Google, with over 2 billion monthly active users worldwide. Android helps Google collect personal user information, activity on the mobile phone, and location coordinates. Section 3 showed how frequently Android sends Google user location and device-related information passively, i.e., without direct user knowledge.

3. The Chrome browser helps Google collect user data from both mobile and desktop devices, with over 2 billion active installs worldwide.[43] Section 3 described how the Chrome browser col-

---

43 Frederic Lardinois, "Google says there are now 2 billion active Chrome installs," *TechCrunch* (Nov. 10, 2016), https://techcrunch.com/2016/11/10/

lects personal information (e.g., when a user completes online forms) and sends it to Google as part of the data synchronization process. It also tracks webpage visits and sends user location coordinates to Google.

4. Android and Chrome send data to Google even without *any* user interaction. Experiments in section 3 showed that a dormant, stationary Android phone running Chrome in the background communicated location information to Google 340 times during a 24-hour period. In fact, location information constituted 35% of all data samples sent to Google. In contrast, Google cannot collect any appreciable data on an iOS Apple device with Safari (where neither Android nor Chrome were used) in the absence of user interaction with the device.

5. Google can use advertising identifiers (which are purportedly "user anonymous" and collect activity data on apps and third-party webpage visits) to connect with a user's Google identity. This connection happens via passing of device-level identification information to Google by Android devices, as discussed in section 4. Likewise, the DoubleClick cookie ID is another purportedly "user anonymous" identifier that Google can connect to a user's Google account.

6. After a user starts interacting with an Android phone, passive communication to Google server domains increases significantly, even when the user runs no prominent Google apps. This increase is driven by data activity from Google's publisher and advertiser products. The results presented in section 5 suggest that even if a user does not interact with any key Google applications, Google still collects considerable information through its advertiser and publisher products.

7. While using an iOS device, if a user decides to forgo the use of *any* Google product (i.e., no Android, no Chrome, no Google applications), and visits only non-Google webpages, the number of times data is communicated to Google servers still remains surprisingly high. This communication is driven purely by advertiser/publisher services. An experiment in section 5 shows how the total magnitude of data communicated to Google servers from an iOS device is approximately half of that from an Android device.

---

google-says-there-are-now-2-billion-active-chrome-installs/.

Google's data collection practices are particularly problematic in this age of surveillance capitalism. As shown in this paper and related studies, if you use Android mobile devices Google tracks your movements, whether you like it or not.[44] If you use popular products like Chrome, Gmail, and Search, Google also knows who you are and what you do, whether you like it or not. Likewise, if you use the Google Photos app, then Google knows who your friends and family are, whether you like it or not. In the words of former Google CEO Eric Schmidt, "We know where you are. We know where you've been. We can more or less know what you're thinking about."[45] Eric Schmidt has also pointed out that "Your digital identity will live forever . . . because there's no delete button,"[46] demonstrating yet another reason why Google's vast trove of collected data on their users is particularly unsettling.

## Appendix: Related Work on Google's Data Collection Practices

Table 12.1. Summary of other studies relating to Google's data collection practices

| Title | Relevant Findings |
| --- | --- |
| AP Exclusive: Google tracks your movements, like it or not | Google is tracking users' location even when location services are disabled. |
| Australian Regulator Investigates Google Data Harvesting from Android Phones[47] | Google "harvests" about 1GB of data from Android devices per month. |
| How to keep Google from Owning Your Online Life[48] | It is hard for the average consumer to avoid Google products. |

---

44   Ryan Nakashima, "AP Exclusive: Google tracks your movements, like it or not," *AP* (August 13, 2018), https://apnews.com/828aefab64d4411bac257a07c1af0ecb.

45   Andrew Orlowski, "Google's Schmidt: We know what you're thinking," *Register* (October 4, 2010), www.theregister.co.uk/2010/10/04/google_ericisms/.

46   Yasha Levine, "Googles for Profit Surveillance Problem," *Pando* (December 16, 2013), pando.com/2013/12/16/googles-for-profit-surveillance-problem.

47   Anne Davis, "Australian Regulator Investigates Google Data Harvesting from Android Phones," *Guardian* (May 13, 2018), www.theguardian.com/technology/2018/may/14/australian-regulator-investigates-google-data-harvesting-from-android-phones.

48   David Pierce, "How to Keep Google from Owning Your Online Life," *Wall Street Journal* (May 8, 2018), www.wsj.com/articles/how-to-keep-google-from-owning-your-online-life-1525795372.

| Title | Relevant Findings |
| --- | --- |
| Google Tracking Phones Even When They Are Disconnected?[49] | Google tracks phones even when phones are "disconnected" (no SIM cards, airplane mode, Wi-Fi off). |
| Google Collects Android Users' Locations Even When Location Services Are Disabled[50] | Google collects Android location when location services are turned off. |
| Google Is Permanently Nerfing All Home Minis Because Mine Spied on Everything I Said 24/7[51] | The Google Home mini was saving recording when the device was not activated with "OK Google" (Google claims to have resolved the issue). |
| Online Tracking: A 1-Million-Site Measurement and Analysis[52] | Google can track users ~80% of websites using its cookies. |
| Why Do Android Smartphones Guzzle the Most Data?[53] | Android devices consume more data (2.2GB/month) than other smartphones. |
| Data Leakage from Android Smartphones[54] | Android passes anonymous IDs along with devices IDs such as Mac address and IMIE. |

49 Brett Larson, "Google Tracking Phones Even When They Are Disconnected?," *Fox News* (February 11, 2018), http://video.foxnews.com/v/5731183327001/?#sp=show-clips.

50 Keith Collins, "Google Collects Android Users' Locations Even When Location Services Are Disabled," *Quartz* (November 17, 2017), https://qz.com/1131515/google-collects-android-users-locations-even-when-location-services-are-disabled/.

51 Artem Russakovskii, "Google Is Permanently Nerfing All Home Minis Because Mine Spied on Everything I said 24/7," *Android Police* (October 10, 2017), www.androidpolice.com/2017/10/10/google-nerfing-home-minis-mine-spied-everything-said-247/.

52 Steven Englehardt and Arvind Narayana, "Online Tracking: A 1-Million-Site Measurement and Analysis," *ACM CCS* (2016), http://randomwalker.info/publications/OpenWPM_1_million_site_tracking_measurement.pdf.

53 Brian Chen, "Why Do Android Smartphones Guzzle the Most Data?," *New York Times* (December 31, 2013), https://bits.blogs.nytimes.com/2013/12/31/why-do-android-smartphones-guzzle-the-most-data/.

54 Lasse Øverlier, "Data Leakage from Android Smartphones," *Norwegian Defense Research Establishment* (June 6, 2012), available at www.ffi.no/no/Rapporter/12-00275.pdf.

# Contributors

CLIFFORD B. ANDERSON is Associate University Librarian for Research and Digital Strategy at the Vanderbilt University Library. He holds a secondary appointment as Professor of Religious Studies in the College of Arts & Science at Vanderbilt University. He is the co-author (with Joseph C. Wicentowski) of *XQuery for Humanists* (2020) and is the editor of *Digital Humanities and Libraries and Archives in Religious Studies* (2022).

EDWARD DAWSON is Assistant Professor of Practice of German and faculty affiliate in the Center for Digital Research in the Humanities at the University of Nebraska-Lincoln. Recent publications on environmental humanities and media studies include an ecological reading of Christoph Ransmayr's novel *Cox oder der Lauf der Zeit* in *The German Quarterly* and a chapter on the infrastructure of digital humanities work in *Right Research: Modelling Sustainable Research Practices in the Anthropocene* ed. Geoffrey Rockwell, Chelsea Miya, and Oliver Rossier.

JOHANNES ENDRES is Professor of Art History and Comparative Literature at the University of California, Riverside. He is a specialist of German literature of the 18th and 19th centuries and of the interdisciplinary methodologies of the study of images and texts. Recent publications include two volumes on Friedrich Schlegel and essays on Leonardo da Vinci, Johann Wolfgang von Goethe, Heinrich von Kleist, and Hans Blumenberg. Currently, he is working on a history of "Style" as an interdisciplinary concept of the study of image, music, and text.

ROLF J. GOEBEL is Distinguished Professor of German, Emeritus, University of Alabama in Huntsville. His current research focuses on German modernism and on intersections of sound/music, philosophy, media technologies, and literary aesthetics. His publications include *Constructing China: Kafka's Orientalist Discourse* (1997); *Benjamin heute: Großstadtdiskurs, Postkolonialität und Flanerie zwischen den Kulturen* (2001); *A Companion to the Works of Walter Benjamin* (editor, 2009), and *Klang im Zeitalter technischer Medien: Eine Einführung* (2017).

BORIS GROYS is Professor of Russian and Slavic Studies at New York University. He has written extensively on modern and contemporary art. His publications include *Art Power* (2008), *On the New* (2014), *In the Flow* (2016), and *Logic of the Collection* (2021).

MICHAEL KNOCHE is a Library Scientist and Germanist living in Weimar, Germany. He was Director of the Herzogin Anna Amalia Bibliothek/ Klassik Stiftung Weimar from 1991 to 2016. His research focuses on library theory and history and German literary history around 1800, centering around the role of libraries and literature in the past and present. His latest book publications include: *Auf dem Weg zur Forschungsbibliothe: Studien aus der Herzogin Anna Amalia Bibliothek* (2016), *Die Zukunft des Sammelns an wissenschaftlichen Bibliotheken* (2017, edited), *Die Idee der Bibliothek und ihre Zukunft* (2018). His blog is "Aus der Forschungsbibliothek Krekelborn" https://biblio.hypotheses.org/.

PETER M. McISAAC is Associate Professor of German Studies und Museum Studies at the University of Michigan. His research focuses on the intersections of literature and museums, the Wunderkammer, the cultural history of popular anatomical exhibitions from the Panoptikum to Body Worlds, and digital humanities analyses of German-speaking monthly magazines. He is the author of *Museums of the Mind: German Modernity and the Dynamics of Collecting* (2007) and co-editor of *Exhibiting the German Past: Museums, Film, and Musealization* (2015, with Gabriele Müller). His articles have appeared in *German Studies Review*, *The German Quarterly*, *Seminar*, *Monatshefte*, *Literatur für Leser*, *German Life and Letters*, und *The International Journal of Cultural Policy*.

DOUGLAS C. SCHMIDT is the Cornelius Vanderbilt Professor of Computer Science, Associate Provost for Research Development and Technologies, Co-Chair of the Data Science Institute, and a Senior Researcher at the Institute for Software Integrated Systems at Vanderbilt University. Prof. Schmidt's research covers a range of software-related topics facilitate the development of mission-critical middleware for distributed real-time embedded (DRE) systems and mobile cloud computing applications. He has published 650+ technical papers and books that have been cited 44,500+ times and his h-index is 87.

ROBERTO SIMANOWSKI is Associated Member of the Excellence Cluster *Temporal Communities* at Freie Universität Berlin and served as Professor of Media Studies at Universität Basel and City University of Hong Kong. He has published widely on aesthetics, culture, and politics of digital media. His recent books include *The Death Algorithm and Other Digital Dilemmas* (2018), *Facebook Society: Losing Ourselves in Sharing*

*Ourselves* (2018), and *Data Love: The Seduction and Betrayal of Digital Technologies* (2016).

ERIN L. THOMPSON is an Associate Professor at John Jay College of Criminal Justice (City University of New York). She researches the intersections between cultural heritage, law, and crime, including the ethics of digitization of cultural property. Her books are *Possession* (2016), a history of the private collecting of Greek and Roman antiquities, and *Smashing Statues* (2022), on controversies over American monuments.

JESSICA WALTHEW is a conservator at Cooper Hewitt Smithsonian Design Museum where she works across the Product Design and Decorative Arts and Digital Collections. Her recent publications include "Planning for the Future Right Now: Riskscapes in Conserving Contemporary Design" in *Journal of the American Institute for Conservation*, 60:2–3 (2021) 115–27, and "Conserving active matter in contemporary design" in *Living Matter: The Preservation of Biological Materials in Contemporary Art*, ed. Rachel Rivenc and Kendra Roth (Getty 2022).

NIKOLAUS WEGMANN is Professor of German at Princeton University. His research areas are German literature from the eighteenth century to the present and the history and theory of cultural techniques. His recent publications include "Ästhetik der Skalierung," eds. Carlos Spoerhase, Steffen Siegel, and Nikolaus Wegmann, in *Zeitschrift für Ästhetik und Allgemeine Kunstwissenschaft* (ZÄK), Sonderheft 18 (2020).

CHRISTOPH ZELLER is Professor of German and European Studies at Vanderbilt University. His research focuses on literature, media, and culture, centering around philosophical concepts and their impact on individuals and groups. He has published essays and books on the intersection of literature, art, and technology, including "From Object to Information: The End of Collecting in the Digital Age" (2015), *Literarische Experimente: Medien, Kunst, Texte seit 1950* (edited, 2012), and *Ästhetik des Authentischen: Literatur und Kunst um 1970* (2010).

# Index

Printed in the United States
by Baker & Taylor Publisher Services